SAFEGUARDING ADULTS

SAFEGUARDING ADULTS

KEY THEMES AND ISSUES

GILLIAN MACINTYRE, AILSA STEWART
AND PEARSE McCUSKER

 macmillan international HIGHER EDUCATION   palgrave

First published 2018 by
PALGRAVE

Palgrave in the UK is an imprint of Macmillan Publishers Limited, registered in England, company number 785998, of 4 Crinan Street, London, N1 9XW.

Palgrave® and Macmillan® are registered trademarks in the United States, the United Kingdom, Europe and other countries.

ISBN 978–1–137–38100–2 paperback

This book is printed on paper suitable for recycling and made from fully managed and sustained forest sources. Logging, pulping and manufacturing processes are expected to conform to the environmental regulations of the country of origin.

A catalogue record for this book is available from the British Library.

A catalog record for this book is available from the Library of Congress.

CONTENTS

1

Introduction

Pearse McCusker, Glasgow Caledonian University;
Gillian MacIntyre, University of Strathclyde; Ailsa Stewart,
University of Strathclyde

Safeguarding adults is a rapidly evolving area of professional practice that has been subject to significant policy and legislative development over the last decade in the United Kingdom (UK) and Northern Ireland (NI). This book aims to critically engage with those developments and to encapsulate some of the emerging approaches to safeguarding adults in contemporary practice. Addressing multi-disciplinary working with a range of stakeholders, including social workers, health practitioners, the police, service users and carers, and wider communities, the book combines conceptual thought and key messages from research and practice experience to provide what we hope will be a valuable resource for students on qualifying and post-qualifying social work and health courses and related disciplines. It also serves as a timely resource to support the continuing professional development of health, social care and allied professionals involved in this ethically contentious area of practice.

Adult safeguarding can be considered to be a continuum incorporating within its parameters a range of interventions and safeguards to prevent adults from coming to harm (Stewart, 2016) including compulsory treatment at one end and provision of traditional welfare supports at the other. This may include those who are unable to protect themselves by virtue of mental disorder, learning disability, physical disability and/or physical frailty. Consequently a number of legislative avenues may be drawn upon to ensure protection, often creating a complex and interactive legislative framework for practitioners to navigate.

Already, therefore, complex and contested in terms of definitions and application, adult safeguarding has been further problematised by significant legal developments both nationally and internationally, most notably 'Cheshire West' (The Supreme Court, 2014) and the United Nations Convention on the Rights of Persons with Disabilities (CRPD)

(United Nations, 2006). The former refers to a UK Supreme Court judgement that clarifies what constitutes deprivation of liberty for adults who may lack capacity to make decisions, representing a wholesale change in thinking and requiring new legislative provision to ensure compliance – as illustrated by the introduction of Deprivation of Liberty Safeguards in England and Wales (Social Care Institute for Excellence [SCIE], 2015) and more recent proposals by the English Law Commission to reform this system and introduce Liberty Protection Safeguards (Law Commission for England and Wales, 2017) to combat the increase in illegal deprivation cases. Much wider in scope, the CRPD amounts to a paradigm shifting international legal mandate for achieving equality before the law for people with disabilities (Spandler et al., 2015). Its influence is beginning to be felt in policy and legal developments closer to home, for example, in the Adult Safeguarding: Prevention and Protection policy in Northern Ireland (Department of Health, Social Services and Public Safety [DHSSPS], 2015). CRPD enshrines equality before the law and autonomy over decision making regardless of the perceived level of disability, reorienting the focus of statutory interventions and professional practice from assessing capacity to facilitating supported decision making. Both of these legal developments reflect the highly disputed and ethically difficult nature of seeking to protect adults from harm, whilst also upholding their human rights. They provide context for the sense of urgency policy makers and legislators across the four jurisdictions in the UK have shown to keep pace.

This is reflected in the introduction of numerous pieces of legislation across the UK such as the Care Act 2014 in England and the Social Care (Self-Directed Support) (Scotland) Act 2013, which arguably represent the biggest change to the way in which adult social care will be delivered since the onset of community care. These developments place the emphasis firmly on co-production, adopting an asset-based approach where the starting point is based on the strengths that an individual brings as well as the existing sources of support that they have to draw on. With a focus on preventative rather than crisis driven work, these developments arguably offer greater opportunity to provide personalised support to enable individuals to enhance their wellbeing. Yet these shifts also require a greater understanding of risk and ability to consider adult safeguarding across a range of settings within a broad and complex legislative framework, as set out in various documents such as the *Making Safeguarding Personal* guidance, published by the Local Government Association in 2014.

While statutes and policies are essential for defining the parameters of adult safeguarding and establishing the degree and limits of States' responsibilities in relation to it, they represent only a part of the activity required to realise the central aim of protecting adults from harm. Indeed there appears to be a significant gap in providing a cohesive discourse that explores the multi-disciplinary nature of this emerging field of practice. Consequently, the aim of this book is to encourage readers to engage with some of the key conceptual themes associated with safeguarding adults across the jurisdictions and their application to practice, it is consequently not a legal textbook. Readers are, therefore, invited to consider barriers to and ways of developing ethical and anti-oppressive safeguarding practice that promote the rights of individuals whilst providing appropriate support and protection from harm and are guided to references for explicit legal frameworks.

The book comprises two main sections. Part 1 provides an overview of some of the emerging themes and issues in the field of adult safeguarding. While some consideration of key legislative and policy developments across the UK and NI is necessary in order to set the context for further discussion, the aim is not to examine these in depth, as previously noted, but rather to use them as a contextual framework in order to unpack and explore central themes. This will include providing the reader with an overview of safeguarding work with adults exploring this concept in order that further consideration of issues and dilemmas can take place. Part 1 also provides critical analysis of concepts such as 'risk', 'abuse', 'harm' and 'capacity', setting this against some of the challenges involved in intervening in the lives of adults. This section ends with an in-depth exploration of the multi-disciplinary nature of adult safeguarding, drawing attention to professional roles and responsibilities.

Part 2 of the volume explores the key concepts and issues identified in Part 1 as they relate to people who use services. While it is recognised that classifying people by the services they use is not without its problems, this approach allows the reader to develop a more nuanced understanding of how some of the ethical dilemmas and tensions identified apply to particular service user groups or areas of practice. Concepts of risk and capacity, for example, will play out in different ways when working with different groups of service users, as will decisions about appropriate thresholds for intervention. Readers are thus given the opportunity to consider the different knowledge and skills required to work across various relevant areas of practice, and case examples will demonstrate the multi-disciplinary and ethically challenging nature of this work. The particular user groups discussed in Part 2 represent some of those likely to be subject to safeguarding concerns, but this is not an exhaustive list. There are highly relevant areas of safeguarding practice, including work with older people, substance misuse and intimate partner violence, which are referred to only briefly here and require further exploration. Neither should it be assumed that all adults in the groups covered in this volume are at risk of harm or likely to be subject to safeguarding. Indeed the discriminatory nature of such assumptions is one of the themes that run throughout the Chapters.

Readers are invited to take messages from each Chapter and consider how these might apply to their own professional contexts. To this end, each Chapter draws on rich case study material taken directly from the authors' own practice or personal experience and ends with implications for practice. While each Chapter shares the aim of encouraging readers to use this material to make sense of the key issues within each Chapter, the way in which the case study material is presented within each Chapter depends very much on the authors' own backgrounds.

One of the primary aims of this volume was to have relevance to a diverse audience, including service users and carers, students, practitioners and academics alike. Spanning the four countries of the UK, the authors bring knowledge and expertise of adult safeguarding across a range of service user groups and disciplines. While their own work and experiences may be situated within a particular country or with a particular service user group, their contributions to the volume have applicability across the jurisdictions. One consequence of seeking views from a wide range of contributors is that the book presents a multiplicity of opinion on the question of safeguarding and on issues relating to personal and professional experiences, and the service user groups discussed. As such, the definitions and language used in the Chapters often reflect profession-specific or personal perspectives, and the editors have welcomed this diversity rather than seeking to work from agreed terms or meanings. Thus, ideas about highly contested terms, including disability, ageing and mental health and distress may be read as reflecting the respective writers' particular sets of knowledge and values, including the degree to which they encapsulate social or medical models of disability.

That said, we have taken several noteworthy decisions in relation to terminology. The term 'vulnerable adults' has been rejected on the grounds that it places the locus for potential harm with the individual rather than within the wider social context that surrounds them. In Scotland, the preferred terminology refers to 'adults at risk of harm' and this is gaining currency across other jurisdictions. Conversely, the term 'adult protection', which is used in Scotland, is less common in England, Wales and Northern Ireland, perhaps reflecting discomfort with overtones of paternalism or being considered too narrow for the consideration of such a broad legislative and practice framework. Instead, in these jurisdictions, 'adult safeguarding' is the given definition and consequently is the one used predominantly throughout the text; where authors have chosen to use 'adult protection' for specific reasons, this has been left unchanged. This discussion on terminology helps encapsulate the potential benefits of each country learning from one another in relation to aspects of adult safeguarding as practices, laws and policies develop over time. It also illustrates the consistent process of change that this hitherto neglected area of practice is now engaged in, which this volume seeks to contribute to in critically reflective and reflexive ways. A brief synopsis of each Chapter is now provided, drawing out particular and shared themes that will hopefully be of value to the reader.

In Chapter 2, Ailsa Stewart and Gillian MacIntyre introduce the reader to some of the key concepts of relevance in any discussion of adult safeguarding across the UK. These include 'power', 'choice', 'vulnerability', 'harm', 'abuse' and risk. They argue that the reader should appreciate the contested and potentially discriminatory nature of these concepts. They draw on a range of academic literature in order to provide the reader with the conceptual underpinnings for the remainder of the book. They argue that those adults who are most likely to be subject to safeguarding measures are also most likely to experience power imbalances and structural inequalities and are less likely to be deemed to have capacity to make their own choices and decisions. They warn against making judgements about people's capacity based on a simple label or diagnosis and highlight the need to take the individual's broader social context into account when making decisions with regard to safeguarding. They discuss the concept of risk and highlight the shift towards an increasingly risk-averse society where the focus is on making defensible decisions. They draw on research that suggests a risk enablement approach is required to overcome potentially paternalistic approaches to safeguarding. The Chapter ends with a number of key questions or dilemmas for the reader to consider during the remainder of the book.

A core tension within adult safeguarding, that of upholding individual rights to autonomy while also protecting citizens from harm, forms the central debate of Chapter 3, written by Kathryn Mackay. It poses key questions about and explores the scope of State responsibilities for the care and protection of citizens and how these are influenced by society, the media and, increasingly, by the marketisation of health and social care. It helpfully delineates the distinctive features and benefits of safeguarding legislation across the UK and NI before providing analysis of the varied responses citizens might expect to receive depending on where they live. It thus contextualises adult safeguarding within wider political ideology, critiquing the myopic responses of governments to failures in protecting people from harm and questioning what safeguarding can actually encompass in increasingly individualised societies.

In Chapter 4, Ailsa Stewart and Gillian MacIntyre explore the complex and challenging area of safeguarding where the capacity of the adult is unclear or unknown. Concepts such as capacity and bounded rationality are drawn upon to consider the demanding and ethically complex decisions that practitioners are required to make. This discussion is situated with a UK safeguarding context and draws on relevant legislative and

policy frameworks to identify a spectrum of possible thresholds for intervention. The promotion of the human and citizenship rights of adults
is central to the exploration of how practitioners make determinations
about those thresholds for intervention within safeguarding practice.
The potential for conflict between the aims of the legislation and the promotion of these rights is therefore a key area for discussion. Case studies
are used to draw out learning for practitioners and to illustrate some of
the challenges in practice. The Chapter concludes by underscoring the
importance of a safeguarding framework that is flexible and interactive in
nature to ensure that ethically appropriate practice is promoted.

Chapter 5, written by Kaye McGregor, Eileen Niblo and Michael
Preston-Shoot, sets the scene for many of the volume's discussions by
addressing one of the key themes within adult safeguarding, that of multi-
disciplinary working. It compares the policy and legal frameworks that
relate to how agencies work together to safeguard adults from harm across
the UK, highlighting gaps that have been found to impede effective practice. The discussion identifies training, operational practice and strategic
leadership as central to developing more effective multi-disciplinary
working. It then uses a case study to explore these and other related factors
that convey the 'messy realities' and uncertainties that are encountered
in much of adult safeguarding practice. The case study illustrates that
despite these difficulties, effective multi-disciplinary working, including
shared ownership of decision making and imaginative thinking that goes
beyond conventional resource delivery, can help facilitate better outcomes for adults at risk of harm.

Chapter 6, written by Jim Campbell, Gavin Davidson and Graham
Morgan, considers issues around safeguarding those with mental distress.
The Chapter begins by setting out the legislative context across the four
countries of the UK, identifying points of similarity and difference in relation to compulsory measures, including the use of community treatment
orders alongside the range of patient safeguards including mental health
tribunals, access to independent advocacy, advance statements or directives and the role of the 'named person' (outlined in the Mental Health
(Care and Treatment) (Scotland) Act 2003). The Chapter also considers
the complex issue of impaired capacity as a result of mental distress and
considers the extent to which individuals are supported to make decisions
in line with the CRPD. The various legislative frameworks that support
or impede the supported decision-making process are considered, and a
proposal for a unified mental health and capacity framework in line with
developments in Northern Ireland is discussed. The Chapter also explores
the views of people with experience of mental distress around detention,
capacity and safeguarding highlighting an acknowledgement of the need
for compulsory measures in certain circumstances.

Chapter 7, written by Claire Pearson and Martin Kettle, considers some of the particular issues around safeguarding older adults. Beginning with a review of research evidence, it highlights the complexity of relationships that may often be felt as both abusive and caring, which presents particular ethical challenges for professionals in striking a balance between protection from harm and the potential erosion of key personal and social supports. Acknowledging a dearth of research relating to older people abuse, it then reports on findings from a focus group carried out-with carers, providing rich and honest insights into the lived experiences of caring set against the legal framework. A particular finding problematises the breadth of definitions and cultural appreciations of 'harm', making it very difficult to differentiate between behaviours that might be considered 'understandable reactions' to the stresses that invariably arise in the caring role and those that overstep a legally delineated boundary. The Chapter concludes with a number of recommendations that may inform safeguarding interventions, including the role of motivation as a potential means of classifying harm, by differentiating between malice of forethought and actions that have no ill-intent.

Chapter 8, written by Robert Jenkins and Alan Middleton, considers adult safeguarding as it relates to people with learning disabilities. It addresses assumptions of 'vulnerability' in this context, acknowledging the potential for discrimination by adopting paternalistic approaches, whilst at the same time highlighting the greater risk of abuse people with learning disabilities face compared with the general population. It contextualises these and other related notions in a series of case studies, which serve to illustrate the challenges adults with learning disabilities face in having their rights to safety upheld. It also considers the organisational and cultural barriers that impede professionals in carrying out their related legal and professional responsibilities in ethically sound ways. The case studies convey the day-to-day dilemmas encountered by people who provide support to adults with learning disabilities, which in some instances may involve reaching a 'least worst' outcome. They discuss a number of key ethical issues, including sexuality, sexual health and the right to have children that are often poorly addressed in supporting adults with learning disabilities to lead fulfilling lives. Throughout, the case studies underscore the importance of adopting supported decision-making approaches with adults with learning disabilities in developing safeguarding arrangements that meet their self-identified needs. The discussion ends with recommendations that should enable professionals to critically review practices and identify anti-oppressive approaches to communication and intervention with people with learning disabilities.

In Chapter 9 Pearse McCusker and Jackie Jackson explore safeguarding as it relates to adults experiencing self-harm and/or suicidal behaviours.

It considers the question of whether these life experiences, which are often linked to wider social, economic or health factors, should fall under the ambit of safeguarding law. It sets out policy initiatives designed to reduce suicide and self-harm across the UK and NI and draws upon a range of research, including adult protection committee reports in Scotland, to explore the prevalence of suicide and self-harm and some of the particular barriers facing service users and professionals in finding humane and accessible ways of responding to experiences of distress. The Chapter also reports on findings from a multi-disciplinary focus group, highlighting the particular needs of people who frequently present with self-harming and/ or suicidal behaviours, and acknowledges links between this and personality disorder. It explores some of the themes raised therein through a case study and illustrates how effective multi-agency working, combined with informed understandings of the origins of trauma, can help develop more humanitarian services and helpful professional responses.

Chapter 10, written by Andrew Molodynski and Frank Reilly, pays particular attention to the question of adult safeguarding in institutional contexts, further exploring and allowing comparison with this subject as raised in Chapters 7 and 8. It highlights some of the serious failings in adult safeguarding across a range of institutions in recent years and identifies the key types of abuse that have taken place. In seeking to learn from these failures in care, it outlines a series of approaches for militating against institutional abuses occurring at organisational, cultural and individual professional levels, in turn providing a very helpful checklist for agencies and practitioners to assess current working practices.

The conclusion to the volume draws out common themes across the preceding Chapters and considers their significance for the future development of adult safeguarding practice.

References

Department of Health, Social Services and Public Safety (DHSSPS). (2015) *Adult Safeguarding: Prevention and Protection in Partnership*, Belfast: DHSSPS. Available at https://www.health-ni.gov.uk/sites/default/files/publications/dhssps/adult-safeguarding-policy.pdf.

Law Commission for England and Wales. (2017) *Mental Capacity and Deprivation of Liberty Summary*, London: HMSO.

Local Government Association. (2014) *Making Safeguarding Personal: Guide 2014*, London: LGA.

Social Care Institute for Excellence (SCIE). (2015) *At a Glance 43: The Deprivation of Liberty Safeguards*. Available at http://www.scie.org.uk/publications/ataglance/ataglance43.asp.

Spandler, H., Anderson, J. and Sapey, B. (eds) (2015) *Madness, Distress and the Politics of Disablement,* Bristol: Policy Press.

Stewart, A. (2016) *The Implementation of the Adult Support and Protection (Scotland) Act (2007)*, Glasgow: University of Glasgow.

The Supreme Court. (2014) *JUDGEMENT: P (by his litigation friend the Official Solicitor) (Appellant) v Cheshire West and Chester Council and another (Respondents); P and Q (by their litigation friend, the Official Solicitor) (Appellants) v Surrey County Council (Respondent).* Available at https://www.supremecourt.uk/decided-cases/docs/UKSC_2012_0068_Judgment.pdf.

United Nations. (2006) *United Nations Convention on the Rights of Persons with Disabilities.* Available at http://www.un.org/disabilities/convention/convention.shtml.

PART 1

Safeguarding Adults: Theoretical Perspectives

2

Safeguarding Adults: Key Issues and Concepts

Ailsa Stewart and Gillian MacIntyre, University of Strathclyde

The expectation of care, treatment, support and protection for those unable or unwilling to secure or seek it for themselves is a fundamental right in a civilised society (Stewart, 2016; Ash, 2015). The way in which society supports individuals to secure this right either individually or through state intervention is the basis for many actions under adult safeguarding. This broad area of policy and legislation is therefore an acknowledgement by governments that they have a duty towards adults who may be at risk of harm and who may be unable to safeguard themselves due to a variety of factors including poor mental health, cognitive impairment, disability or physical infirmity (Greenfields et al., 2012; Johns, 2007; SCIE, 2006). The acceptance and language of this requirement in the social policy and legislative landscape of the UK gained particular currency with the election of the New Labour administration in 1997 when more detailed consideration of vulnerability, risk, harm and safeguarding became commonplace (Ash, 2015). A re-evaluation of this discourse has taken place over the last five years resulting in greater consideration of the relationship between the individual and the State and a potential limitation or withdrawal of the State's intervention in the lives of its citizens as part of the drive towards self-care and self-management (Ash, 2015). Adult safeguarding is therefore an evolving and dynamic area of practice that often reflects the prevailing political ideology with regard to the extent to which individual rights and responsibilities promote or negate the requirement for state intervention.

What is adult safeguarding?

Adult safeguarding can be considered a continuum concerned with a range of functions and criteria (Mandelstam, 2009). Safeguarding is consequently a broad term used across the UK, although not extensively

in Scotland (see below) to encompass a variety of procedures and interventions for adults who require support to protect themselves (Mackay,
2011). The term has also been used to include adults who require different levels of intervention from community care support services, from
home care support to compulsory measures such as detention in hospital,
without their consent, for medical and therapeutic treatment (Ash, 2015).
This is reflected in the Law Commission (2011: 109) definition, which
delineates between safeguarding and protection by suggesting that adult
safeguarding is part of a general approach to assessment and service delivery while adult protection focuses on the action taken to intervene and
investigate when abuse or harm are identified.

Adults can therefore be subject to safeguarding under a range of legislation and policy, for example the Mental Capacity Act 2005 (MCA) in
England and Wales, the Mental Health Act 2007 (MHA) in England and
Wales and the Care Act 2014 (CA) in England, and this term has encompassed activity to protect adults at risk of harm and/or abuse either from
themselves or others. Safeguarding could also be used to describe actions
under the three key pieces of legislation in Scotland that correspond with
the English legislation. Those adults who lack capacity are considered
under the Adults with Incapacity (Scotland) Act 2000 (AWIA), those with
mental disorder under the Mental Health (Care and Treatment) (Scotland)
Act 2003 (MHCTSA) and those adults who are determined to be at risk of
harm under the Adult Support and Protection (Scotland) Act 2007 (ASPA)
although at times these legislative avenues can overlap and interact
(Keenan, 2012; Calder, 2010). Corresponding legislation in Wales is the
Social Services and Well-being (Wales) Act 2014. In Northern Ireland, an
integrated policy and legislative framework has emerged encompassing all
aspects of care, support, protection and treatment currently reflected in
the *Adult Safeguarding: Prevention and Protection in Partnership* policy document (DHSSPS, 2015), alongside other relevant guidance. The finer detail
of these frameworks and the distinctions between them are discussed
throughout this volume. It is appropriate here, however, to consider what
is meant in the UK by the term adult safeguarding.

Defining adult safeguarding

Contemporary adult safeguarding frameworks across the UK have
been driven by a combination of factors. These include a number of
high-profile cases of harm and abuse, either perpetrated by or experienced
by someone with a defined vulnerability or identified need for care and
treatment alongside the evolution of the community care agenda and
the increasing numbers of adults with support needs living within the

community (Mandelstam, 2009). This has included, for example, the Miss X case in Scotland (Scottish Executive, 2004) where a woman with learning disabilities was subject to physical and sexual assault over many years without being appropriately protected. Responses to the challenges presented by these issues have been underpinned by political ideology, the lobbying of interest groups and available resources. For example, New Labour acknowledged the State's responsibility to care for particular groups within society such as those experiencing mental distress; this, combined with lobbying by interest groups such as the disability movement to support community interventions for those experiencing specific conditions, influenced the development of the existing framework (Ash, 2015). As resources have diminished during times of austerity, a focus on self-care and self-management alongside a shift in political ideology (influenced by the growth of neo-liberalism that considered the welfare state as inefficient, ineffective and paternalistic) has developed, although the extent of this influence differs across the UK with devolved government.

Adult safeguarding frameworks across the UK therefore vary and are based on both policy and legislative responses to the *'problem'* of how to ensure adults are provided with care, treatment, support and protection when required. Ash (2015) has argued that in England, Wales and Northern Ireland the term adult safeguarding is used to denote a broad focus on an individual's welfare and the prevention of harm and abuse. In Scotland, however, the term adult support and protection is more commonly used to denote the prevention of harm and abuse (Mantell and Scragg, 2008), a much narrower focus. The focus within this volume is the former, considering an umbrella approach to safeguarding adults that encompasses a range of interventions and legislation as noted in the introduction.

In exploring the evolution of adult safeguarding, therefore, it is appropriate to make distinctions between those who require care and treatment and those who require support and protection. This is not to suggest that there is no overlap between these groups, and often people require an integrated approach (Ash, 2015) (see also Chapter 6 in this volume). Different groups with different needs will therefore require different safeguarding approaches to protect their interests, ranging from the provision of support with daily living tasks to supported and substitute decision making and compulsory treatment for those in need of care and treatment. To illustrate this continuum it is useful to consider what is often termed the triangle or hierarchy of protection in Scotland, which has different tariffs of intervention across the three legislative frameworks, outlined above. The triangle shape reflects the different levels of tariff, with the interventions that determine the most coercive treatment for the smallest group of people at the pinnacle (Figure 2.1).

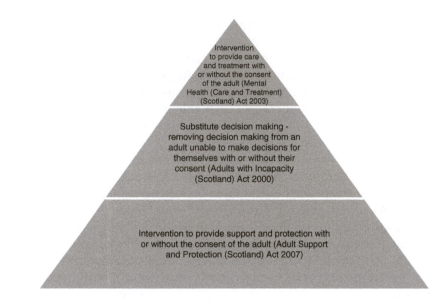

Figure 2.1   Triangle of protection (Mackay, 2012)

Adult safeguarding can therefore be viewed as a continuum or hierarchy of possible interventions available to provide a range of health
and welfare interventions to a broadly defined group of adults likely to
include older people, people with learning disabilities, people with physical disabilities and people with mental health problems. It should be
noted however that belonging to one of these groups does not automatically mean that someone will be at risk of harm.

Key concepts within adult safeguarding

A number of key concepts interact within adult safeguarding, and an understanding of each alongside an understanding of the impact they have on each
other is essential in exploring the main challenges within this area of practice.

Power

The nature and use of power within neo-liberal societies which reject the
notion of state intervention at the expense of individual responsibility
such as the UK has been the subject of significant academic discourse
(see, for example, Giddens and Sutton, 2013; Foucault, 1984; Lukes,
1974) and is considered a universal phenomenon reflected in almost all
forms of human interaction (Harrison, 2010). Power has been defined

variously but with key tenets consistent throughout, including the capacity to modify the conduct of individuals through the use of punishment or rewards (Sayce, 2016; Ash, 2015). The use of power is therefore linked to many other central concepts in understanding how society organizes and manages its citizens, such as choice, vulnerability and harm (Giddens and Sutton, 2013). The relationship between these various concepts and how they interact with one another is important in the consideration of human situations and in particular the extent to which adult safeguarding can be imposed upon citizens and the potential abuses of power within any process. Power is not merely embedded in social structures; rather it can be described as a network entrenched in individual belief systems that incorporate all aspects of daily life (Foucault, 1984). Citizens develop their own constructs of what is normal and abnormal, and this can influence society as a whole depending upon their individual authority.

Lukes (1974) in his influential work on power discusses the three faces of power whereby face one suggests that the person who wins the debate or argument has power. In faces two and three attention is given to those who have the power to set the agenda hence influencing what is debated or discussed in the first place and those who are in a position to influence or manipulate the views of others thus having most power. Arguably one function of government is to use power to set laws and exert authority on behalf of its citizens. Weber (1922, cited in Giddens and Sutton, 2013) defined power as the ability to control others despite their opposition, with the most direct form of power being coercion. In the context of adult safeguarding, Pilgrim (2014) notes that care imposed on an individual can be considered coercive and a potential abuse of power.

Discourse surrounding power relations has largely focused on how this knowledge can help us explain and understand the oppression of certain groups within society (Webb, 2006), based on race, gender and disability for example. The concept of relational power on the other hand focuses on how people use their power to influence the behaviour of others through their social relationships (Arendt, 1971). This is important in considering adult safeguarding and the right of the State to intervene in the lives of its citizens. By attributing inherent characteristics to a group of adults to construct a definition, in this case of vulnerability, the power and consequent authority of the State is used to shape the lives of a group of its citizens involving the use of coercion where necessary.

Choice

Bandura (2001) has argued that the essence of humanness is having the power and capacity to control the nature and quality of one's life and consequently to make appropriate choices to affect that life. He posited that the interaction between human and personal agency means people are producers as well as products of social systems, feeding into societal structures and being influenced by and becoming products of those same structures. His social cognitive theory distinguishes between three modes of agency: 'direct personal agency, proxy-agency that relies on others to act on one's behest to secure desired outcomes, and collective agency exercised through socially coordinated and interdependent effort' (Bandura, 2001: 13). To be an agent requires intentionally making things happen through individual action. The essential aspects of agency enable individuals to play a part in their own development and change over time, for example securing rights and undertaking responsibilities. We can make links here to the continuum of support and protection discussed above by considering the inter-dependent nature of supported decision making for example, or the ways in which people make decisions on behalf of someone subject to compulsory care and treatment.

Harre (1983) has suggested that it is not people but their constituent parts, particularly their psychological processes, that orchestrate their courses of action including the choices they make in the world. For human beings to effectively navigate a complex world full of challenges, they require the ability to make realistic judgements about their own capabilities, anticipating the consequences of different events and courses of action. They need to be able to evaluate opportunities and challenges and adjust their behaviours accordingly. The ability to develop and effectively use reflective capabilities is imperative for human progress and in particular to promote protection of the individual. Therefore those unable to exercise choice and understand their actions and their consequences are more likely to be subject to adult safeguarding measures such as substitute or supported decision making or some form of care and treatment.

Decision making

> Without a phenomenal and functional consciousness people are essentially higher-level automatons undergoing actions devoid of any subjectivity or conscious control. Nor do such beings possess a meaningful phenomenal life or a continuing self-identity derived from how they live their life and reflect upon it.
>
> (Bandura, 2001: 3)

As noted above power is often exerted through decision making and authority, which also exhibits choice; these three concepts are consequently inextricably linked. Underpinning the ability to exert one's power and affect choice is the decision-making process. Decision making involves various elements of cognitive functioning. It brings together the ability to assess a situation, decide on a course of action and to implement the action required to reach the goal. This requires a level of cognitive functioning, which it has been argued changes across the life-course, arguably making those in later life or those experiencing significant life disruptions such as mental distress less able to make rational choices (Stewart, 2016; Rowe et al., 2012). Of course, this is a contentious and potentially discriminatory viewpoint and recent work around the implementation of the United Nation Convention on the Rights of Persons with Disabilities (UNCRPD) for example aims to challenge this. The UNCRPD can be viewed as a statute signalling a paradigm shift in conferring equal human rights and fundamental freedoms on all people with disabilities. Of particular relevance to adult safeguarding, capacity and mental health laws are Articles 12 and 14. Article 12 enshrines equal recognition before the law (i.e. that people with disabilities have legal capacity on an equal basis with others in all aspects of life), which confers a duty on countries to provide people with disabilities with adequate support to ensure they can exercise their rights. Article 14 refers to the liberty and security of people with disabilities and stipulates that the existence of disability alone cannot justify deprivation of liberty.

Substitute decision-making legislation in the UK includes within its definition of incapacity the ability to make, communicate, remember and understand the consequences of decisions, linking the two concepts. There are specific tests in law (MCA, 2005; AWIA, 2000) that must be carried out to establish capacity where it is in doubt. Using these definitions, a legal decision can be reached that an adult lacks capacity to make decisions and empowers someone else to make decisions for them, having proxy-agency. Legal capacity, however defined, to make decisions about one's own life can be the difference between having State-sponsored intrusion in one's life or not (Stewart, 2012). By removing an element of choice for adults through the introduction of a compulsory element to the provision of care, treatment, support and protection of adults, it could be argued that a paternalistic approach has been adopted. This suggests that the intervention of the State in the life of an adult, without their consent, defended or motivated by a claim that the intervention ensures that the adult will be cared for, supported or protected from harm, is acceptable. Indeed, proponents of a libertarian approach (focused on a belief of free will for all) to paternalism (for example, Thaler and Sunstein, 2003) view it as inevitable and desirable that public institutions will influence the behaviour of individuals, while also respecting their freedom or choice. They argue that intervention is unavoidable where opinions and decisions are ill informed or influenced by external factors, as could be illustrated by many adults subject to adult safeguarding procedures.

Yet all adults make decisions at some point over the life-course that may be considered ill informed. However, it is the ability of the State to intervene to challenge these decisions or ameliorate their consequences that distinguishes those likely to be subject to safeguarding measures from the rest of the population (Sherwood-Johnson, 2013).

Vulnerability

Vulnerability is a contested concept with a variety of interpretations (Daniel and Bowes, 2010). As all adults may be considered vulnerable at various points throughout the life-course (Beckett, 2006), this universality needs to be considered within any definition. Sherwood-Johnson (2013) created three categories of concern with regard to vulnerability; firstly, the debate over definition; secondly, to whom it is applied; and thirdly, the use of the term vulnerable as an exclusionary term given the potential for all adults to be deemed vulnerable at some point in their life, as explored by Beckett (2006).

Discourse regarding vulnerability has often been concerned with the definition of the term: for instance, whether it describes a particular individual or the situation within which the individual may be living (Wishart, 2003), or whether it can be conflated with prejudice and hate in explaining crime against disabled people (Roulstone et al., 2011). Brown (2011) explored a concern that the term vulnerable can be used by professionals and indeed policy makers to describe individuals without a clear understanding of the definition they are drawing upon. This has significant implications for individuals given that there can be both practical and personal consequences to being judged to be vulnerable in a range of particular contexts (Roulstone et al., 2011). Harbison et al. (2012), for example, noted that assuming that all older people are vulnerable creates a stigmatised perception of the capacity of older people.

Fineman (2008) argued that it is unrealistic to develop policies based on an invulnerable, rational citizen with different policies for those who do not meet this standard, as this does not reflect the human experience. In particular, the likelihood that different situations and circumstances across the life-course are likely to make someone vulnerable suggests that vulnerability should be considered to be a fluid state (Daniel and Bowes, 2010; Beckett, 2006). There are strong parallels here with ideas about inter-dependence and an ethic of care, which have been drawn upon to challenge conceptions of autonomy and independence that underpin a variety of UK social policies (Anderson and Honneth, 2009; Ferguson, 2007). In addition, perspectives arising from the independent living movement and the social model of disability suggest that disability is caused by the way society is organised, rather than by a person's impairment or difference (Kittay, 1999; Reindal, 1999).

Some theorists have considered the ways in which vulnerability can be differentiated from harm and exploitation (Goodin, 1985). Goodin (1985) for example, argued that it is the perceived vulnerability of any adult that results in the provision of support in whatever form, rather than a voluntary commitment from the adult. Welfare provision provided on a society-wide, universal basis is a way of discharging broader State responsibilities in a more morally acceptable dependency relationship as it means that particular individuals are less likely to be singled out and labelled, thus reducing the potential for stigma and discrimination. This is reflected in the development of legal provision which has extended to include not just those who lack mental capacity but those who may be under duress or whose decisions may be viewed as endangering them or others, as in the ASPA in Scotland (Sherwood-Johnson, 2012).

Alongside this, the association of vulnerability with some 'inherent' factors has itself been challenged. Hasler (2004) argued that being ascribed as vulnerable has led to an association with the need for professional 'care'. Many people with disabilities have rejected these arguments in respect of the need for State intervention and in particular safeguarding (Hough, 2012; Hollomotz, 2009; Wishart, 2003) and have been particularly critical about being categorised as vulnerable and/or in need of care, treatment, support and protection, because they associate this with deficit, paternalism and stigma (Brown, 2011). It can also be argued that vulnerability has a significant subjective component (Spiers, 2000), and that people's own views of themselves and their situations are relevant to its definition (Dunn et al., 2008).

The term vulnerable, as it is applied in adult safeguarding, can be viewed as vague yet all encompassing, limiting the choice of adults to make their own decisions. The importance of concepts of power, choice and capacity can clearly be seen in the way in which vulnerability is constructed and applied. Those who are considered vulnerable are likely to be those with little power, with limited choices available to them and whose capacity to make decisions is deemed questionable. Being labelled as vulnerable can therefore stigmatise the adult and lead to inappropriately paternalistic interventions. Fitzgerald (2008) argues that there is no such thing as a 'vulnerable' adult; that it is the circumstances, environment, opportunity and other people that invariably create vulnerability, thereby creating the potential for harm and abuse. Considering the use of language that may disempower adults (by eroding their rights as citizens, for example) is therefore clearly important in adult safeguarding.

Harm and abuse

Adult safeguarding policy and legislative frameworks developed around the concept of vulnerability inevitably take a deficit approach by instilling the vulnerability within the adult (Sherwood-Johnson, 2013). Protecting individuals from and supporting them to protect themselves from harm and abuse form the core of what contemporary health and social services aim to offer society. Johnson et al. (2010), in a review of literature which used a comparative lifespan approach to harm and abuse, noted that comparisons between abuse of older people and children were more likely to take place rather than between older people and those experiencing domestic violence. This may be due to parallel concerns about levels of inherent vulnerability accepted in older people and children, whereas those most likely to experience domestic violence or intimate partner violence appeared to be made vulnerable by external factors. Viewing older adults as inherently vulnerable and therefore in need of care and protection from harm and abuse in the same way as children can be viewed as potentially discriminatory, as discussed above.

The importance of resilience (defined by Rutter, 1987, as the mechanisms that protect people from the psychological risks associated with adversity) as a protective factor in preventing harm and/or abuse in adults has also been the subject of academic discourse, although this has principally been focused on work with children (Rolf and Johnson, 1999). This is not to suggest that those adults who demonstrate resilience do not experience challenges in dealing with adversity, rather that they have effective ways of coping with challenges (Klohnen, 1996). Diel and Hay (2010) outlined the importance of resilience for adults in dealing with daily stress. Coping does not, however, necessarily equate with an ability to protect oneself, and there is limited evidence to suggest that those who demonstrate resilience in their daily living are more able to protect themselves from harm and abuse. Friborg and colleagues (2003) did, however, include resilience amongst the protective factors that aid in the prevention of psychiatric disturbance.

Definitions of abuse remain contested, and there have been suggestions that we need different definitions for different areas, for example for care management, research and legislation (Bennett et al., 1997). Brown (2003: 5) argued that the dynamics of abuse are complex and that the factors to be considered include:

> ➤ 'the nature (and underlying intent) of the relationship between the potential abuser and the "at risk" adult; for example, the process of "grooming" in respect of a vulnerable adult;

> the process used to gain and maintain access to the vulnerable adult; for example, a perpetrator using the workplace to gain access to "at risk" adults;

> the degree or severity of the harm to the vulnerable adult (including psychological elements);

> the degree of continuing risk to the vulnerable adult or other "at risk" adults in the setting; for example, when an accused member of staff continues to have access to the vulnerable adult;

> situations where there might be multiple components of vulnerability; for example, sexual abuse between service users;

> the need to consider the situation where a conflict of interest might occur; for example, where an attorney may be connected to a family member and have their objectivity compromised.'

(Brown, 2003: 5)

Agreement on what constitutes abuse is therefore unlikely to be universal or to remain static, given the fluid nature of acceptable and unacceptable behaviours (Stewart, 2011). Our understanding of abuse and abusive behaviour is also likely to be affected by local and cultural factors, including existing practice and procedures; consequently, a range of definitions are inevitable (Penhale et al., 2000). Having a fixed definition of abuse could in fact be considered to be unhelpful and inappropriate if it does not reflect contemporary societal norms, although how likely this is to be achieved is questionable.

The terms abuse and harm can be considered linked but also separate across the safeguarding continuum. In the ASPA in Scotland, for example, the term harm is preferred to abuse, given the subtle differences in intentionality associated with both terms (with abuse being viewed as intentional, while harm can potentially be perpetrated unintentionally). Sherwood-Johnson (2012) noted some considerable challenges with this change of terminology and argued that the ASPA continues to make unhelpful and stigmatising assumptions about disabled people, older people and people with mental health problems. She argued that including within the three-point test for intervention under the ASPA (Section 3(i)) the terms disabled people, older people and people experiencing mental disorder could perpetuate discriminatory and stigmatizing views about these groups.

Risk and thresholds of intervention

Underpinning all of the discussions above around power, capacity, choice, vulnerability and abuse is the concept of risk. Arguably one's understanding of this concept and the extent to which it can be applied to an individual or group will directly influence the extent to which any intervention into that individual's life or the lives of the group members can be justified or otherwise. Yet, like all of the other concepts introduced in this Chapter, risk is a socially constructed and contested notion. According to Stalker (2003) there is no universally agreed definition of risk, although it is often used to refer to undesirable events or outcomes with Warner suggesting that it refers to a 'particular adverse event [that] occurs during a stated period of time or results from a particular challenge' (1992: 2, cited in Stalker, 2003: 213). Stalker also suggests that understandings of risk vary according to the service user group being discussed, arguing that risk is often equated to vulnerability for older adults or people with learning disabilities but is more often associated with danger in discussions around offenders or those who use mental health services.

According to Stalker (2003) there are a number of different ways in which risk can be understood and conceptualised. Drawing on the work of Jaeger et al. (2001) she argues that a scientific approach to risk based on probability calculations assumes that risk is something objective that can be measured using psychometric risk assessment tools based on rational behaviour theory. Beck (1992) on the other hand argues that risk is something that is socially constructed. In his seminal work on the 'risk society', he has argued that society is no longer stratified along traditional lines of class, gender and so on (although these are still relevant) but instead can best be understood in terms of the ability that one has to negotiate risk. Those with greater resources to draw on in terms of social and cultural capital as well as those with a high number of protective factors are more able to negotiate risk successfully. It follows that those who have traditionally been marginalised, such as those with learning disabilities or mental health problems who therefore have less social and cultural capital and other protective factors to draw on, are more likely to experience risk adversely and therefore are more likely to be viewed as needing protection. Beck (1992) argues that society has become increasingly risk averse and preoccupied with reducing the likelihood of risk by introducing more sophisticated ways of predicting its probability. The result, in this context, has been the introduction of a range of statutory measures aimed at reducing risk and therefore protecting those individuals perceived to be vulnerable from harm.

Conversely, while this notion of a 'risk society' and increasingly risk-averse culture has been used to legitimise state intervention in the lives of its most marginalised citizens, the concept of risk has also been closely associated with neo-liberalism and the corresponding shrinkage of state responsibility for individuals and families. Indeed, Ferguson (2007) has argued that neo-liberalism has resulted in 'privatisation by the back door' whereby individuals and families are increasingly responsible for managing risk for themselves. This, Ferguson contends, is something that would previously have been considered the responsibility of the State (Ferguson, 2007) and of social work in particular. Neo-liberalism has resulted in the development of a culture whereby individuals are blamed for failing to protect themselves from risk should they get into difficulties. This is closely linked to greatly reduced budgets during times of austerity, which has resulted in services being targeted at those most in need via the introduction of ever stricter eligibility criteria. In these circumstances, need is often associated with those considered to be most at risk (Ferguson, 2007). For those who use mental health services in particular this often involves consideration of those deemed to be a risk to others as well as to themselves (Pilgrim and Rogers, 1999).

Despite this retraction of state responsibility, professionals find themselves increasingly focused on risk assessment and risk management and this can create further complexity given that different professionals' understanding of risk is greatly influenced by their own professional training and background. Correspondingly, they also have different thresholds for intervention and differing understandings as to when it is appropriate to intervene in the life of an individual. Decision making in this regard is largely determined by the undertaking of risk assessments, which assume that risk is something that can be viewed objectively and measured, as discussed above (Stalker, 2003). Critics of this approach suggest that an emphasis on using tools to measure risk has the potential to undermine professional judgement and decision making (O'Sullivan, 2010; Evans and Harris, 2004; Parton, 1996) as discussed more fully in Chapter 4 of this volume. Further, the shift from clinical to actuarial methods of risk assessment suggests that predictions of future risk can be made using statistical methods. Such an approach, while useful in many circumstances, clearly has the potential to be discriminatory and may result in overly restrictive interventions being introduced to manage or control behaviour. It certainly has the potential to contribute to the risk-averse culture that is arguably a dominant feature of many organisations currently (Mitchell and Glendinning, 2007).

While approaches to risk management vary across agencies and professions, in many cases practice has become increasingly defensive. Parton (1996) argues that making a *defensible* decision has become more important than making the *right* decision. Referring to social work, Stalker (2003) has suggested that in the literature, risk management is often characterised as the profession 'watching its own back'. This has resulted in an overly procedural approach being adopted whereby social workers have become more concerned with managing risk than with tackling social problems. This has been exacerbated by the many high-profile cases (usually involving children) where decision making by social workers (and other professionals) has been scrutinised and often found to be lacking. Serious case reviews and negative media coverage have thus generated a fear of being held responsible should an adverse outcome occur and, according to Stalker (2003), act as a strong disincentive to risk taking.

It can be argued therefore that current conceptualisations of risk and the consequent ways in which it is assessed have taken a very individualised approach which focus on shifting responsibility to the individual and blaming them for any increased risk. To counteract this, Stalker (2003) argues that a social model of risk is required. Drawing on the work of Gurney (2000) and Parsloe (1999) she argues that current approaches to risk focus on individual behaviour rather than the broader social, economic and political factors that can create or contribute to risk. Gurney (2000) argues that responsibility for risk taking and allocating blame when things go wrong varies according to how far risk is seen as being a result of social structures or is attributed to individual behaviour. Indeed, to avoid adopting an overly discriminatory approach, it would appear important to acknowledge the broader social context within which an individual operates and the likely impact this will have on risk. In addition, it would seem essential to avoid making decisions based purely on an individual's status as a particular type of 'service user'. For example, older people should not be prevented from taking risks purely on the basis of age, and those with learning disabilities should not be assumed as unable to make decisions for themselves as a result of their learning disability. Indeed, it is important to remember that risk taking can lead to many benefits and positive outcomes and can be an empowering experience for individuals, although the decision about acceptable and unacceptable levels of risk taking introduces another layer of complexity. For example, if taking a particular risk may be viewed as beneficial for one person but at the expense of another, decisions have to be made about whose outcome and whose aspirations are more important, resulting in a significant ethical dilemma (Stalker, 2003).

Discussion: dilemmas to consider throughout the book

It is hoped that this Chapter has raised for the reader a number of questions and dilemmas that should be kept in mind as they read the following Chapters. The central debate that runs throughout adult safeguarding work is the extent to which individual autonomy can be promoted at the same time as protecting that individual from harm, should that be required. Both of these values are important but are often difficult to merge. They raise a number of questions for practitioners for which there are no easy answers. As the reader progresses through this volume they might find it useful to bear the following questions in mind, alongside their own:

> How is vulnerability conceptualised and understood? To what extent is this based on individual characteristics or broader social and structural factors?

> Who decides which risks are acceptable and on what basis are these decisions being made?

> At what point does an individual's need for protection override their right to make choices?

> What power dynamics are at play and how do these impact on the decision-making process?

> Whose views should take precedence when there is a conflict of interest and how is this decided?

In addressing these questions it is important to consider the extent to which those individuals who are likely to be subject to adult safeguarding measures are involved in the decision-making process. Stalker (2003) advocates strongly for the rights of service users to be involved in decisions affecting their own life, but the extent to which this happens varies according to the nature and level of perceived risk and the perceived capacity of the individual to make decisions and understand their consequences. The 'right to take risks' has become increasingly prominent in discussions around risk. For example, a report published by the Joseph Rowntree Foundation in 2012 highlighted the view of service users that they should have the right to 'weigh up' the risks of undertaking a particular endeavour or activity, trying to find the balance between benefits and risks. All too often however, people felt excluded from this decision-making process and gave examples about not being included in assessments of risk. People felt that decisions were made without them and often by people not directly affected by the risk (Faulkner, 2012). This clearly has implications not only for the accuracy of any risk assessment undertaken but also on the dignity and rights of those involved. While legislation and policy across the four jurisdictions of the UK sets out the ways in which service users should be involved in decision-making processes, the likelihood of this occurring varies across jurisdictions and often by service user group. For those with experience of the criminal justice system for example, it is likely that the rights of victims and the public will always take priority over the rights of perpetrators (Kemshall and Pritchard, 1997), and with many examples of risk assessments not being shared with service users it can be difficult to see how meaningful involvement in the decision-making process can be promoted (Faulkner, 2012).

Likewise, for those service users with learning disabilities in particular, but also for those with mental health problems and older adults, questions can be raised about their ability to make choices that are in their best interests, prompting an often paternalistic approach to support. Decisions about capacity are clearly set out in legislation, as discussed earlier in this Chapter, and for those lacking in capacity, clear processes for substitute decision making are set out in statute. More recently, questions have been raised about the appropriateness of substitute decision making, particularly in the wake of the (UNCRPD), and there has been a shift towards a model of supported decision making, which, it can be argued, is more in line with principles of participation and service user involvement.

This model acknowledges individuals as experts in their own experience who have the right to make decisions about issues affecting their life. Individuals often have many years of experience of negotiating and managing risks in their lives and have likely developed their own coping strategies and identified a range of protective factors to draw on. These should be acknowledged during the decision-making process. This should be done in partnership with professionals who bring knowledge and expertise based on their own professional training and experience. Bringing these different sets of knowledge and expertise together requires the development of trusting relationships between those who use services and the professionals who support them. Developing these relationships is not without its challenges, and professional boundaries can often act as a barrier to developing meaningful relationships (Reamer, 2003). These challenges alongside the increasingly risk-averse culture in which professionals operate are likely to combine to create even greater distance between professionals and those who use services. Using the principles of co-production outlined by Molodynski and Reilly later in this volume might help to overcome these barriers promoting a more meaningful model of supported decision making.

Carr (2010) suggests that transformative change is required at an organisational level, incorporating a risk enablement approach into ongoing developments around self-directed support and safeguarding. She defines risk enablement as promoting independence, choice and control while at the same time balancing a duty of care and ensuring people stay safe. She suggests that:

> 'all risk enablement approaches should be person-centred focusing on the perspectives and understanding of the person using the service

> front line practitioners should be supported by organisational culture and systems that allow them to spend time with people and to focus on their safety concerns and achieving their chosen outcomes rather than going through unnecessary auditing processes

> personalisation and safeguarding policies need to be more closely aligned and inform each other. They should be underpinned by the principle of person-centred practice and the promotion of choice, control, independent living, autonomy and staying safe

> organisations need to foster a culture of positive risk taking that will support front line practitioners to work in a risk-enabling way with the person using the service

> duty of care decisions should be made in a shared and informed way, with transparent, shared responsibility'.

(Carr, 2010: vii)

Conclusion

This Chapter has aimed to introduce the reader to the key concepts of relevance in the world of adult safeguarding – namely power, choice, capacity, vulnerability, abuse and risk. During the course of the Chapter it will have become clear that this is a complex and dynamic area with many contested definitions and competing understandings. It will also have become apparent that the concepts are socially constructed and are likely to change over time and place. For example, our understanding of what makes someone vulnerable and consequently when it is appropriate or acceptable to intervene in their lives has changed over time. These understandings have been influenced by a range of political, economic and social factors including the shift from institutionalisation to community care and the recent financial crisis, which has led to an increase in eligibility criteria in an attempt to ration service provision.

The social construction of vulnerability and risk has significant consequences for those who are deemed to be so. For example, everyone makes decisions that at times can be considered foolish or which may have negative consequences or outcomes. However, it is only those who are deemed to be vulnerable or 'at risk' where it is viewed as legitimate to intervene. This is particularly harmful when whole groups of people are considered vulnerable on the basis of a particular characteristic such as age or learning disability, as it can lead to overly interventionist and risk-averse practice that can lead to stigma and discrimination. Instead it is more helpful to broaden our understanding to take a whole population approach that has as its starting point an acknowledgement that there is no such thing as a vulnerable adult. Rather it is people's situations – their broader social and political context combined with their individual characteristics and situations – that make them vulnerable.

Implications for practice

> A clear understanding is required of all possible options for adult safeguarding, using the breadth of legislation available. Constructing adult safeguarding as a continuum will aid in this process.

> Clarity over the conceptual framework used by staff for decision making will promote consistent decision making.

> Organisational guidance should be focused on thresholds for intervention to promote clarity and consistency of approach.

> Anti-discriminatory practice should be considered a key principle in implementing safeguarding approaches.

References

Anderson, J. and Honneth, A. (2009) 'Autonomy, vulnerability, recognition, and justice', in Christman, J. and Anderson, J. (eds), *Autonomy and the Challenges to Liberalism* (pp. 127–149), Cambridge: Cambridge University Press.

Arendt, H. (1971) Thinking and moral considerations. *Social Research,* 38(3): 417–446.

Ash, A. (2015) *Safeguarding Older People from Abuse: Critical Contexts to Policy and Practice*, Bristol: Policy Press.

Bandura, A. (2001) Social cognitive theory: An agentic perspective. *Annual Review of Psychology*, 51: 1–26.

Beck, U. (1992) *Risk Society: Towards a New Modernity*, London: SAGE.

Beckett, A. (2006) *Citizenship and Vulnerability: Disability and Issues of Social and Political Engagement*, Basingstoke: Palgrave Macmillan.

Bennett, G., Kingston, P. and Penhale, B. (1997) *The Dimensions of Elder Abuse: Perspectives for the Practitioner*, Basingstoke: Macmillan.

Brown, H. (2003) What is financial abuse? *The Journal of Adult Protection*, 5(2): 3–10.

Brown, H. (2011) The role of emotion in decision-making. *The Journal of Adult Protection*, 13(4): 194–202.

Calder, B. (2010) *A Guide to the Adult Support and Protection (Scotland) Act 2007*, Dundee: Dundee University Press.

Carr, C. (2010) *Enabling Risk: Ensuring Safety: Self-directed Support and Personal Budgets, SCIE Report 36*, London: SCIE.

Daniel, B. and Bowes, A. (2010) Re-thinking harm and abuse: Insights from a lifespan perspective. *British Journal of Social Work*, 41(5): 820–836.

Department of Health, Social Services and Public Safety (DHSSPS). (2015) *Adult Safeguarding: Prevention and Protection in Partnership,* Belfast: DHSSPS.

Diel, M. and Hay, E. (2010) Risk and resilience factors in coping with daily stress in adulthood: The role of age, self-concept incoherence, and personal control. *Developmental Psychology*, 46(5): 1132–1146.

Dunn, M., Clare, I. C. H. and Holland, A. J. (2008) To empower or to protect? Constructing the 'vulnerable adult' in English law and public policy. *Legal Studies*, 28(2): 234–253.

Evans, T. and Harris, J. (2004) Street-level bureaucracy, social work and the (exaggerated) death of discretion. *British Journal of Social Work*, 34(6): 871–895.

Faulkner, A. (2012) *The Right to Take Risks: Service Users Views of Risk in Adult Social Care,* York: Joseph Rowntree Foundation.

Ferguson, I. (2007) Increasing user choice or privatising risk? The antinomies of personalization. *British Journal of Social Work*, 37(3): 381–403.

Fineman, M. (2008) The vulnerable subject: Anchoring equality in the human condition. *Yale Journal of Law and Feminism*, 20(1): 1–23.

Fitzgerald, G. (2008) 'No Secrets, safeguarding adults and adult protection', in Pritchard, J. (ed.), *Good Practice in Safeguarding Adults*, London: Jessica Kingsley.

Foucault, M. (1984) *The Foucault Reader*, New York: Random House.

Friborg, O., Hjemdal, O., Rosenvinge, J. H. and Martinussen, M. (2003) A new rating scale for adult resilience: What are the central protective resources behind healthy adjustment? *International Journal of Psychiatric Research Methods*, 12(2): 65–76.

Giddens, A. and Sutton, A. (2013) *Sociology*, Cambridge: Polity Press.

Goodin, R. E. (1985) *Protecting the Vulnerable: A Re-analysis of Our Social Responsibilities*, Chicago: University of Chicago Press.

Greenfields, M., Dalrymple, R. and Fanning, A. (eds) (2012) *Working with Adults at Risk from Harm,* Maidenhead: Open University Press.

Gurney, A. (2000) 'Risk-taking', in Davis, M. (ed.), *The Blackwell Encyclopaedia of Social Work*, Oxford: Blackwell.

Harbison, J., McKinley, P. and Pettipas, D. (2012) Older people are subjects not objects: Reconsidering theory and practice in situations of elder abuse and neglect. A critique of assumptions underpinning responses to the mistreatment and neglect of older people. *Journal of Elder Abuse and Neglect*, 24(2): 88–103.

Harre, R. (1983) *Personal Being: A Theory for Individual Psychology*, Cambridge: Harvard University Press.

Harrison, B. (2010) *Power and Society: An Introduction to the Social Sciences* (13th edition), Boston: Thompson Higher Education.

Hasler, F. (2004) 'Disability, care and controlling services', in Swain, J., French, S., Barnes, C. and Thomas, C. (eds), *Disabling Barriers – Enabling Environments*, London: SAGE.

Hollomotz, A. (2009) Beyond vulnerability: An ecological model approach to conceptualizing risk of sexual violence against people with learning difficulties. *British Journal of Social Work*, 39(1): 99–112.

Hough, R. E. (2012) Adult protection and 'intimate citizenship' for people with learning difficulties: Empowering and protecting in light of the No Secrets review. *Disability and Society*, 27(1): 131–144.

Jaeger, C., Renn, O., Rosa, E., and Webler, T. (2001) *Risk, Uncertainty, and Rational Action*, London: Earthscan.

Johns, R. (2007) Who decides now? Protecting and empowering vulnerable adults who lose the capacity to make decisions for themselves. *British Journal of Social Work*, 37(3): 557–564.

Johnson, F., Hogg, J. and Daniel, B. (2010) Abuse and protection issues across the lifespan: Reviewing the literature. *Social Policy and Society*, 9(2): 291–304.

Keenan, T. (2012) *Crossing the Acts: The Support and Protection of Adults at Risk with Mental Disorder; Across the Scotish Legislative Frameworks*, Brimingham: Venture.

Kemshall, H., and Pritchard, J. (1997) *Good Practice in Risk Assessment and Risk Management 2*, London: Jessica Kingsley Publishers.

Kittay, E. (1999) *Love's Labor: Essays on Women, Equality and Dependency*, New York: Routledge.

Klohnen, E. C. (1996) Conceptual analysis and measurement of the construct of ego-resiliency. *Journal of Personality and Social Psychology*, 70: 1067–1079.

Law Commission. (2011) *Adult Social Care*, London: The Stationery Office.

Lukes, S. (1974) *Power: A Radical View*, London: Palgrave Macmillan.

Mackay, K. (2011) Compounding conditional citizenship: To what extent does Scottish and English mental health law increase or diminish social citizenship? *British Journal of Social Work*, 41(5): 931–948.

Mackay, K. (2012) A parting of the ways? The diverging nature of mental health social work in the light of the new Acts in Scotland, and in England and Wales. *Journal of Social Work*, 12(2): 179–193.

Mandelstam, M. (2009) *Safeguarding Vulnerable Adults and the Law*, London: Jessica Kingsley.

Mantell, A. and Scragg, T. (2008) *Safeguarding Adults in Social Work*, Exeter: Learning Matters.

Mitchell, W. and Glendinning, C. (2007) *A Review of the Research Evidence Surrounding Risk Perceptions, Risk Management Strategies and Their Consequences in Adult Social Care for Different Groups of Service Users*, Working Paper No. DHR 2180 01.07, York: University of York Social Policy Research Unit.

O'Sullivan, T. (2010) *Decision Making in Social Work*, Basingstoke: Palgrave Macmillan.

Parsloe, P. (1999) *Risk Assessment in Social Care and Social Work, Research Highlights in Social Work, Number 36*, London: Jessica Kingsley Publishing.

Parton, N. (1996) `Social work, risk and "The Blaming System"', in N. Parton (ed.), *Social Theory, Social Change and Social Work*, London: Routledge.

Penhale, B. and Parker, J. with Kingston, P. (2000) *Elder Abuse*, Birmingham: Venture Press.

Pilgrim, D. (2014) *Key Concepts in Mental Health,* London: SAGE.

Pilgrim, D. and Rogers, A. (1999) *A Sociology of Mental Health and Illness,* Buckingham: Open University Press.

Reamer, F. (2003) Boundary issues in social work: Managing dual relationships. *Social Work,* 48(1): 121–133.

Reindal, S. M. (1999) Independence, dependence, interdependence: Some reflections on the subject and personal autonomy. *Disability & Society*, 14(3): 353–367.

Rolf, J. and Johnson, J. (1999) 'Opening doors to resilience intervention for prevention research, in Glantz, M. and Johnson, J. (eds), *Resilience and Development. Longitudinal Research in the Social and Behavioral Sciences: An Interdisciplinary Series* (pp. 229–249), New York: Spring Science and Business Media.

Roulstone, A., Thomas, P. and Balderston, S. (2011) Between hate and vulnerability: Unpacking the British criminal justice system's construction of disablist hate crime. *Disability and Society*, 26(3): 351–364.

Rowe, M., Clayton, A., Benedict, P., Bellamy, C., Antunes, K., Miller, R., Pelletier, J. F., Stern, E. and O'Connell, M. J. (2012) Going to the source: Creating a citizenship outcome measure by community-based participatory research methods. *Psychiatric Services,* 63(5): 445–450.

Rutter, M. (1987) Psychosocial resilience and protective mechanisms, *American Journal of Orthopsychiatry,* 57(3): 316–331.

Sayce, L. (2016) *From Psychiatric Patient to Citizen Revisited*, London: Palgrave.

Scottish Executive. (2004) *Investigations into Scottish Borders Council and NHS Borders Services for People with Learning Disabilities: Joint Statement from the Mental Welfare Commission and the Social Work Services Inspectorate.* Available at http://www.gov.scot/Publications/2004/05/19333/36719 [accessed 29 September 2017].

Sherwood-Johnson, F. (2012) Problems with the term and concept of abuse: Critical reflections on the Scottish Adult Support and Protection study. *British Journal of Social Work*, 42(5): 833–850.

Sherwood-Johnson, F. (2013) Constructions of vulnerability in comparative perspective: Scottish protection policies and the trouble with 'adults at risk'. *Disability and Society*, 28(7): 908–921.

Social Care Institute for Excellence (SCIE). (2006) *Adult Services Practice Guide: Dignity in Care.* London: SCIE.

Spiers, J. (2000) New perspectives on vulnerability using emic and etic approaches. *Journal of Advanced Nursing*, 31(3): 715–721.

Stalker, K. (2003) Managing risk and uncertainty in social work : A literature review. *Journal of Social Work*, 3(2): 211–233.

Stewart, A. (2011) 'Adult protection in the UK: Key issues for early career social workers', in Taylor, R., Hill, M. and McNeil, F. (eds), *Early Professional Development for Social Workers*, Birmingham: Venture.

Stewart, A. (2012) *Supporting Vulnerable Adults: Citizenship, Capacity and Choice. Policy and Practice*, Edinburgh: Dunedin Academic Press.

Stewart, A. (2016) *The Implementation of the Adult Support and Protection (Scotland) Act (2007)*, Glasgow: University of Glasgow.

Thaler, R. and Sunstein, C. (2003) Designing better choices, *American Economic Review,* 93(2): 175–179.

Webb, S. A. (2006) *Social Work in a Risk Society*, Basingstoke: Palgrave Macmillan.

Wishart, G. (2003) The sexual abuse of people with learning difficulties: Do we need a social model approach to vulnerability? *Journal of Adult Protection,* 5(3): 14–27.

Statutes

Adults with Incapacity (Scotland) Act (AWIA) (2000) Edinburgh: Blackwell.

Mental Capacity Act (MCA) (2005) London: HMSO.

3

The UK Policy Context for Safeguarding Adults: Rights-Based v Public Protection?

Kathryn Mackay, University of Stirling

Adult safeguarding policy is an acknowledgment by governments that they have responsibilities towards a range of adults who may be at risk of harm and who may be unable to safeguard themselves due to poor mental health, cognitive impairment, disability or physical infirmity. It is multi-agency in nature as it requires engagement by social care, police, health, housing and regulatory agencies. It also overlaps with other policy streams such as domestic violence. However this Chapter narrows down its exploration of the context to the core functions of the identification, investigation and possible intervention into the individual lives of adults at risk of harm. This means looking at its situation within general social care and health provision and examining its interaction with mental capacity and mental health legislation for adults who may require compulsory legal orders to support and protect them. Underlying this complex area of law and policy are questions around if, when, why and how governments choose to intervene in the lives of adults (Stewart, 2012; Mackay, 2008). For example, what responsibility does a government have towards its adult citizens with care and support needs? How do governments balance individual human rights with protection of that adult or of others? Such questions lead us to look not only at political views but also at the views of society at large and the attention the media gives to adult safeguarding.

As a result, describing what is a complex and at times contradictory policy context is not easy. Devolution across the UK has added to this complexity where laws and policy now differ between England, Northern Ireland, Scotland and Wales though the issues they aim to address are the same. This Chapter first briefly sets out the different national structures relevant to this subject area. Second it explores the challenges of balancing individual rights with public protection and then third it provides an overview of some of the key similarities and differences in terms of rights, support and protection across the four countries. The Chapter draws to a close with consideration of the emerging themes in this policy context and their implications for future change across the UK.

UK devolution: approaches to welfare services

The UK Parliament in Westminster continues to have reserved powers for key policy areas such as immigration, taxation, out-of-work benefits and pensions. Functions such as housing, health and social care services have been devolved to the Assemblies of Wales and Northern Ireland and the Parliament in Scotland. These three countries have different historical paths, which cannot be detailed here but they have led to varied patterns of devolved powers. Whilst all four countries have policy responsibility for adult safeguarding, only Scotland and Northern Ireland have fully devolved powers in relation to mental health and mental capacity law – and the policies that evolve from these. Differences in Scotland are further increased because its legal practice is founded on Scots law, which has developed differently to the rest of the UK. For example, until now Scotland has had a tradition of using Sheriff courts or tribunals as the decision-making body for long-term mental health or mental capacity orders. In contrast, the rest of the UK use an administrative process within health trusts or local authorities for the majority of these orders. There are also differences in how health and social services are structured. Northern Ireland's health and social services have been integrated since the 1970s, whereas structural integration has been much slower in the rest of the UK, though Scotland is currently structurally merging social care and health services around local partnerships as a result of the Public Bodies (Joint Working) (Scotland) Act 2014. The integration of health and social services has enabled Northern Ireland, the smallest of the UK countries, to create a national adult safeguarding board that commissions adult safeguarding services from the different regional health and social care trusts. The potential impact of this is that it might better standardise responses across the country, but it also potentially creates better links between different policy streams at a national as well local level. However Northern Ireland is a much smaller country and there is no empirical evidence to confirm whether integrated services lead to closer ties between adult safeguarding and other policy areas.

One cannot avoid considering the impact of the market model within health and social care where services more generally are commissioned by both health boards and local authorities. This may have contributed to the diversity of local provision in a relatively economically stable UK in 1990s and early 2000s. However, currently the purchasing of services is focused on cost savings, with a deterioration in the breadth and quality of the services offered (Jones, 2014; Ferguson and Lavalette, 2013; Oliver and Barnes, 2012). In the past ten years more social services and health care services have been put out to tender and the pace has increased since 2010, when long-term cuts in public expenditure became the chosen method of the UK government to reduce debt incurred in the banking financial crisis in 2008. These varied approaches to welfare provision and the long-term cuts in public spending set the backdrop to the consideration of individual rights to autonomy but also to support and protection.

Individual rights and public protection

Adult safeguarding is often framed as taking either an individual rights-based or public protection approach. Yet frontline adult safeguarding practice is often a 'foggy borderland' (Mackay et al., 2012: 201) where there are all sorts of conflicting priorities, views and wishes between agencies, practitioners, families and the adult at risk of harm, but also within the person themselves. A mother being abused by her son who lives with her may want the harm to stop but at the same time can't ask him to leave because she feels responsible about his becoming homeless. A practitioner wants to empower a service user to make decisions about how to live their life but at the same the practitioner has a legal duty to inquire into reported harm.

There are different types of rights within law, policy and literature: human rights and rights for persons with disabilities (CRPD); rights set out by the disability movement to independence and integration (Oliver and Barnes, 2012) and citizenship rights (Lister, 2003). What they share is a concern for defining the status of a person in relation to society and to the government. Civil rights can be negative: the right not to be killed or not to be wrongly detained. They can also be positive, sometimes described as social rights, such as free access to health care or equality of opportunity. However these positive or social rights have been steadily eroded since the 1980s. They are being replaced with prescribed individual legal rights such as the right to a referral to a service and the right to complain about subsequent decisions and services (Preston-Shoot, 2010; Harris, 2009; Rummery, 2002). This development reflects the increasingly neo-liberal orientation in UK political and policy discourse: the independent citizen who takes responsibility for their life and makes what might be described as rational decisions about their health and welfare (Clarke et al., 2007). Neo-liberalism views the welfare state as inefficient, ineffective and paternalistic, and therefore develops policies that promote the use of markets in service delivery to create self-reliance in the citizen.

This individualisation of responsibility, as well as choice, is reflected in the self-care and self-management service developments across health and social care.

From the 1980s onward the disabled people's movement won some key arguments in terms of promoting equality of access to work and wider society, as well as arguing for disabled people to have the independence to control their own support in everyday life. These developments are evidenced within disability discrimination legislation, disability welfare benefits and the creation of the independent living fund. However more recently there has been a retraction from this level of support, in particular the closure in England and Wales of the independent living fund and the abolition of standalone disability welfare benefits. This means that making a reality of the vision of integrated living will become increasingly dependent on families' economic and personal resources, or their ability to 'shout loudest' for support (Oliver and Barnes, 2012; Morris, 2011). Therefore whilst there might appear to be a profusion of rights, as set out in the CRPD, these are to varying degrees constrained by availability of personal, family, community and welfare agency resources.

This individualised approach to rights, underpinned by the assumption that adults will be self-reliant (Clarke et al., 2007) means that adult safeguarding issues tend to capture less of the government's and society's attention than child welfare and protection. However, one topic has risen to public attention recently: the ill-treatment, neglect and avoidable death of people within hospitals and care homes (see Chapter 10). It might be argued that it only became a high-profile issue when the abuse of patients in Mid Staffordshire NHS Hospital and Winterbourne View (private) Hospital came fully into the public view via newspaper and television coverage. However, this revealed that relatives and occasionally staff had raised individual concerns with the health trust and national regulators over a sustained period of time beforehand (Francis, 2013; Flynn, 2012). It was this failure to address individual cases of abuse that became a question of failure to protect the public more generally. The UK Parliament's response has been to require improvements to the national regulators, NHS management and commissioning performance and to extend the offence of ill-treatment and wilful neglect to all adults in health and social care settings. Yet these are all very specific interventions which do not really address what are seen as inherent problems in service provision that have been raised in previous inquiries over a long period of time, including frontline working conditions, underfunding and cultures that sustain mediocre care and devalue both staff and patients (Mandelstam, 2014).

There are fundamental questions to be asked about how much, as a society, we value disabled people, older people or people with mental distress. There are also emerging concerns over disability hate or 'mate' crimes (Quarmby, 2011). More generally some disabled people have reported sensing a change in the way they are treated in everyday interaction in their communities (Faulkner, 2012). Whilst the media has played a positive role in raising awareness of what are called hate or mate crimes and institutional abuse, there does not appear to be a consistent groundswell of political will to address the wider structural problems.

Not all media attention is positive in terms of promoting an adult's right to safety and support in their own community. For example, people with mental distress, to some extent, are still viewed as a potential threat to their family, community and to the wider public (Pilgrim, 2007). There have been different responses, across the UK, to the pressure asserted by some sections of the media to tighten up mental health law and practice in response to statistically very rare yet very violent crimes committed by a person with a personality disorder or serious mental illness. The Westminster government appeared to take much more cognisance of 'public pressure' than the alliance of service user, legal and professional groups that viewed the government's proposed reforms as prioritising public protection over individual rights (Pilgrim, 2007). In effect it is now much easier in England and Wales than in Scotland to detain someone in a hospital or supervise them in the community as a result of these public protection concerns.

There is also the CRPD challenge to mental health law, that it is in and of itself discriminatory and that the power to detain and impose interventions should be 'de-linked from the disability and neutrally defined so as to apply to all persons on an equal basis' (Fennell, 2010: 49). This argument has had more of an influence in Northern Ireland as we will see in the next section. However the CRPD also challenges us to consider the validity of adult safeguarding legislation, particularly vis–á-vis domestic violence, because impairment of the individual is part of the definition of an adult at risk of harm and the focus is on the victim as opposed to the perpetrator (Sherwood-Johnson, 2013).

A final point about rights is that providing safeguards for adults subject to compulsory measures is expensive and this was felt to be a key reason why the Westminster government resisted implementing most of the recommended improved legal safeguards in mental health law (Fennell, 2010; Pilgrim, 2007). These tensions around rights, protection and resources need to be borne in mind as we move on to consider the policy context in more detail.

Rights, support and protection across the UK

The UK countries currently share the same overarching legal framework, as illustrated in Figure 3.1, wherein every adult at risk of harm has assumed human rights and access to justice and protection under pre-existing criminal and civil law. It then becomes increasingly specialised in terms of social welfare, adult safeguarding and upwards to mental capacity and mental health legislation.

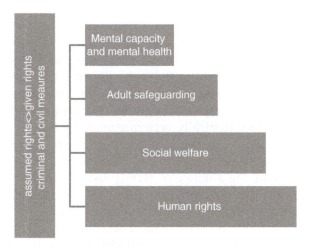

Figure 3.1   UK Legal framework

What we will see is that the four UK countries populate this framework differently. However a general trend that one can see is that the more one moves up through what might be described as a ladder of intervention, the more assumed rights to liberty and autonomy become constrained, and conversely the more legal safeguards and rights to representation are built in. Human rights have already been discussed, so this section starts with social welfare and moves up through each rung of the ladder.

Social care

There continues to be a duty for social care services across the UK to assess anyone who may have care and support needs, and thereafter to consider whether support should be provided to meet any identified needs. Whilst some policies concern discrete groups such as people with dementia, others are about welfare in general. There are clear policy aims in all four countries around:

➤ Personalised approaches based on people's desired outcomes,

➤ Direct payments: money in lieu of services to meet assessed needs so the person or their proxy can arrange and manage their own support, and

➤ Support for carers.

There have also been attempts to improve accountability of services through:

➤ Registration and inspection of social and health care services and

➤ Regulation of social and health care workers.

Whilst the four countries have similar aims, they have different laws that underpin their approaches (see Figure 3.2)

A new feature in 2014 was the introduction of national eligibility criteria for providing services or receiving direct payments in regulations that flow from the Care Act 2014 (England), Social Services and Well-being

	England	N. Ireland	Scotland	Wales
Social Care	Care Act 2014	Various – yet to be consolidated	Social Care (Self-directed Support) (Scotland) Act 2013	Social Services and Well-being (Wales) Act 2014
Adult Safeguarding	Within above statute	Adult Safeguarding: Prevention and Protection in Partnership 2015 (policy)	Adult Support and Protection (Scotland) Act 2007	Within above statute
Mental Capacity	Mental Capacity Act 2005	Mental Capacity Act (Northern Ireland) 1986	Adults with Incapacity (Scotland) Act 2000	Mental Capacity Act 2005
Mental Health	Mental Health Act 1983 as amended by the 2007 Act	Mental Capacity Act (Northern Ireland) 1986	Mental Health (Care and Treatment) (Scotland) Act 2003, updated by the Mental Health (Scotland) Act 2015	Mental Health Act 1983 as amended by the 2007 Act

Figure 3.2   Law across the UK at a glance

(Wales) Act 2014, and the Social Care (Self-directed Support) (Scotland) Act 2013. Whilst this makes eligibility more transparent, it also emphasises that funds are dedicated more towards significant levels of need or risk of admission to hospital or care, as in the example of Scotland's ensuing statutory guidance for self-directed support (Scottish Government, 2014a).

Whilst everyone with possible care and support needs still has the right to an assessment, the combination of cuts and introduction of restrictive eligibility criteria are likely to mean that people with what are described as moderate needs or less may not receive any funded ongoing support or direct payments. This statutory guidance also requires local authorities to consider how they might fund preventative services and those practitioners in undertaking assessments to work creatively with services users to consider how they might achieve their desired outcomes. However, it is hard to avoid the overall impression that the positive words of the policy documents are somewhat out of synch in communities where local mainstream resources are themselves struggling to survive. As a result, it may prove too challenging to fund both preventative adult safeguarding initiatives as well as meet and address high-level need within the same pot of money.

Adult safeguarding

Only a brief overview of the differences and similarities in adult safeguarding policies will be considered here, specifically in relation to the wider context, as other Chapters in this volume provide much more detail around practice. Up until the Care Act 2014 and the Social Services and Well-being (Wales) Act 2014, Scotland was the only country to have legislation that focused on adult support and protection. However, Scotland continues to have, arguably, the most interventionist approach, with powers around investigation and protection orders. Wales has established slightly wider powers than England, though these have not gone as far as Scotland with seven-day removal or banning orders. One reason for this divergence in balancing individual rights with duties to protect might be that England, in particular, took a more civil libertarian view and was less swayed by arguments that protective powers uphold rights in the longer term even if they might seem compromised in the short term (Stewart, 2012). In Northern Ireland there is interest in critically reviewing the existing provision and considering the need for further statutory powers (see *A review of the adult safeguarding framework in Northern Ireland, the UK, Ireland and Internationally*, 2014, commissioned by the Commissioner for

Older People for Northern Ireland). In the meantime, a revised adult safe-guarding policy has been published (DHSSPS, 2015).

In addition, there are differences in the definitional thresholds between the countries. All countries explicitly state that risk of as well as actual harm, abuse or neglect is grounds for investigation. This suggests that there is a preventative duty across the UK, but the terminology thereafter varies: the term *abuse or neglect* is used in Wales and England; Northern Ireland uses *abuse, exploitation* or *neglect*; and Scotland has the most open term *harm* on its own. Scotland's experience suggests that it is important to avoid overly defining what constitutes harm or abuse in order to focus on the unique combination of factors that occur around each adult at risk of harm (Scottish Government, 2014b), and England's and Northern Ireland's new guidance stress this point. Whilst both English and Welsh statutes state non-eligibility for services does not exclude anyone from adult safeguarding, there is a potential danger that limited resources, managerial practices and workload stress will lead to defensive gatekeeping practice (Ash, 2013; Ellis, 2011).

These small differences, in the current climate, might potentially leave adults at risk of harm in England with the least safeguards and practi-tioners with least scope to proceed with investigations where they may not have access to the adult concerned as a result of non-eligibility for other services. While early research indicates the value of the new English measures (Preston-Shoot and Cornish, 2014; Mackay et al., 2012), one may question the extent to which a stricter civil libertarian approach at a national policy level is potentially divorced from the complexities of adults' lives, and the harm they might face as well as the demands of adult safeguarding practice. However, whilst Scottish adult safeguarding law contains protection orders, these require the agreement of the adult concerned to be effective. Therefore, most ongoing protection plans are agreed on a voluntary basis with the adult concerned. This means a minority of adults with significant learning disabilities or with mental distress may require some form of compulsory intervention under mental capacity or mental health law in order to effectively address the harm.

Mental health and mental capacity

Mental health and mental capacity has also been an area of significant policy change in the last 30 years. Large-scale hospitals have been closed and more support has become available in communities. However, the legal framework in the UK remained outdated with underlying assump-tions that capacity was an all-or-nothing condition and that treatment of those legally classified as having a mental disorder was based upon hospitalisation. The term mental disorder is defined differently across the UK, but all definitions include mental illness, learning disability and personality disorders. Major reviews were conducted across the UK in the late 1990s, and the influence of human rights can be seen in the ensuing reforms. Whilst England and Wales, and Scotland continue to develop mental capacity and mental health law separately, Northern Ireland's recently implemented Mental Capacity (Northern Ireland) Act 2016 based on the recommendations of the Bamford Review (Northern Ireland Executive, 2008), represents one piece of legislation that will cover both. Its principle aims are to avoid the labelling of those who experience significant mental distress and to develop an 'all-health approach' based on an adult's capacity to make decisions.

Comparisons between UK countries are complex in this arena, not just because of the two-versus-one statute debate but also because the countries have different legal traditions around when to use courts or tribunals for approving compulsion orders. For example, England and Wales had pre-existing mental health tribunals for three-year reviews and appeals. However, the Westminster government did not accept the review's recommendation to extend their remit to the approval of the original application for long-term orders. This remains an internal administrative process within health trusts. In contrast, Scotland already had external scrutiny because long-term orders were approved within Sheriff courts. However, its review led to the creation of mental health tribunals as a more humane venue for both patients and their family. There is also likely to be much more change in the next few years. This section therefore provides an introduction to three of the key challenges around supporting and protecting people where decisions may be need to be taken on their behalf: substitute decision making for those who lack capacity, deprivation of liberty and treatment orders for those defined as having a mental disorder.

Mental capacity and substitute decision making

An adult is presumed to be capable of making decisions unless it can be demonstrated that capacity is lacking to:

- understand (an issue or an action),
- articulate one's opinion,
- take action to address the issue or instruct someone else to do so, or
- retain the memory of one's decision.

If, prior to losing capacity, provisions have not been made to give financial and welfare decision-making powers to another person, problems can occur in supporting wellbeing on a daily basis. There are also bigger, more one-off decisions around a person, such as moving house, or moving into supported accommodation or care homes, that need to be considered. Capacity is no longer viewed as an all-or-nothing condition, and practice is evolving, albeit unevenly, to support people to make decisions where possible, in line with the principles of the CRPD. This should isolate those specific areas in which a person lacks capacity and therefore limit substitute decision making by a third party more effectively than in the past. There are concerns however that perhaps practitioners and direct care staff may not fully appreciate this expectation and require advice and training to fully develop their supported decision-making skills (Boyle, 2008).

The legal measures by which substitute decision making is authorised vary across the UK. Scotland was the first to modernise this area of law with the Adults with Incapacity (Scotland) Act 2000, but its reliance on welfare and court-granted welfare and financial guardianship and intervention orders for people who have already lost capacity means that applications are increasing year on year, putting pressure on social work and court resources (Mental Welfare Commission, 2014). Additionally, the statute did not adequately address deprivation of liberties (to be considered in the next section). The Scottish Law Commission (SLC) (2014) have identified that medical and social work staff have conflated the issue of where someone lives with the issue of deprivation of liberty. This they argue can be seen by the number of patients who remain in hospital waiting for legal orders to be granted before they can move to a care home when these orders may not be required to lawfully move the person.

The SLC is seeking a more proportionate response, which means some decisions may be made without the need for guardianship, but at the time of writing the Scottish Government have not responded to their proposals. This idea of proportionality can be seen within the Mental Capacity Act 2005 for England and Wales and the Mental Capacity (Northern Ireland) 2016 Act. Their approach is tiered in the sense that there is, or will be, protection from liability of decisions made on behalf of an adult who it is believed lacks the capacity at that time. As such, a friend, relative or worker could, without recourse to a more formal legal process, act in the adult's best interests. There should, however, be an assessment of capacity carried out by a prescribed practitioner as a safeguard. However formal authorisation through each country's respective administrative or court system is, or will be, required where there is a conflict of opinion about the proposed action or where the action is more significant such as withholding life sustaining sustenance, accessing banks accounts and depriving a person of their liberty.

Deprivation of liberty

A key concern of late was that laws across the UK are not in line with human rights in terms of providing safeguards against unlawful deprivation of liberty for those adults who lack capacity and preventing care staff from acting unlawfully in restraining an adult. Deprivation of liberty orders (DOLs) were first introduced in England and Wales and have become contentious due to the complexity of the application process itself, the geographical variations of their use, examples of inappropriate use and divergent court appeal judgements (Care Quality Commission, 2013). At the time of writing, the Law Commission for England and Wales (2015) are consulting on proposals that will replace DOLs with a 'protective care' approach which will be more proportionate in light of the above concerns. Part of the debate around DOLs is whether there should or could be one test to fit all circumstances. The danger here is that it might focus attention on more easily measureable factors such as a locked door in a care facility.

It is possible that this debate has benefited Northern Ireland in devising its Mental Capacity Act, and the Scottish Law Commission's recent proposed legal changes. Northern Ireland has kept with the idea of deprivation of liberty, but stresses its nature will vary between individuals and context. In contrast, the Scottish Law Commission (2014: 4) are recommending the use of an alternative concept of '*significant restriction of liberty*' because this recognises that the factors that might constitute it are of '*degree or intensity, not of nature or substance*'. Whilst debates go on between lawyers, policy makers and other stakeholders about restructuring the law, the difficult dilemmas around how and when a person might be appropriately restrained in the interests of their welfare continue for families, and social care and health staff.

Detaining and supervising someone with a mental disorder

As noted above, the modernisation of mental health law in the early 2000s has caused a divergence of approaches between the UK countries. Northern Ireland has dispensed with its mental health law in favour of an all-encompassing Mental Capacity Act, whilst the Westminster government was seen to produce a public safety approach in contrast to the more rights-based approach taken by the Scottish Parliament (Fennell, 2007; Pilgrim, 2007). One common thread is that all countries have accepted the need for community-based care and treatment orders to prevent unnecessary hospitalisation. However, there are concerns in England and Wales, in particular, that their use is being extended beyond those they were intended for (Care Quality Commission, 2011). This again raises questions about the balance of individual rights and potential risk of harm.

Part of the reason for this may be that Westminster rejected the recommended additional criteria of significantly impaired decision-making ability, over and above evidence of mental disorder and risk to self or others, whereas Scotland adopted it. After the new legislation was implemented, rates of compulsion continued to rise in England and Wales but began to fall in Scotland (Mackay, 2011), although in more recent years rates of compulsion have increased in Scotland also, but at a much slower rate than in England and Wales. This would seem to imply that where there are fewer external controls, welfare professionals may act more paternalistically. However, the law on its own may not be the sole cause of greater rates of detention (McLaughlan and Cardell, 2013) and the wider context may also be significant. For example, the mental health service context in England and Wales has been described as one of chronic underfunding where there is little scope for the preventative work that might reduce the need for compulsory measures (Pilgrim, 2012).

Rights of the individual

The above changes in mental health, mental capacity and adult safeguarding law have led to more participation and representation rights for adults. These are meant to act as a series of checks and balances on the use of professional power. For example, each statute has principles which should guide practitioners in terms of involving the adult as much as possible in decision-making processes and making any intervention the least restrictive possible. There are rights to advocacy, but these seem rather unevenly applied across the UK and between statutes. Scotland has taken a more universal approach which might be seen as improving the voice of the person in any assessment/investigation and intervention. Up until recently, Scottish advocacy services had scope to work with a range of people and types of provision were quite varied. However, in more recent years funding has focused more on meeting those who might be subject to compulsory measures (Stewart and MacIntyre, 2013), suggesting reality might be falling short of aspiration.

In contrast, contracts for advocacy in England and Wales are delivered in what might be a divisive way: there are independent mental capacity advocates (IMCAs) and then independent mental health advocates

(IMHAs) who focus mainly on those subject to compulsory orders. There are further constraints in that the IMCA role has been ring-fenced for certain types of decisions such as serious medical treatment decisions, change of accommodation, adult protection concerns and deprivation of liberty orders. In addition, IMCAs should generally only get involved where the person does not have an appropriate friend or relative to support them. Advocacy in adult safeguarding is also much more prescribed. Again here we might be seeing the wider influence of spending cuts but also the view that families and friends should speak for the adult rather than the adult having an independent voice as a right. Some relatives, however, may be more protective of the person and therefore may wish to see them in a supervised environment where risk can be reduced. Also speaking up for another person against professionals can be a daunting task. These developments around advocacy may sit somewhat more uneasily if the CRPD becomes a more significant motivator. Its focus on equality of access and justice are not just about courts and one-off decisions but also about administrative decision-making processes within social care and health services.

Conclusion

The context of adult safeguarding across the four UK countries, whilst sharing commonalities, is also contradictory and raises questions about which approaches might better uphold an individual's rights to autonomy and liberty whilst also supporting and protecting them. There are also positive and perhaps worrying underlying trends that can be discerned. The positives are around greater clarity about how human rights might be better protected and how people can be better supported in communities and avoid group living arrangements if they so choose. These are initiatives that can increase a person's control over their own lives and minimise the scope for professionals to have power over them – for example, an adult having control of their own support arrangements. In addition, there is a greater understanding around the nature of capacity and of supporting decision making wherever possible. One has to remember, however, that laws and policies on their own may not achieve change in frontline practice (Brammer, 2014; Preston-Shoot, 2010) and currently health and social care services are under immense pressures of demand on the one hand, and continued cuts to welfare spending on the other. This means that whilst policies may talk of personalisation and independence, eligibility criteria may leave little room for preventative work that might reduce harm and abuse as well as promote social integration. More widely, there does appear to be what might be called an emerging insensitivity towards adults who might find themselves in vulnerable situations even though many of the reasons for this will lie in societal inequalities and poverty. Disabled and older people who have personal or family resources can meet the extra support costs that impairments engender. In contrast, those who rely on welfare benefits and services are increasingly subject to scrutiny, not only by policy makers but also members of the public (Faulkner, 2012). To challenge this, we need to question the underpinning assumption of the self-reliant citizen with research that demonstrates the inter-dependent nature of everyday living and care-giving whether that be by friends, family, neighbours or paid workers (Rabiee, 2013). In the meantime, we are facing the reality in the UK that based on where an adult at risk of harm lives, they may be more (or less) likely left to cope on their own, be subject to institutional ill-treatment or neglect and have less recourse to supported decision making and rights to representation through advocacy.

Implications for practice

➤ UK adult safeguarding legal frameworks vary in terms of levels of intervention.

➤ Reduced public sector funding in the wake of austerity has significant implications for the provision of preventative adult safeguarding services.

➤ These include significant variations in provision depending on geographical location.

➤ Adequately funded advocacy support is an important safeguard in ensuring the voices of people who need protection are heard, but there is considerable variation in provision across the UK.

References

Ash, A. (2013) A cognitive mask? Camouflaging dilemmas in street-level policy implementation to safeguard older people from abuse. *British Journal of Social Work*, 43(1): 99–115.

Boyle, A. (2008) The law and incapacity determinations: A conflict of governance. *The Modern Law Review*, 71(3): 413–463.

Brammer, A. (2014) *Safeguarding Adults*, Basingstoke: Palgrave Macmillan.

Care Quality Commission. (2011) *Monitoring the Mental Health Act in 2010/2011,* London: Care Quality Commission.

Care Quality Commission. (2013) *Monitoring the Use of Mental Capacity Act Deprivation of Liberty Safeguards in 2011/12,* London: Care Quality Commission.

Clarke, J., Newman, J., Smith, N., Vidler, E. and Westmarland, L. (2007) *Creating Citizen-Consumers: Changing Publics and Changing Public Services,* London: SAGE.

Department of Health, Social Services and Public Safety (DHSSPS). (2015) *Adult Safeguarding: Prevention and Protection in Partnership,* Belfast: DHSSPS.

Ellis, K.(2011) Street-level bureaucracy' revisited: The changing face of frontline discretion in adult care in England. *Social Policy & Administration,* 45(3): 221–244.

Faulkner, A. (2012) The right to take risks. *Journal of Adult Protection,* 14(6): 287–296.

Fennell, P. (2007) *Mental Health Law: The New Law,* Bristol: Jordan Publishing Limited.

Fennell, P. (2010) 'Institutionalising the community: The codification of clinical authority and the limits of rights-based approaches', in McSherry, B. and Weller, P. (eds), *Rethinking Rights-Based Mental Health Laws* (pp. 13–50), Oxford: Hart Publishing Limited.

Ferguson, I. and Lavalette, M. (2013) Crisis, austerity and the future(s) of social work in the UK. *Critical and Radical Social Work,* 1(1): 95–110.

Flynn, M. (2012) *Winterbourne View Hospital: A Serious Case Review,* South Gloucestershire Safeguarding Adults Board.

Francis, R. (2013) *Report of the Mid Staffordshire NHS Foundation Trust Public Inquiry,* London: The Stationery Office.

Harris, J. (2009) 'Customer-citizen in modernised social work', in Harris, J. and White, V. (eds), *Modernising Social Work: Critical Considerations* (pp. 67–88), Bristol: The Policy Press.

Jones, R. (2014) The best of time, the worst of times: Social work and its moment. *British Journal of Social Work,* 44(3): 485–502.

Law Commission for England and Wales. (2015) *Mental Capacity and Deprivation of Liberty A Consultation Paper,* London: HMSO.

Lister, R. (2003) *Citizenship, Feminist Perspectives* (2nd edition), Houndmills: Palgrave Macmillan.

Mackay, K. (2008) The Scottish adult support and protection legal framework. *The Journal of Adult Protection,* 10(4): 25–36.

Mackay, K. (2011) Compounding conditional citizenship: To what extent does Scottish and English mental health law increase or diminish social citizenship? *British Journal of Social Work,* 41(5): 931–948.

Mackay, K., Notman, M., McNicholl, J., Fraser, D., McLaughlan, C. and Rossi, S. (2012) What difference does the Adult Support and Protection (Scotland) 2007 make to social work service practitioners' safeguarding practice? *Journal of Adult Protection,* 14(4): 197–205.

Mandelstam, M. (2014) Wilful neglect and health care. *Journal of Adult Protection*, 16(6): 342–354.

McLaughlan, K. and Cardell, S. (2013) 'Doing what's best, but best for whom? Ethics and the mental health social worker', in Carey, M. and Green, L. (eds), *Practical Social Work Ethics: Complex Dilemmas Within Applied Social Care* (pp. 111–130), Farnham: Ashgate Publishing Ltd.

Mental Welfare Commission. (2014) *Adults with Incapacity Monitoring 2013–14*, Edinburgh: Mental Welfare Commission.

Morris, J. (2011) *Rethinking Disability Policy*, York: Joseph Rowntree Fund.

Northern Ireland Executive. (2008) *Delivering the Bamford Vision: The Response of the Northern Ireland Executive to the Bamford Review of Mental Health and Learning Disability*, Belfast: Northern Ireland Executive.

Oliver, M. and Barnes, C. (2012) *The New Politics of Disablement*, Tavistock: Palgrave Macmillan.

Pilgrim, D. (2007) New 'mental health' legislation for England and Wales: Some aspects of consensus and conflict. *Journal of Social Policy*, 36(1): 79–95.

Pilgrim, D. (2012) Lessons from the Mental Health Act Commission for England and Wales: The limitations of legalism-plus-safeguards. *Journal of Social Policy*, 41(1): 61–81.

Preston-Shoot, M. (2010) 'The more things change, the more they remain the same? Law, social work and counteracting discrimination', in Long, L. A., Roche, J. and Stringer, D. (eds), *The Law and Social Work: Contemporary Issues for Practice* (pp. 55–75), Basingstoke: Palgrave Macmillan.

Preston-Shoot, M. and Cornish, S. (2014) Paternalism or proportionality? Experiences and outcomes of the Adult Support and Protection (Scotland) Act 2007. *The Journal of Adult Protection*, 16(1): 5–16.

Quarmby, K. (2011) *Scapegoat: Why We are Failing Disabled People?*, London: Portobello Books.

Rabiee, P. (2013) Exploring the relationships between choice and independence: Experiences of disabled and older people. *British Journal of Social Work*, 43(5): 872–888.

Rummery, K. (2002) *Disability, Citizenship and Community Care: A Case for Welfare Rights?*, Aldershot: Ashgate Publishing.

Scottish Government. (2014a) *Statutory Guidance to Accompany the Social Care (Self-directed Support) (Scotland) Act 2013*, Edinburgh: Scottish Government.

Scottish Government. (2014b) *Adult Support and Protection (Scotland) Act 2007: Revised Code of Practice*, Edinburgh: Scottish Government.

Scottish Law Commission. (2014) *Report on Adults with Incapacity*, Edinburgh: SLC.

Sherwood-Johnson, F. (2013) Constructions of vulnerability in comparative perspective: Scottish protection policies and the trouble with 'adults at risk'. *Disability and Society*, 28(7): 908–921.

Stewart, A. (2012) *Supporting Vulnerable Adults: Citizenship, Capacity and Choice, Policy and Practice in Health and Social Care No. 13,* Edinburgh: Dunedin Academic Press.

Stewart, A. and MacIntyre G. (2013) *Advocacy: Models and Effectiveness, IRISS Insight, Number 20.* Available at http://www.iriss.org.uk/sites/default/files/iriss-insight-20.pdf [Accessed 28 September 2014].

4

Safeguarding Adults With and Without Mental Capacity

Gillian MacIntyre and Ailsa Stewart, University of Strathclyde

Adult protection and safeguarding can be considered as a continuum with functions and criteria ranging from compulsory detention in hospital to the provision of traditional welfare supports, contained within a suite of policy and legislation in the UK (SCIE, 2015). As discussed in Chapters 2 and 3, across the four jurisdictions of the UK these frameworks vary considerably but commonly provide agreed criteria for care, treatment, support and protection for adults who may claim these rights or have them imposed upon them (Carr, 2014; Sherwood-Johnson, 2012; Stewart, 2012). The range of adults for whom safeguarding may apply is therefore considerable and is likely to include those who retain capacity, those who lack capacity and those where the level of capacity is not known. This may include, but is not limited to, people with learning disabilities, those with mental health problems, older adults and those with dementia. The types of harm from which adults may be at risk is extensive but can be broadly categorised as psychological harm, financial harm, sexual harm and/or exploitation, physical harm, self-neglect or self-harm (Scottish Government, 2011; Cooper et al., 2008; O'Keeffe et al., 2007).

This Chapter aims to consider adult safeguarding where:

- an adult has been found to lack mental and or legal capacity or

- an adult's level of capacity is either unknown, unclear or fluctuating.

Concepts of capacity and incapacity are explored from a theoretical, legal and practice perspective and consideration given to the ways in which practitioners construct their understanding of the limits of service users' capacity to make decisions and what may influence this process. The Chapter discusses issues that arise in relation to the assessment of capacity and potential substitute decision-making procedures from a multi-jurisdictional perspective within the UK. In addition, the ways in which practitioners can balance the tensions and dilemmas that are apparent in this complex area of work are also explored. Case studies are provided to draw out key messages for students and practitioners working in this area. The case studies are drawn from research undertaken in Scotland to explore the knowledge practitioners' draw upon in making decisions within the relevant safeguarding framework (Stewart, 2016), however the messages from these cases studies are transferrable to other contexts. The Chapter concludes by raising key areas for consideration in the development of safeguarding practice.

Spectrum of adult safeguarding

Across the four countries of the UK, different terminology is used to describe the variety of frameworks and practices aimed at preventing harm and dealing with the consequences of harm that has been perpetrated against adults. Safeguarding is the broad term used across the UK (although not extensively in Scotland, as indicated in the introduction to this book) to encompass a range of procedures, interventions and supports for adults who require support to protect themselves (Mackay, 2011). This term has also been used to include the consideration of adults who require different levels of intervention from basic community care support services, ranging, for example, from home care support to compulsory measures such as detention in hospital for medical and therapeutic treatment. Consequently, adults can be subject to safeguarding under a range of legislation and policy across the UK. This includes the Mental Capacity Act 2005, the Mental Health Act 2007 and the Care Act 2014 in England, the Social Services and Well-being (Wales) Act 2014, the Mental Capacity Act (Northern Ireland) 2016, the Adult Safeguarding: Prevention and Protection in Partnership policy (Northern Ireland) 2015, as well as the Adults with Incapacity (Scotland) Act 2000, the Mental Health (Care and Treatment) (Scotland) Act 2003 and the Adult Support and Protection (Scotland) Act 2007. The term safeguarding has also encompassed activity to protect adults at risk of harm and/or abuse either from themselves or others.

Safeguarding therefore provides care, treatment, support and protection for those who have capacity as well as those who do not. Definitions of capacity vary across the UK but all are broadly concerned with the ability of an individual to make decisions about matters affecting their lives. In the past this lack of capacity may have been considered to be due to a particular condition (e.g. mental disorder); however, more recently the focus has shifted in human rights terms to consider the individual rather than the condition (see for example, Shtukaturov v Russia, 2008). Across the UK, functional definitions of capacity focus on the decision-making process. In England for example, the definition given under the Mental Capacity Act 2005 suggests that *a person is unable to make a decision for himself if he is unable: (a) to understand the information relevant to the decision, (b) to retain that information, (c) to use or weigh that information as part of the process of making the decision, or (d) to communicate his decision (whether by talking, using sign language or any other means)* (Mental Capacity Act 2005, Section 3(1a-d)).

In Scotland 'incapable', for the purposes of the Adults with Incapacity (Scotland) Act 2000 is defined as being incapable of:

➣ acting; or

➣ making decisions; or

➣ communicating decisions; or

➣ understanding decisions; or

➣ retaining the memory of decisions.

in relation to any particular matter due to mental disorder or inability to communicate because of physical disability. The core aspects are therefore broadly similar.

Once an adult has been assessed as lacking capacity, policy and legislation across the UK is concerned with providing practitioners with a framework to support the adult to make decisions or to make decisions on the adult's behalf (substitute decision making). This is a complex process as capacity is neither static nor an all-encompassing concept but should be determined on an issue-by-issue basis. An individual may lack capacity to make decisions in relation to some aspects of their life but may retain capacity in others (Davidson et al., 2015).

It can be argued that intervention in the lives of adults who retain capacity potentially compromises their assumed right to self-determination, although this is a complex and contested area of law (Stewart, 2016). This may also breach individuals' rights under European human rights law and the UN Convention on the Rights of Persons with Disabilities in particular. This conflict will be considered later in this Chapter. This sets up a complex and challenging environment for practitioners to operate within, where often there is a lack of clarity with regard to the adult's level of capacity during the process of assessment and consequent intervention. It is often, therefore, those at the margins, where capacity is unknown or unclear, for whom intervention is most challenging.

Capacity and incapacity

The interaction between capacity and incapacity is critical in considering intervention within a safeguarding framework. Citizens within the UK are assumed to have capacity unless assessed otherwise (Patrick, 2001). This assumption brings with it an understanding that retaining capacity means one is less likely to experience intervention imposed externally by the State in relation to decision making (Stewart, 2012). Adults likely to be subject to intervention under adult safeguarding procedures, consequently, can be considered in two groups: those with capacity where interventions are likely (but not exclusively) to require the consent of the adult and those without capacity where interventions may be imposed on the adult without consent. The former group can be subject to intervention under Section 35 (3) of the Adult Support and Protection (Scotland) Act 2007 if evidence is provided to the Sheriff that the Adult has been subject to undue pressure to withhold their consent, this extends the group for whom this Act may be used. However, any use of Section 35 (3) to override or ignore the lack of consent of the adult still does not come with the power to detain or treat the adult against their will. This power requires practitioners to consider circumstances that may impact on the adult's ability to make decisions, drawing in concepts such as undue pressure and bounded rationality.

Assessing capacity

There are specific tests in law that must be carried out to establish capacity where it is in doubt. These legal tests are underpinned by medical assessments, alongside legal determinations (Patrick, 2001). Using the definitions of capacity outlined above, a legal decision can be reached that an adult lacks capacity to make decisions themselves and enables someone else to make decisions for them (i.e. proxy-agency). Legislation and policy across the four countries of the UK have increasingly formalised the assessment of capacity and have increased the expectation that health care, social work and legal practitioners should be competent in assessing capacity (Nicholson et al., 2008). Specific legislation is now in place in all four countries to determine whether an adult has the mental and/or legal capacity to make decisions (Duffy et al., 2015).

Practitioners face a number of issues and dilemmas when assessing capacity and Bennett (2010) has highlighted the importance of considering the 'best interests' of the adult when making such assessments. 'Best interests' under the Mental Capacity Act 2005 must be considered when making any determination about a person's capacity and must not be made merely on the basis of a person's age or appearance or 'a condition of his, or an aspect of his behaviour, which might lead others to make unjustified assumptions about what might be in his best interests' (Mental Capacity Act, 2005, C9 3(1b)). In Scotland the concept of 'best interests' is considered to be overly paternalistic and therefore any determination regarding capacity and all subsequent interventions must be considered to be of *benefit* to the adult as contained within the principles underpinning the triangle of protection including the AWIA 2000, (Scottish Government, 2008).

In recognition of the issues and dilemmas faced, guidance has been issued to support practitioners to assess capacity from a number of sources. The British Medical Association (BMA), for example, have produced a toolkit that is designed to be used by doctors in England and Wales when working with patients who may lack capacity (BMA, 2008). While in Scotland, the Scottish Government issued guidance relating to communication and assessing capacity (Scottish Government, 2008). The guide considers how individual decision making can be supported before going on to consider the assessment of capacity in a number of areas including money, property and personal care. The guide also considers issues that might arise when assessing the capacity of those from specific groups, including those with neurological conditions, those with dementia and those with a learning disability (Scottish Government, 2008). In Northern Ireland great emphasis is placed on supporting adults to make decisions for themselves. This will be discussed in more detail later in the Chapter.

It can be seen therefore that capacity is a fluid concept that can change over time and is dependent upon the individual in question, the support they have in place to make decisions as well as the particular issue or decision in question. Policy and legislation has been put in place across the UK to support adults to make decisions or to provide mechanisms to make decisions on their behalf. This structured approach to safeguarding adults involves the removal of choice to a greater or lesser extent, and some might argue that this represents a paternalistic approach (Sherwood-Johnson, 2012). The arguments for and against this approach are well rehearsed in Chapter 2; however, the decision to intervene in the life of an adult or to promote their freedom of choice represents the key dilemma faced by health and social care practitioners when working with those who may lack capacity or be considered to be at risk of harm.

Limits to capacity

We might assume that an adult who has been assessed as having capacity will remain free from intervention; however, retaining capacity does not always ensure a lack of safeguarding intervention in an adult's life, although in the majority of safeguarding procedures consent will be required as exemplified by the Adult Support and Protection (Scotland) Act 2007, notwithstanding Section 35(3) discussed above (where undue pressure can be evidenced). Reflecting on the concept of bounded (or limited) rationality introduced by Simon (1972, 1978) in exploring capacity and decision making can be helpful in considering the validity of any such intervention in the life of an adult who retains capacity. Bounded rationality suggests that rationality in decision making is limited by a variety of factors including the information available to make the decision, the cognitive limitations of the individual's mind and the finite amount of time available to make decisions. Simon (1972, 1978) argued that only part of our decision making is rational and that as humans we are likely also to draw upon emotional or irrational elements to make decisions, such as our relationships with others (e.g. family members) (see Case Study A for an example). In considering the impact of this approach to decision making, Stewart (2012) considered how this influenced professional decision making in the context of adult safeguarding and added the impact of any undue influence or pressure to this model, including influence or pressure from family members or others, particularly where there are concerns about capacity. Consideration of undue influence and its impact on rational decision making forms an accepted part of our legal system. Mandelstam (2009) discussed the various ways in which undue influence can be brought to bear upon decision making and its impact on legal frameworks. He noted that undue influence could be summarised as occurring when:

> The adult being exploited has capacity (if not, they cannot be unduly influenced).

> The adult is influenced to enter into a transaction or behaviours not of his or her own free, informed will.

> The undue pressure can be either expressed or presumed.

(Mandelstam, 2009: 223)

Presumed undue influence relies on a relationship of trust and confidence where the trust is being breached. The result of this abusive and/or harmful relationship will be a situation that disadvantages the vulnerable person or at least creates a situation that requires explanation (Mandelstam, 2009).

Capacity compromised in this manner forms the basis for much intervention under the safeguarding banner. Drawing on the work of Bandura (2001) it can be argued that a lack of capacity in one area of decision making does not necessarily dictate a lack of capacity in all decision making, creating what can be described as situational capacity as discussed previously. A Court of Appeal judgement in England in 2012 discussed two types of incapacity: mental incapacity as defined under the Mental Capacity Act 2005 and incapacity derived from other circumstances (situational), especially influenced by other people (DL v A Local Authority & Ors, 2012). The case focused on the elderly parents of a violent and aggressive son who had been either unable or unwilling to protect themselves from his behaviour. This judgement states that the local authority can intervene in a situation where an adult is either unable or unwilling to protect themselves. The judge noted that:

> I do not accept that the jurisdiction ... is extensive and all-encompassing, or one which may threaten the autonomy of every adult in the country. It is ... targeted solely at those adults whose ability to make decisions for themselves has been compromised by matters other than those covered by the Mental Capacity Act 2005.
>
> (DL v A Local Authority & Ors, 2012)

The impact of undue influence can be seen specifically in the Adult Support and Protection (Scotland) Act 2007, the powers within which can only be used with the consent of the adult unless undue influence or pressure as defined within the Act can be identified. In such cases, the adult's consent, or lack of it, can be overridden by a Sheriff. The Adult Support and Protection (Scotland) Act 2007 therefore accepts that undue influence can lead to an adult being unable or unwilling to give their consent for appropriate support and protection (Patrick and Smith, 2009) and that without the intervention available within the Act the adult would render themselves at risk of being harmed or exploited. This is exemplified in Case Study A below. Safeguarding legislation in other jurisdictions (e.g. the Care Act 2014 in England and Wales) also consider the impact of undue influence on the decision-making ability of the adult. The fine detail of the implementation of the Social Services and Well-being (Wales) Act 2014 and the Adult Safeguarding: Prevention and Protection in Partnership policy 2015 in Northern Ireland remains unclear at the time of writing. It appears, however, that there will be consideration of the impact of undue influence on decision making further acknowledging potential limits to decision making.

Case study A

Catherine was 75 and was subject to a removal order (a protection order available under the Adult Support and Protection (Scotland) Act 2007 (ASPA) which facilitates the removal of an adult to a place of safety for the purposes of assessment, support and protection) without her consent under the ASPA following concerns that

▶

◀

the conditions she was living in at home were not fit for human habitation. Alongside this, Catherine was discovered emaciated and malnourished and there was no edible food in the house. It was also <u>unclear</u> whether she had capacity to make her own decisions, and there was concern that she was subject to undue pressure from her son Adam. Her older son Peter provided evidence of undue influence being exerted by his brother on his mother, who he felt was unable and unwilling to protect herself. Evidence from professionals witnessing Adam's controlling behaviour was also provided to the Sheriff and a removal order under the ASPA was granted without her consent.

Practitioners working with Catherine explored their understanding of capacity, bounded rationality and the impact of undue influence and pressure in making a determination about her ability to say no to her son and how her relationship with him may have impacted on her willingness to protect herself, leaving her at risk of harm.

Implementation of the ASPA therefore draws upon professional understanding of concepts of capacity, bounded rationality and undue influence to enable the provision of support and protection to a range of adults including those who appear unable or unwilling to protect themselves but who nonetheless retain capacity to make decisions for themselves. Once Catherine was provided with support and protection, it was clear she had capacity to make decisions for herself. Medical evidence suggested that had intervention under the ASPA not taken place, Catherine would have died within a number of weeks from malnutrition.

Capacity, adult safeguarding and human rights

Patrick and Smith (2009) discuss the potential impact of the use of Section 35 of the ASPA (as described above) on the human rights of adults. They suggest that despite the historical use of undue influence in the UK for setting aside the decisions of an adult, Section 35 of the ASPA takes this concept a stage further. They argue that by enabling the setting aside of an adult's consent to an order applied for under the ASPA by a third party, despite the adult declaring they have not been unduly influenced, there is the potential for the adult's human rights to be breached under Article 8 of the European Convention on Human Rights (ECHR) which sets out the adult's right to a private life (Patrick and Smith, 2009). Conversely, the right to live free from harm is also enshrined in the ECHR (Article 3), and safeguarding can be viewed as one way of ensuring that this right is upheld (Greenfields et al., 2012). These separate rights contained within the ECHR can therefore be considered to be in conflict within a safeguarding paradigm, and it is at the intersection of these rights that much adult safeguarding work takes place, creating further dilemmas for practitioners and families (Stewart, 2016).

Reflecting on the position of the English courts discussed above and the argument developed by Patrick and Smith (2009), Scottish law appears to have ensured the State's ability to protect adults at risk of harm where their ability to protect themselves is reduced for a number of reasons, including compromised or unknown levels of capacity. Despite the ability of local authorities to apply for an order that does not have the consent of the adult, once the order is enacted it can still be difficult to enforce. For example, once a removal order under Section 14 of the Act is in place, as in the case of Catherine, and the adult is removed from an unsafe situation, they can immediately return home if they do not wish to remain in the place of safety. There are no compulsory measures to detain someone without their consent, even through the use of Section 35, which allows for the withholding of consent by the adult to be overridden by a Sheriff where sufficient evidence exists that they have been subject to undue pressure to do so. To do so would represent a deprivation of the liberty of that adult. Whilst this may limit the usefulness of Section 35, it may also ensure that any potential breach of the adult's human rights, including deprivation of liberty, is reduced at the same time as offering protection.

Supported decision making and human rights

A recent general comment (a mechanism used to clarify rights within specific human rights treaties) issued by the United Nations (UN) (2013) on Article 12 of the Convention on the Rights of Persons with Disabilities (CRPD) (United Nations, 2006) suggests that there are no circumstances under which those who have mental capacity to make their own choices should have this limited and that even when mental capacity is compromised, supported decision making should be preferred to substitute decision making. Supported decision making involves working with those who may have limited capacity to make decisions and exercise their legal capacity. Specific decisions are addressed, weighed and concluded by the individual, drawing on the support of others who might include friends, family or other trusted individuals. According to the United Nations (FRA, 2013):

> The individual is the decision maker; the support person(s) explain(s) the issues, when necessary, and interpret(s) the signs and preferences of the individual.

> Even when an individual with a disability requires total support, the support person(s) should enable the individual to exercise his/her legal capacity to the greatest extent possible, according to the wishes of the individual.

Davidson et al. (2015) suggest that it is helpful to think of supported decision making on a continuum with complete autonomy at one end and substitute decision making at the other, with legal capacity being maximised as one progresses towards complete autonomy (Bach and Kerzner, 2010, in Davidson et al., 2015). Chartres and Brayley (2010, in Davidson et al. 2015) identify a number of different types of supported decision making where more or less formal agreements and arrangements are in place.

These renewed discussions around supported decision making and the statement by the United Nations potentially present significant challenges to existing policy and legislation where it is possible to make decisions on behalf of those lacking capacity, such as the Adults with Incapacity (Scotland) Act 2000 and the Mental Capacity Act 2005 in England. Some commentators argue that supported decision making should be considered as a potential alternative to guardianship, while recognising the limitations to current models of supported decision making (Kohn et al., 2012). Indeed, there is limited evidence to suggest that supported decision making as it currently stands has achieved its potential to promote the autonomy of individuals while at the same time protecting them from harm (Kohn et al., 2012; see also Davidson et al.'s 2015 rapid evidence review which suggests that further research in this area is needed).

Citizenship and human rights

The overlap and potential conflict between safeguarding frameworks and broader human rights more generally has been of concern for some time and most obviously since the CRPD took effect in 2008 (Bartlett, 2012). It has been argued that the social model of disability had a significant influence on this declaration, and it was considered to be a significant advance in the rights for people with disabilities (Kayess and French, 2008), many of whom may be considered within adult safeguarding frameworks. Although recently Degener (2016) has argued that in fact a human rights model of disability underpins the CRPD extending the social model to encompass, for example, civil and political rights as well as economic, cultural and social rights. Article 16 of the CRPD highlights the right of individuals with disabilities to freedom from exploitation, violence and abuse in any setting and insists on government policy that ensures that instances of exploitation, violence and abuse against persons with disabilities are identified, investigated and, where appropriate, prosecuted. This could clearly cover a number of areas relevant for adult safeguarding. Consequently, consideration must be given to the potential for individual rights to be compromised when exploring opportunities for the provision of support and protection.

Also worthy of consideration are the rights adults have as citizens. There are a considerable number of definitions and concepts of citizenship that continue to cause debate, although there is a common thread which is generally perceived to be the balancing of rights and responsibilities (Lawson, 2001). The context of those rights and responsibilities differs throughout the various concepts, as does the balancing of those elements, which are often described as a conditional relationship (Mackay, 2011; Beckett, 2006). Politicians often use the term citizen to outline the responsibilities of their populations in a framework of equality (for example, a view of good citizens producing social capital through employment, social networks and other contributions to a broader society). The State provides care and protection when required but in return the individual is responsible for living a 'good life' as a citizen; as Lister (1998) described it, acting as a citizen rather than simply being a citizen.

Despite the range of models and concepts of citizenship relevant in considering the support and protection of adults, the conditional approach to citizenship (acting as a citizen) has been most prominent in the UK in recent times (Mackay, 2011). It is useful to consider the impact of limited or 'fragile citizenship' rights on adults at risk of harm. Use of adult safeguarding interventions may be more likely on those unable to claim their rights as citizens (Stewart, 2016). This might include those with limits to their capacity as a result of learning disability, mental disorder, poverty and social isolation.

The above context therefore suggests that practitioners working in adult safeguarding must balance a range of complex rights and responsibilities to ensure adults are empowered to protect themselves where possible or risk eroding their citizenship and breaching human rights. Safeguards to protect the rights of adults are therefore crucial in any intervention considered to support and protect an adult at risk of harm. Mechanisms for protecting the rights of adults vary across the different jurisdictions (Mandelstam, 2009), however commonly they include independent oversight of decisions, access to independent advocacy and a number of principles to guide practitioner intervention, including ensuring that any intervention is of benefit to the adult, that the adult's wishes are taken into account and that the least restrictive option to secure protection is used.

Challenges in safeguarding adults at the intersection of capacity/incapacity

As considered in detail in other Chapters within this volume, the key challenge in providing support and protection to adults is to balance freedom and choice with risk and protection (Preston-Shoot and Cornish, 2014; Sherwood-Johnson, 2012; Stewart, 2012; Mackay, 2011). By reducing the power of individuals by removing or compromising choice and control in their lives or reducing these aspects of daily living, there is a danger of paternalistic models evolving which reduce citizenship rights or increase their fragility for this group of adults (Stewart, 2016). Consideration must therefore be given by practitioners as to how to safeguard adults while promoting their right to self-determination, regardless of capacity, in a way that protects their rights both under UK and human rights legislation. In Scotland all legislation must be human rights compliant, consistent with the demands of the Scotland Act (1998); however, as previously discussed there is the potential for emerging interpretations of applied human rights to be compromised by the existing adult safeguarding framework. These significant issues also apply to other jurisdictions within the UK.

An increase in focus on evidence and justifiable decision making has been linked to risk aversion in social work practice and this has considerable implications for adult safeguarding (Coulshed and Orme, 2006). Ash (2013), in exploring the dilemmas for practitioners in safeguarding adults in Wales, found that the majority of staff prioritised self-determination over protection, particularly where there were resource constraints. This study drew on interviews and focus groups with social workers and managers as well as reviewing data from local adult safeguarding cases. Bergeron (2006) further suggested that the concept of self-determination was over-simplified in social work and in the elder abuse literature as a reason for non-intervention in cases of abuse. Sexton (2009) found that each agency had its own priorities and drivers of what constitutes independence and protection. These findings suggest that social workers *do* prioritise the rights and wishes of the adult, but perhaps to the detriment of their overall wellbeing in cases of continuing harm. This must be considered in the context not only of defensible practice whereby practitioners must be able to draw on appropriate evidence to justify their decisions but also of 'defensive practice' (Whittaker and Havard, 2015). Defensive practice occurs where safety is the primary consideration, the argument being that social work has shifted from a concern with 'need' to responding to 'risk'. It is argued that social work is practiced within a risk society (Beck, 1992) that has resulted in increasingly 'defensive and morally timid social work practice' (Whittaker and Havard, 2015: 3). This creates yet further dilemmas for social work and health care practitioners as they seek to promote self-determination while at the same time reduce risk.

Using Scotland as an example, Case Study B illustrates how the protection of an individual's rights and an acknowledgement of existing skills and strengths can support and protect an adult at risk of harm, despite lack of clarity over the adult's capacity.

Case study B

Laura was a female service user, age range 20–30. She was considered to be a parent with learning disabilities (assessed as mild) who required support in relation to practical and domestic daily living tasks and independent travelling, however, there was often ambiguity about whether or not her learning disability impacted on her capacity to make decisions and her capacity was assessed on a number of separate occasions. She presented as having difficulty making complex decisions especially regarding sexual relationships and their appropriateness. The assessment of Laura suggested that she engaged well with her child, who was cared for by another family member, but was unable to prioritise the child's needs above her own.

Laura was the subject of an adult protection referral due to concerns expressed by her family and the police about her sexual relationships following a number of incidents culminating in her disappearance from the family home and subsequent admission to hospital following an alleged sexual assault. An ASPA inquiry and investigation were undertaken and it was identified that Laura could be considered an adult at risk of harm as defined within the Act. Laura would not agree to any intervention under the ASPA and could make well-reasoned arguments about why she behaved in the way that she did. Such was the coherency of her argument that some staff expressed uncertainty over whether or not she did in fact have a learning disability. Staff had to consider the following with regard to assessing Laura's decision-making ability:

➢ Acknowledging that making unwise choices did not necessarily indicate that Laura lacked capacity (Mandelstam, 2009).

➢ Avoidance of assuming an innate lack of capacity in Laura simply because of her learning disability (Keywood et al., 2009).

➢ Consideration of whether Laura was able to withhold her consent in an informed manner (Patrick and Smith, 2009).

> Acknowledging that if Laura lacked capacity, her ability to determine the extent of the harm would be compromised. (Greenfields et al., 2012)

Whilst an assessment of Laura's capacity was sought and her IQ was re-tested, an Adult Protection Plan was put in place to aid in the ongoing protection of Laura within the limits that she had set and the confines of what the legislation allowed, all of which required her consent. This facilitated inter-agency collaboration including effective information sharing about her progress and ongoing contact with Laura and her family. Laura was subsequently assessed as lacking capacity, with medical evidence suggesting she had learned rote answers to questions about her risky behaviour which had masked the true extent of her cognitive abilities. A guardianship order was subsequently sought and granted under the appropriate substitute decision-making legislation.

There was a clear benefit to Laura with the use of the Adult Protection Plan in that it facilitated a holistic understanding of her situation across key stakeholders without being intrusive. Laura was aware of all aspects of the plan and contributed to its development. This collaborative approach reflected the principles of the legislation, promoted Laura's rights and empowered her to continue to make decisions for herself whilst providing an element of support and protection.

Determining the extent to which, legally, Laura had capacity to make decisions for herself was a significant challenge within this case, and practitioners had to draw upon a range of knowledge to analyse and understand the extent to which she was able to make her own decisions. The assumption of capacity clearly determined practice, and there is evidence in the above example that practitioners were keen to promote Laura's rights by ensuring that all practical steps had been taken to enable her to protect herself before considering whether or not her capacity in making those decisions could be compromised.

Conclusion

This Chapter has considered the ways in which adults who retain or lack capacity can be protected from harm via a range of safeguarding frameworks across the UK. Safeguarding those with and without capacity is both complex and challenging. The concept of incapacity can be diagnostic (based on the type of condition someone has) or functional (based on the decision being made) and it can fluctuate on a daily basis as well as on an issue-by-issue basis. The concept is by no means static, and therefore the policy or legislative framework must also be flexible to ensure that adults receive the appropriate support or protection at the right time.

The interaction between different elements of the safeguarding framework is evident in the challenges facing practitioners, particularly where the threshold between capacity and incapacity are unclear, and practitioners face a number of key tensions and dilemmas when working in this area. These dilemmas relate primarily to protecting an adult from harm (with or without their consent) while at the same time promoting their right to self-determination and a private life as enshrined in human rights legislation.

To date, much legislation across the UK (with the exception of Northern Ireland) has focused on substitute decision making where procedures are put in place to make decisions on behalf of a vulnerable adult (albeit such intervention is based upon a clear set of protective principles). However, in recent times developments at a European level have raised questions around the extent to which substitute decision making is human rights compliant. The UN Convention on the Rights of Persons with Disabilities has argued that supported decision making is the most appropriate way to safeguard the autonomy of people with disabilities whose capacity may be impaired, suggesting that other measures may be overly paternalistic or in breach of an individual's human rights. Yet evidence of the effective use of supported decision making is currently lacking (Davidson et al., 2015), suggesting that further research is necessary.

The Chapter has considered the ways in which practitioners can balance the tensions and dilemmas that are apparent in this complex area of work and has explored decision-making processes. Legislative criteria, principles and professional codes of practice all provide a framework to support practitioners to make decisions, but these must be set within the context of a risk society with its associated need for defensible (and often defensive) practice within an organisational context that is often bound by resource constraints. While the case studies have shown that effective practice can ensure that individual citizenship and human rights are upheld, this places significant demands upon practitioners. Effective, consistent support and supervision of staff is required to ensure practitioners are able to appropriately resolve the tensions and dilemmas for those adults whose capacity is either unknown or compromised.

Implications for practice

> Awareness of the relevant codes of practice and legislative options is necessary to promote a rights-based approach.

> Whilst there is need for defensible decision making that may undermine professional judgement, regular supervision is crucial to ameliorate the impact on professional practice.

➤ An understanding of the functional and diagnostic approaches to capacity will enable appropriate supported and substitute decision-making pathways to be considered.

References

Ash, A. (2013) A cognitive mask? Camouflaging dilemmas in street-level policy implementation to safeguard older people from abuse. *British Journal of Social Work*, 43(1): 99–115.

Bandura, A. (2001) Social cognitive theory: An agentic perspective. *Annual Review of Psychology*, 51: 1–26.

Bartlett, P. (2012) The United Nations Convention on the Rights of Persons with Disabilities and mental health law. *Modern Law Review*, 75(5): 752–778.

Beck, U. (1992) *Risk Society: Towards a New Modernity*, London: SAGE.

Beckett, A. (2006) *Citizenship and Vulnerability: Disability and Issues of Social and Political Engagement*, Houndmills: Palgrave Macmillan.

Bennett, J. (2010) Assessing mental capacity. *Social Care and Neurodisability*, 1(3): 44–48.

Bergeron, L. R. (2006) Self-determination and elder abuse: Do we know enough? *Journal of Gerontological Social Work*, 46(3–4): 81–102.

British Medical Association. (2008) *Mental Capacity Act Toolkit*, London: BMA.

Carr, S. (2014) National Adult Support & Protection in NHS Accident & Emergency Settings Project, Scottish Government. Available at http://www.scotland.gov.uk/Resource/0045/00453795.pdf.

Cooper, C., Selwood, A. and Livingston, G. (2008) The prevalence of elder abuse and neglect: A systematic review. *Age and Ageing*, 37(2): 51–160.

Coulshed, V. and Orme, J. (2006) *Social Work Practice*, Basingstoke: Palgrave Macmillan.

Davidson, G., Kelly, B., MacDonald, G., Rizzo, M., Lombard, L., Oluwaseye, A., Clift-Matthews, V. and Martin, A. (2015) Supporting decision making: A review of the international literature. *International Journal of Law and Psychiatry*, 38: 61–67.

Degener, T. (2016) Disability in a human rights context. *Laws*, 5(3): 35.

D. L v A Local Authority & Ors, EWCA Civ 253 (2012).

Duffy, J., Basu, S., Davidson, G. and Pearson, K. (2015) *Review of Legislation and Policy Guidance Relating to Adult Social Care in Northern Ireland*, Belfast: Commissioner for Older People in Ireland.

FRA European Union Agency for Fundamental Rights. (2013) *Legal Capacity of Persons with Intellectual Disabilities and Persons with Mental Health Problems*, Vienna: FRA.

Greenfields, M., Dalrymple, R. and Fanning, A. (2012) *Working with Adults at Risk from Harm*, Berkshire: Open University Press.

Kayess, R. and French, P. (2008) Out of darkness into light? Introducing the convention on the rights of persons with disabilities. *Human Rights Law Review*, 8(1): 1–34.

Keywood, K. (2009) Vulnerable adults, mental capacity and social care refusal. *Medical Law Review*, 18(1): 103–110.

Kohn, N. A., Blumenthal, J. and Campbell, A. T. (2012) Supported decision making: A viable alternative to guardianship. *Penn State Law Review*, 117(4): 1111–1154.

Lawson, H. (2001) Active citizenship in schools and the community. *Curriculum Journal*, 12(2): 163–78.

Lister, R. (1998) 'In from the margins: Citizenship, inclusion and exclusion', in Barry, H. C. (ed.), *Social Exclusion and Social Work: Issues of Theory, Policy and Practice*, Lyme Regis: Russell House Publishing.

Mackay, K. (2011) Compounding conditional citizenship: To what extent does Scottish and English mental health law increase or diminish social citizenship? *British Journal of Social Work*, 41(5): 931–948.

Mandelstam, M. (2009) *Safeguarding Vulnerable Adults and the Law*, London: Jessica Kingsley.

Nicholson, T. R. J., Cutler, W. and Hotopf, M. (2008) Assessing mental capacity: The Mental Capacity Act. *British Medical Journal*, 336(7639): 322–325.

O'Keeffe, M., Hills, A., Doyle, M., McCreadie, C., Scholes, S., Constantine, R., Tinker, A., Manthorpe, J., Biggs, S. and Erens, B. (2007) *Prevalence Survey Report: UK Study of Abuse and Neglect of Older People*, London: Comic Relief/ Department of Health.

Patrick, H. (2001) *Mental Health, Incapacity and the Law in Scotland,* Kent: Bloomsbury Professional.

Patrick, H. and Smith, N. (2009) *Adult Protection and the Law in Scotland*, Kent: Bloomsbury Professional.

Preston-Shoot, M. and Cornish, S. (2014) Paternalism or proportionality? Experiences and outcomes of the Adult Support and Protection (Scotland) Act 2007. *Journal of Adult Protection*, 16(1): 5–16.

Simon, H. A. (1972) 'Theories of bounded rationality' in McGuire, C. B. and Radnor, R. (eds), *Decision and organisation*, Amsterdam: North Holland Publishing.

Simon, H. A. (1978) Rationality as process and as product of thought. *American Economic Review*, 68(1): 1–16.

Scottish Government. (2008) *Communication and Assessing Capacity: A Guide for Social Work and Health Care Staff*, Edinburgh: Scottish Government.

Scottish Government. (2011) *Reshaping Care for Older People: A Programme for Change 2011–2021*. Available at http://www.scotland.gov.uk/Topics/ Health/Support-Social-Care/Support/Older-People/ReshapingCare [Accessed 8 January 2015].

Sexton, M. (2009) Fine lines and hard choices: Adult protection and social work ethics. *Ethics and Social Welfare,* 3(1): 79–86.

Sherwood-Johnson, F. (2012) Problems with the term and concept of abuse: Critical reflections on the Scottish Adult Support and Protection study. *British Journal of Social Work,* 42(5): 833–850.

Shtukaturov v Russia, Application no. 44009/05, (2008). Available at http:// www.mdac.info/sites/mdac.info/files/English_Shtukaturov_V_Russia.pdf.

Social Care Institute for Excellence (SCIE). (2015) *Adult Safeguarding: Types and Indicators of Abuse*, London: SCIE.

Stewart, A. (2012) *Supporting Vulnerable Adults: Citizenship, Capacity and Choice, Policy and Practice in Health and Social Care No. 13,* Edinburgh: Dunedin Academic Press Limited.

Stewart, A. (2016) *The Implementation of the Adult Support and Protection (Scotland) Act (2007)*, Glasgow: University of Glasgow.

United Nations. (2006) *United Nations Convention on the Rights of Persons with Disabilities*. Available at http://www.un.org/disabilities/convention/convention.shtml.

United Nations. (2007) From exclusion to reality: Realising the rights of persons with disabilities: Handbook for parliamentarians, Chapter 6: From provisions to practice: Implementing the convention, legal capacity and supported decision making. Available at http://www.un.org/disabilities/default.asp?id=242.

Whittaker, A. and Havard, T. (2015) Defensive practice as 'fear-based' practice: Social work's open secret? *British Journal of Social Work*, 46(5): 1158–1174. doi:10.1093/bjsw/bcv048.

Statutes

Adult Support and Protection (Scotland) Act (2007) Edinburgh: Blackwell.

Adults with Incapacity (Scotland) Act (2000) Edinburgh: Blackwell.

Care Act (2014) London: HMSO.

Mental Capacity Act (2005) London: HMSO.

Mental Capacity Act (Northern Ireland) (2016) Norwich: The Stationery Office.

Mental Health (Care and Treatment) (Scotland) Act (2003) Edinburgh: Blackwell.

Mental Health Act (2007) London: HMSO.

Scotland Act (1998).

Social Services and Well-being (Wales) Act (2014) Cardiff: National Assembly for Wales.

Northern Ireland Adult Safeguarding: Prevention and Protection in Partnership policy document (2015) Belfast: DHSSPS.

5

Multi-disciplinary Working: Moving Beyond Rhetoric

Kaye McGregor and Eileen Niblo, North Lanarkshire Council;
Michael Preston-Shoot, University of Bedfordshire

This Chapter explores adult safeguarding law in practice with respect to multi-disciplinary working. Put another way, it illustrates the outcomes in practice of the law in theory (Jenness and Grattet, 2005), which requires agencies to collaborate operationally and strategically to safeguard adults at risk of harm.

Drawing principally on research and practice experience in Scotland and England, the authors demonstrate well-known barriers to multi-disciplinary working and how they may be overcome. These are further explored in a case study at the end of the Chapter. The architecture of public services across the UK is being redesigned, not least in health and social care, in a search for greater efficiency (in the wake of austerity), integration and delivery through the joint efforts of agencies, which have stakes in respective policy areas (Dudau and McAllister, 2010). The hopeful expectation is that collaborative advantage results from agencies, working in partnership, achieving more than they might do separately.

The legal mandates

Powers and duties regarding multi-disciplinary working, for example to request information or cooperation, are contained in primary legislation and amplified by secondary legislation (regulations) and nation-specific guidance (Preston-Shoot, 2014). The Adult Support and Protection (Scotland) Act 2007 (ASPA), the Care Act 2014 (CA) for England and the Social Services and Well-being (Wales) Act 2014 (SSWB) are all predicated on the requirement for all agencies to work together to ensure the best outcomes for adults at risk. Their genesis, however, differs.

One of the contributory factors in Scotland to setting out the legisla-tion in this fashion was the findings contained within the *Report of the Inspection of Scottish Borders Council Social Work Services for People Affected by Learning Disabilities*. Investigations were carried out by the Mental Welfare Commission (MWC) and the Social Work Services Inspectorate and a joint statement was issued in April 2004 (Social Work Services Inspectorate, 2004). Recommendations included:

> Scottish Borders Council, together with its partners in NHS Borders and Lothian & Borders Police, should ensure multi-agency and multi-disciplinary co-ordination of complex cases at a sufficiently senior level to provide appropriate management oversight, effective information-sharing and accountable practice.

and:

> A Vulnerable Adults Bill should be introduced to complement the protective measures that already exist under the Adults with Incapacity (Scotland) Act 2000 and the Mental Health (Care and Treatment) (Scotland) Act 2003.

The eventual legislation (ASPA, 2007) was informed by the full range of recommendations from the report, which included better information sharing, better inter-agency working and inter-agency training. The ASPA put in place a legal framework that set out definitions, duties and author-ity for public bodies and also promoted rights for the adult. Duties were placed on a range of public bodies, including councils, NHS, police and also national bodies including the MWC, the Care Inspectorate (CI), the Office of the Public Guardian (OPG) and Healthcare Improvement Scotland (HIS). Duties for all public body employees include a duty to report and a duty to cooperate with a Council Officer carrying out an inquiry.

In England and Wales, rather than a major inquiry providing one of the triggers for legislation, locating adult safeguarding within primary legislation as opposed to statutory policy guidance has been premised on the belief that this would make public protection a higher priority for agencies. For this belief there may be some research justification, as the ASPA 2007 does appear to have provided a framework for enhanced multi-agency cooperation and commitment (Cornish and Preston-Shoot, 2013). Both the English and Welsh legislation contain an obligation to share information and a duty to cooperate with Safeguarding Adult Reviews, with further detail contained within secondary legislation and policy guidance (Department of Health [DoH], 2016).

Whilst encouraging multi-disciplinary working and setting out clear expectations on collaboration, the legal mandates are nonetheless weak.

They are essentially permissive rather than directive, crucially in two respects. Partner agencies are encouraged to provide resources for Safeguarding Adult Boards (SABs) or Adult Protection Committees (APCs) and to engage in collaborative activities, such as multi-agency audits, but SABs and APCs cannot compel agencies to participate. These systemic weaknesses mirror those in England and Wales for Local Safeguarding Children Boards (LSCBs) (Preston-Shoot and Pratt, 2014) where the result has been widespread variation in contributions and shortcomings in partnership working from some statutory partners. Indeed, research on the governance of adult safeguarding in Scotland (Cornish and Preston-Shoot, 2013) and in England prior to implementation of the CA 2014 (Braye et al., 2012) uncovered concerns about limited resources for SABs and inadequate participation from statutory partners, most especially health agencies.

Thus, for the law in practice to reflect legislative intentions, adult safeguarding depends on the strategic and operational commitment of those involved. If the legal mandate cannot ensure that the disengaged engage, then it becomes crucial to understand how local authorities and their partners move beyond the rhetoric and overcome familiar barriers to multi-disciplinary working.

Training

One key to successful implementation in practice of the law in theory is training. In keeping with the ASPA 2007, from the outset the majority of adult protection training aimed at staff across Scotland was established on a multi-agency basis. However, as biennial reports from the APCs in Scotland have sometimes recognised, the impact and outcomes of such training have not routinely been evaluated (Cornish and Preston-Shoot, 2013). From experience of developing and presenting such training, there was initially a good degree of scepticism of the usefulness of the legislation:

➢ Many social work staff initially focused on the protection orders included within the legislation, but when realising the requirement of the adult's consent to an application being made to the Sheriff court, or the need to demonstrate 'undue influence' on the adult if not consenting, considered that they would not be of great benefit to the situations they were dealing with.

➢ A number of NHS staff struggled with the concept of having a 'duty to report' when the adult did not wish an adult protection referral to be made, highlighting again the professional challenges that surround notions of autonomy, self-determination and confidentiality.

➤ Representatives from the police had an initial view that the role for them within the legislation would be simply to make referrals, thereafter having very little involvement.

➤ Across the board, there was debate on the usefulness of the three-point criteria and a view that it was not precise enough.

Nine years on, what has been the impact of the legislation and can we evidence multi-disciplinary working? From the authors' experiences of:

➤ developing adult protection procedures,

➤ developing and presenting multi-agency training,

➤ developing and leading multi-agency practitioner fora,

➤ carrying out multi-agency file reading,

➤ carrying out single agency audit,

➤ involvement in awareness raising across local communities,

➤ arranging service user evaluation, and

➤ completing a research study,

we would make the following observations. There is now in place a common language within Scotland of 'adult protection' and 'adult at risk of harm.' At the outset, this was new language, which required to be established, replacing 'vulnerable adults' and 'abuse.' People now attending multi-agency adult protection training from across the public sector and voluntary/independent sector come with an awareness of that language, but perhaps not the detail. This shared language enables and supports discussion of adult protection across the agencies and professions. It has supported work carried out by the APCs in seeking to raise awareness across communities as again the language used is consistent. It is often the case, however, that in referencing 'adult protection', the full title of 'adult support and protection' is neglected, highlighting that one cannot assume that consistent use of language equates to a shared understanding of how legislative principles should be implemented in practice.

The legislation supports frontline workers, and this is borne out at multi-agency practitioner discussions. Despite earlier scepticism, it is noted that the requirement to 'report' when it is 'known or believed' that an adult may be at risk of harm alleviates individual frontline workers of the uncertainty of what they should do, particularly when the adult concerned does not lack capacity and is requesting that the worker take no further action. There may be learning here for practitioners in Wales where the Social Services and Well-being Act 2014 introduces a similar duty. Additionally, reservations about the protection orders have diminished as practitioners, managers and service users have seen both their benefits and their proportional use within a human rights framework (Preston-Shoot and Cornish, 2014).

There does continue to be debate and discussion in respect of the three-point criteria which defines an 'adult at risk of harm'. In particular, there are discussions surrounding the issues of whether a person can 'safeguard' their own wellbeing, property, rights and other interests, and how that could be evidenced. There also exist questions regarding the determination of whether a person has, or requires, a diagnosis of 'disability, mental disorder, illness, physical or mental infirmity'.

These aspects form the basis of discussion at multi-agency training. Those attending are advised to ensure they are aware of their agency's adult protection procedures, which will set out their responsibilities, and also where they can seek support within their organisation in determining whether to make an adult protection referral. This could include speaking to their manager, or the procedures may indicate a staff member or team whose role it is to offer guidance.

That said, for training to be effective, it must be embedded in practice if the knowledge learned and skills acquired are not to decay. Similarly, given the variability of exposure to adult protection work and of knowledge and confidence in using legal rules, learning events are more effective when building on people's baseline knowledge (Cornish and Preston-Shoot, 2013).

Serious case reviews (SCRs) and safeguarding adult reviews (SARs) in England routinely comment on the absence of collaborative working across agencies, with professionals working separately and in isolated silos (Braye et al., 2015; Braye and Preston-Shoot, 2017). Consequently, recommendations about inter-agency communication and collaboration feature prominently, alongside training on such issues as capacity assessments, SAB partner commitment to the SCR/SAR process and the importance of multi-disciplinary meetings to develop a shared and planned approach to complex cases (Braye et al., 2013). There are considerable numbers of people being trained in relation to the CA 2014 and SSWA 2014, a responsibility that SABs should be overseeing, quite probably through sub-groups for training or workforce development, which are already commonplace. Partnership working is central to adult safeguarding and will need to be embedded in this training from the outset. Research (Braye et al., 2012) suggests that the outcomes of training should be evaluated in order to assess effectiveness in terms of impact on practice. Equally, training should cover not just workforce development – knowledge of the law, communication and relationship-building skills, assessment of capacity and of risk, and effective multi-disciplinary working – but also workplace development, the agency context and how organisational systems, such as eligibility criteria, thresholds, management of risk and decision making, availability of guidance and care management structures, affect learning and practice (Braye et al., 2013).

Operational practice

Across Scotland the legislation has led to a much greater awareness and focus on adults who are at risk and are unable to safeguard themselves. This is evidenced by the year-on-year increasing number of adult protection referrals submitted to local social work services. The majority of the adult protection referrals made are from within the main public bodies, referrals from Police Scotland being the largest number. Moreover, research has found that communication across statutory agencies has generally been positive although divergent professional values and poor referral rates from some agencies present a challenge (Cornish and Preston-Shoot, 2013).

This increase in statutory work, in particular for local authority social work services, has had an impact on the management of resources, including staffing. It is important therefore that analysis of referrals received is carried out on a multi-agency basis to provide learning both for those agencies making referrals and with social work services who have the 'duty to enquire.' From such analysis, greater support can be provided in determining if an adult is thought to meet the criteria requiring a referral to be made. Ultimately, however, that determination rests with staff members within the relevant agencies if the adult, in their opinion, meets the three-point criteria.

Whilst the increasing number of adult protection referrals being made can evidence increased awareness across agencies of adult protection and responsibilities under the legislation, it does not indicate the level of multi-agency working in taking forward inquiries and investigations, nor does it indicate the outcomes for adults. From audits of social work records and overview of who is attending adult protection case conferences, there is evidence of information sharing and cooperation across agencies – this is particularly evident in those situations where there are shared concerns about an adult and all are agreed that the person is an 'adult at risk of harm'. This is also borne out by research (Preston-Shoot and Cornish, 2014; Cornish and Preston-Shoot, 2013).

Even when there are shared views that someone is 'at risk', there remain areas where there will be debate across the agencies. One particular focus will be on whether the adult is at risk because of 'lifestyle choice'. An example may be an adult who is thought to be self-neglecting, living in poor environmental conditions. Dismissing such situations as the adult making a 'lifestyle choice' will miss the opportunity of seeking to understand the reasons the adult is in that situation. Such discussions will often make reference to whether the adult has the 'capacity' to make such decisions. The SCR carried out following the death of Michael Gilbert states that:

> with regard to Adult A's decision making it is clear that he was seen by some professionals as having mental capacity with the ability not only to make, but to act on his decisions and assume the consequences. In retrospect, this perception appears to have been formed from a superficial examination of Adult A's conduct, conversations and circumstances.
>
> (Flynn, 2011: 12)

The report goes on to state that:

> the presumption of capacity does not exempt authorities and services from undertaking robust assessments where a person's apparent decision is manifestly contrary to his wellbeing.
>
> (Flynn, 2011: 12)

Other SCRs and SARs in England have identified the challenges of securing multi-disciplinary cooperation, not least around the assessment of mental capacity and of risk (Braye et al., 2013; Braye et al., 2015; Braye and Preston-Shoot, 2017). As challenging for practitioners in England is the absence of a legislative framework that helps them to navigate through those situations where the six principles for safeguarding – empowerment, proportionality, partnership, protection, prevention and accountability – conflict. As research on self-neglect in England (Braye et al., 2013; 2015) has found, respect for autonomy and self-determination sometimes pulls against a duty of care and the promotion of dignity, with practitioners, managers and their agencies having to work together to find a resolution in each unique instance with the individual concerned.

The SCR in respect of Michael Gilbert demonstrates such a situation and the importance of understanding capacity, in human rights terms, as having moved from a 'status-based approach' to a 'functional approach' – that an adult can no longer be presumed to lack capacity solely because of a mental disorder or because they are acting as no prudent person might act. It also illustrates the importance of considering decisional capacity and executive capacity, the latter being the ability to implement decisions and to manage their foreseeable consequences (Braye et al., 2013).

Arrangements for the assessment of someone's capacity to understand across a range of tasks and decisions will be time consuming, both in terms of the process of referral and assessment. This can present challenges to making decisions when it is thought swift action is required to ensure an adult's safety. There may also be disagreements across agencies in respect of the necessity of such assessment. All of this will be part of the necessary multi-agency discussions, keeping the adult and their situation at the centre of discussions (for example, by evidencing supported decision making) and should also influence decisions about which legislation is considered in order to address the adult's situation.

These debates bring to the fore the balancing of the adult's right to self-determination and the duties placed on public bodies to support and protect those thought to be at risk of harm.

Stevens (2013) explores some of the challenges associated with achieving best practice across multi-agency settings and identifies the challenge of balancing the need to empower service users whilst minimising risk and indicating that all agencies need to have a clear understanding of their role. She indicates that whilst having in place a legislative process is an important element, as arguably exists more clearly in Scotland than in either England or Wales, it also requires all practitioners working across the agencies to reinforce that harm is unacceptable and everyone has a responsibility to prevent and report abuse.

These debates may also be informed by a clear commitment to making safeguarding personal (LGA and ADASS, 2014; Klée and Williams, 2013). For cases such as that of Michael Gilbert, the aim is to support people to make difficult decisions using a person-centred, outcomes-focused approach. To be successful, this approach requires the engagement of all partner agencies in planning, understanding the benefits of an outcome focused approach to safeguarding, sharing information, and identifying how the network can assist the individual concerned to achieve their goals as well as making people feel safe.

This brings us back to the legislative framework. Whilst it does not replace professional assessment and professional decision making, it does provide a framework for such processes. It is important for all concerned that they have an awareness of the wider scope of their role in seeking to ensure that their assessment is broadly based, supported by evidence which in turn informs their decision making. It is also important in contributing to the multi-agency discussions that those attending can articulate how they came to such decisions and at the same time listen to others who should have gone through the same processes. It is the sharing and recording of such information which will lead to informed joint and defensible decision making.

Case conferences, network meetings, decision making and management of risk

The primary focus of any adult protection case conference or network meeting is to consider the risk to the adult and how best to keep them safe. Most adult protection case conferences and network meetings, such as the vulnerable adult risk management meeting system used by several local authorities in England, are multi-agency and this offers an opportunity for relevant parties to come together and to share information, tasks and responsibilities in order to protect adults who are at risk of harm. Acknowledgement also has to be given to varying thresholds of agency held by individual workers. While there are many core skills which will be shared and understood, respect for individual skills that exist within each profession is also required. A case conference or network meeting should support a shared understanding of the risks the adult is experiencing and commit to clear decision making, accountability and improved outcomes for the adult at risk of harm, an action plan that is then followed through.

The chairperson has the responsibility of coordinating the information and ensuring everyone's view is heard. Often practitioners can find case conferences daunting as they deliver their assessment and recommendations. It has to be reinforced that while a practitioner may go into a meeting with one view, this is not static. Information from other sources may change that view and offer alternatives, with legislation offering a framework within which to consider what is known.

Those involved in working with people who are at risk should be aware that they are not solely responsible for managing risk. This is not something which is widely quoted among frontline staff and in fact the opposite may be expressed. Despite this feeling sometimes being articulated, the worker is not alone. The whole service has to share the responsibility – from senior management to first-line managers. The need for a wider ownership of risk is necessary and has been recommended by SCRs/SARs, with senior managers expected to chair multi-agency discussions of complex cases and to provide supervision (Braye et al., 2013; 2015). This applies to the person at risk, those posing the risk, their family, partner agencies and organisations involved in their lives, their community and wider society.

This does not mean that frontline workers can ignore their professional and legislative responsibilities nor areas for which they have a part to play, but it is important to acknowledge a much wider constituency of responsibility and ownership and to remind relevant others of this. However, practitioners also need to develop confidence in working in partnership, and especially in challenging the perspectives held by other professionals (LGA and ADASS, 2014; Preston-Shoot, 2014), and this may be one focus for the SAB to take forward, for example through a training sub-group.

There can be difficulties for individual staff members who have concerns about an adult but whose concerns are not shared by their line manager, who may believe that no further action is required. In keeping with professional responsibility, and requirements of registration, the worker must raise their concern at another level of management, stating clearly their understanding of a situation, although practitioners may doubt the support and protection that legislative provisions offer them when they escalate concerns, especially if employers respond negatively (Preston-Shoot, 2014). Multi-agency case conferences reinforce the shared responsibility of protecting adults at risk of harm. Protection plans clearly lay out the task and responsibility of each agency to meet that task. Regular core group meetings and reviews help to monitor progress of the protection plan and the responsibility and accountability of the agencies involved.

Partnership working can also be promoted and sustained by APCs/ SABs through workshops, seminars and case discussions. These too are mechanisms where complex cases can be discussed and a community of practice developed. Spending time developing inter-professional relationships and shared understanding can help practitioners to realise the ambitions of the legal rules with respect to multi-agency working by confronting such challenging issues as values, thresholds and definitions of need, as well as deriving learning for service development from SCRs/ SARs and case law decisions.

Strategic leadership in adult safeguarding

The development of corporate ownership of adult safeguarding falls to SABs in England and Wales, and APCs in Scotland. Legislation (ASPA, 2007; CA, 2014; SSWB, 2014) requires multi-agency working at this senior, strategic level; the focus is not just on frontline working. Collaborative strategic practice requires strong leadership that sustains a shared vision and good interpersonal relationships (Preston-Shoot, 2014). Effective safeguarding must be built on the willingness of partners to align their activities, priorities and organisational cultures to a common goal, and to develop partnership values and collaborative capacity building (Dudau and McAllister, 2010). The history of LSCBs in England and Wales shows that this is by no means easy. LSCBs are required to monitor and evaluate the effectiveness of how local authorities and their partners coordinate their activities to safeguard children. There has been progress in the development of a shared language and vision, but resource constraints, lack of engagement from some partners, weak leadership, reluctance to accept scrutiny, hesitancy to challenge colleagues and difficulties with continuity of membership have frustrated the work of some LSCBs (Preston-Shoot and Pratt, 2014; France et al., 2010) and indeed APCs/SABs (Cornish and Preston-Shoot, 2013; Braye et al., 2012).

Adult protection committees

The ASPA 2007 required all councils to establish APCs, the functions of which are set out in guidance issued by the Scottish Government (2008). Again, picking up on the recommendations made by the Borders Inquiry which included quality assurance and monitoring, a primary function of the Committees is to keep under review the procedures and practice of the public bodies. The Committees also have a significant role in ensuring cooperation and communication within and between agencies and to promote appropriate support and protection for adults (Scottish Government, 2008). A key purpose of having in place an Independent Chair is that they can impartially support and challenge all agencies involved. Unsurprisingly, therefore, the development of multi-disciplinary working processes has been emphasised by APCs, but outcomes have often not been formally evaluated (Cornish and Preston-Shoot, 2013).

Accountability for the Independent Chair and the Committee rests in reporting to local Chief Officers Groups and submission by the Independent Chair of a biennial report to the Scottish Minister. The fourth biennial reports were submitted in October 2016. The main thrust required of the biennial reports is now to indicate what difference multi-agency training and procedures make in terms of outcomes for adults.

Committees can gather a range of materials (e.g. statistical reports, notification of significant incidents or events, multi- and single-agency file reading, as well as engaging directly with practitioners, service users and carers) from which to form a view of how well the agencies are cooperating and working effectively together in seeking to support and protect adults at risk of harm. It is important that Committees are aware that this multi-agency responsibility is increasingly subject to political and public scrutiny (Braye et al., 2012), as evidenced by the screening of the BBC Panorama programme on Winterbourne View Hospital and the media attention which followed the publication of the resultant SCR carried out by Margaret Flynn (2012).

Committees themselves are made up of senior representatives from the statutory bodies which are tasked to play an essential role in adult protection. There may also be representation from the Scottish Fire Service, Scottish Ambulance Service, Crown Office and Procurator Fiscal Services and Trading Standards. It is likely that advocacy services, voluntary organisations and service users and carers will be represented also. Generally, there has been positive engagement by statutory agencies in establishing APCs and setting strategic direction locally for adult protection, although with some criticism about the commitment of health care professionals and the involvement of emergency services, social landlords, housing and independent care homes (Cornish and Preston-Shoot, 2013). Nonetheless, APCs have ensured that a spotlight remains on adult support and protection. The regular reporting to Chief Officers Groups ensures that this area of work remains in focus, as does the requirement to submit biennial reports to the Scottish Government. It has been recognised that there would be great benefit in having access to comparative statistical data across Scotland. There have been attempts to develop a national data set, which has identified variances in recording and also interpretation of adult protection inquiries and investigations as barriers to producing such information. There is a commitment however to respond to the difficulties and compile a Scotland-wide statistical report. APCs are also supported by the regular meetings of Independent Chairs, which leads to a sharing of experiences across Scotland and identification of key issues common to all. Having close links with the Scottish Government provides clear linkages between practice and policy.

Safeguarding adults boards

The CA 2014, together with statutory guidance (DoH, 2016) are clear about the statutory partners (Local Authority, NHS commissioners and the police) that will form the basis of the SABs, together with the requirement to cooperate, to produce an annual plan and an annual report, to commission safeguarding adults reviews and to share information. In England, unlike in Scotland, there are no new powers to protect adults from abuse. In Wales the SSWA 2014 does contain both a duty to report adults at risk and a power of entry. SABs will be responsible for ensuring the effectiveness of the partners in protecting adults at risk. Research will be needed to evaluate the effectiveness of these new legislative arrangements.

The statutory guidance (DoH, 2016) identifies agencies that may be invited to join the SAB alongside the statutory partners. The guidance stresses the necessity of a strong multi-agency framework of cooperation, with SABs promoting joint training, cooperation in learning and applying lessons from safeguarding adult reviews, an open culture, accountability and procedures that clearly outline roles and responsibilities. Unlike in Scotland, there is no requirement for SABs to have an Independent Chair, although this is seen as potentially useful in holding agencies to account. Earlier research had not found overwhelming evidence that supported independent chairing arrangements (Braye et al., 2012). An association of Independent Chairs in England meets quarterly and does have some links to government that enable commentary on policy and practice.

In a review of governance by SABs (Braye et al., 2012), working together could be challenging even where individual members had a strong commitment to contributing to a Board's work and believed in the advantages to be gained from a partnership approach. Barriers included:

> an inadequate understanding of legal rules;

> a clash of cultures, attitudes, priorities and thresholds;

> high-level strategic partnership not always resulting in local collaboration; and

> not every agency or professional group sees adult protection as part of their remit.

Implementation of partnership working at a strategic level was variable, as was understanding of roles and responsibilities across professional networks. Key to the development of SABs appeared to be a history of effective working together; the development of protocols regarding thresholds, information sharing, management of complex cases and the resolution of disagreements; whole system events such as learning seminars; and mutual understanding of the importance of adult safeguarding. Indeed, the characteristics of effective Boards are those where there is an agreed strategic direction, including core values and desired outcomes, clear priorities and effective structures. The culture is reflective with openness to outside scrutiny and challenge. Performance management is evidence-based and learning-oriented. Board membership combines specialist knowledge of safeguarding with positional authority to secure change (Preston-Shoot and Pratt, 2014; Braye et al., 2012).

The future

In looking back to the impact of the ASPA 2007 on multi-agency working, both at operational and strategic level, it is clear from information gathered by APCs, the increasing number of referrals submitted to social work services, and from research (for example, Cornish and Preston-Shoot, 2013) that there is now a much greater awareness of adult protection across agencies, professional groups and increasingly local communities. There is evidence of effective multi-agency working.

There are also the ongoing challenges in multi-agency working as mentioned above, but such debates and discussions are to be expected. The importance in this context is on each staff member involved being aware of not only their role and responsibility but of what informs their practice. Understanding on what basis they form an assessment of any situation and awareness that all involved will have a valid contribution, and ultimately keeping the adult central to all decisions, are required to guide such discussions.

Similar considerations apply in England and Wales although here, at both operational and strategic levels, positive multi-disciplinary working may have been developed as much in spite of legislation as because of it. Implementation of the CA 2014 and SSWA 2014 brings fresh challenges of securing sufficient seniority in SABs to ensure corporate responsibility for developing and monitoring procedures and practice, and of ensuring that all partners are fully involved in complex cases. Perennial issues, such as information sharing and silo working, will not simply evaporate because of new legal rules. Since SABs will not be able to impose either strategic direction or operational practices on partner agencies, much will continue to depend on the relationships that are developed.

There are moreover current policy and structural changes, which may bring challenges to the progress made so far. This includes the recent restructuring of police in Scotland, resulting in the creation of Police Scotland, and of probation services in England. The challenge here is of a major partner within adult protection undergoing change which may suit a national organisation or aspect of political social policy but may not fit in with local arrangements.

Taking forward the requirements of the Public Bodies (Joint Working) Act 2014 in Scotland and progressing the integration of health and social care across the rest of the UK will also bring structural change. As well as placing further demands on managers within the agencies in establishing the new arrangements, and uncertainty for staff across the agencies in respect of their roles and responsibilities, it will be important that this does not detract from the progress that has been made in respect of adult protection. Finally, the ongoing priority of widening access to self-directed support and individual budgets is likely to lead to a greater number of direct payments and recruitment of personal assistants, which will add another dimension to adult protection – balancing the rights of the adults with the responsibilities of the public bodies.

Case Study – Mr Smith

The following case study is designed to explore some of the above noted issues in adult safeguarding and to reflect some of the ethical dilemmas that practitioners face. While illustrating the limitations of statutory intervention, it also demonstrates the potential of effective multi-professional practice for achieving better outcomes for adults at risk of harm.

Mr Smith is a 65-year-old man who, prior to his current circumstances, was married with two children. He owned an engineering business and was an active and respected member of his community. He owned his own home and had an active social and family life. Unfortunately Mr Smith began to drink alcohol on a regular basis and outwith the normal social boundaries. This eventually resulted in the loss of his family, business and home. He moved around various homeless units, and as his alcohol use increased his options for stable accommodation continued to reduce. At the time of referral to social work Mr Smith was living in a caravan, which was located in a local scrap yard and belonged to an old business acquaintance, Mr Black.

Mr Black contacted social work services one afternoon expressing concern that Mr Smith had lost a significant amount of weight as he was not eating properly, drinking regularly and his physical health was deteriorating. He also described him as being in a neglectful state, appearing physically unable to care for himself. Mr Smith had refused to allow him to contact his general practitioner (GP) and he was unclear what to do. Mr Black was also concerned about his living conditions and he felt unable to evict him as he had nowhere else to live. Mr Black stated that the caravan had no running water, no cooking facilities and the toilet was blocked. Mr Smith was using the scrap yard's toilet facilities, although there had been occasions when he had been incontinent. Staff on site were buying him food from the local snack van, and although his alcohol intake had reduced, as he was no longer able to go out or shop for himself, his physical health remained poor.

Mr Black reported that Mr Smith was able to communicate but was on occasions quite confused, thinking he was going to work or had to collect his children from school. Two social workers visited Mr Smith to undertake an assessment and to encourage him to accept medical attention, however he refused saying he was fine. Given the significant risk to Mr Smith's poor physical health and home circumstances, his inability to safeguard his own wellbeing through poor understanding of his situation and his current infirmity, as set out in the three-point criteria of the Adult Support and Protection (Scotland) Act 2007 (ASPA), a decision was taken that all future interventions would be managed under the ASPA 2007. This provides a legislative framework which can support staff and share decision making; however, it does not take away from professional judgement and the need for robust assessment.

Mr Smith refused a medical assessment or support. Social workers and other professionals within the safeguarding field regularly face the dilemma of wanting to protect and improve the individual's life while trying to balance their rights to make informed choices and to live with reasonable risks. For Mr Smith there appeared to be very few protective factors in place to keep him safe other than Mr Black, who on further discussion was feeling overwhelmed with the responsibility.

The question of capacity is another area where practitioners can regularly struggle. Mr Smith's conversation moved from thinking he was still married and working to knowing he lived alone and his home circumstances were poor. Had Mr Smith remained consistently confused, workers would have been able to justify to themselves and others that overriding his right to remain at home was in his best interests. As illustrated here, however, periods of lucid conversation may support a view that the adult is making a 'lifestyle choice' which removes the need for workers to take action they are not confident in.

Capacity laws across the world have, in human rights terms, largely moved from a 'status-based approach' to a 'functional approach' (Shtukaturov v Russia, 2008). Whereas in the past, in many contexts, an individual was presumed to lack capacity because of a mental disorder, today such an assumption is no longer valid – it depends on the individual circumstances. Essentially, intervening in the private life of an individual (e.g. in their financial affairs) or interfering with their physical integrity (e.g. through a medical procedure) without their consent is a serious infringement of their right to respect for private, family and home life. As with any infringement of that right it must pass three tests – it must be legal (according to the law), necessary (the least restrictive alternative) and proportionate to the pursuit of a legitimate aim. These tests must be passed in each instance, meaning that assessments of decision-making capacity should be individualised and not applied as blanket policies.

It could be argued that 'interfering' in Mr Smith's life was necessary and proportionate, but was it legal? Yet failing to protect him from self-harm could also be seen as ignoring his right to dignity, respect and a reasonable quality of life that everyone is entitled to. Mr Smith's physical health needed further assessment, and unfortunately in these circumstances the Adult Support and Protection (Scotland) Act 2007 does not offer emergency powers. While it may offer the power to transfer an adult to a suitable place for assessment or interview, it does not confer the right to detain the person should they wish to leave. It was acknowledged that Mr Smith was not willing at this time to consider admission to hospital or another care setting that would support his care and medical needs.

Consideration was also given to using the Mental Health (Care and Treatment) (Scotland) Act 2003. A mental health officer (MHO) and Mr Smith's local GP agreed to visit urgently. Mr Smith was assessed for detention under the Act, however as he presented more lucidly at interview his GP refused to detain him. The Mental Health (Care and Treatment) (Scotland) Act 2003 states that for Mr Smith to meet the criteria for detention he (a) has to have a mental disorder and because of that mental disorder his decision-making ability is significantly impaired;

(b) it is necessary to be detained in hospital for the purpose of determining what medical treatment should be given to the patient and (c) if not detained, there could be significant risk to the health and safety of the adult or any other person. It could be argued that Mr Smith's decision to live in squalid conditions or neglect his physical health needs was due to his decision-making ability being significantly impaired and that while at the time of interview he appeared more lucid, previous knowledge of his confused state might have been verified by others. At the very least, a detention under this Act would have allowed for further assessment of his mental health and potentially identified a mental disorder. It could also be debated that Mr Smith would be at significant risk were he not detained in hospital and that appropriate treatment was available. There was, however, no evidence of a mental disorder at the time of interview and consequently it would be illegal and a deprivation of Mr Smith's liberty to detain him without all the legal criteria being met. The difficulty the practitioners faced was how to protect Mr Smith when his quality of life was so poor. There was also the dilemma of serious harm happening to him before workers could put supports in place that he would accept.

In practice, an urgent multi-agency case conference was convened by social work the next day and fortunately key partners, including representatives from social work and housing services along with health professionals, were engaged. This level of cooperation can vary and impact significantly on the information shared and the decisions made.

The primary focus of any adult protection case conference is to consider the risk to the adult and how best to keep them safe. Consideration has to be taken of the risks and protective factors already in place, what can be built on, as well as any new protective factors that need to be put in place.

The vast majority of adult protection case conferences are multi-agency and this offers an opportunity for sharing of information, tasks and responsibilities in order to protect adults who are at risk of harm. Acknowledgement also has to be given to varying thresholds of agency and individual workers. While professionals have many core skills that they share and understand, they also have to respect each other's individual skills that make them unique to their own profession. A case conference should help move towards a shared understanding of the risks the adult is experiencing and commit to clear decision making, accountability and improved outcomes for the adult at risk of harm.

The chairperson has the responsibility of coordinating the information and ensuring everyone's view is heard. They will also have the responsibility of ensuring that the decisions taken at the meeting are distributed to all partners and taken forward. Often practitioners can find case conferences daunting as they deliver their assessment and recommendations.

It has to be reinforced that while practitioners may go into a meeting with one view, this is not static. Information from other sources may change their view and offer alternatives they were not aware of.

The Adult Support and Protection (Scotland) Act 2007 highlights that risk enablement, is not one person's business. It sets out a range of responsibilities and duties on a number of statutory organisations (Public Bodies in the Act) – Councils, NHS, the police, inspection agencies and the Mental Welfare Commission – which gives them a very clear role in reducing the risk to 'adults at risk'. It also very clearly identifies the person's own rights and responsibilities in the situation, as the adult needs to consent to any action deemed necessary to protect them; though, as stated earlier, it is important to establish if it is thought that the adult has the 'capacity' to make such decisions.

Adult Support and Protection multi-agency case conferences reinforce the shared responsibility of protecting adults at risk of harm. Protection plans clearly lay out the task and responsibility of each agency to meet that task. Regular core group meetings and reviews help to monitor progress of the protection plan and the responsibility and accountability of the agencies involved.

The four key decisions of the case conference were:

➤ To continue supporting Mr Smith under Adult Support and Protection legislation as it offered a framework where both staff and Mr Smith would be supported and protected.

➤ Health and social work staff would again visit Mr Smith to discuss options to look at his health and social care needs.

➤ Further discussion with police to consider possible options available to remove Mr Smith to a place of safety.

➤ Environmental Services to be contacted for information on the legalities of Mr Smith residing in the caravan.

A further visit to Mr Smith highlighted that both his physical health and living conditions had deteriorated. While he continued to refuse support, Mr Smith was advised he could no longer live in the caravan due to the insanitary conditions and he reluctantly agreed to alternative accommodation as long as it was not a hospital. Mr Smith was of the view that if he went into hospital he would not come out. As professionals, when faced with crisis it is easy to feel frustrated that your attempts to improve the person's life can seem unwanted or even obstructive; however, looking beyond Mr Smith's initial refusal of support, his fear of hospitals was an understandable influencing factor.

This situation highlights the importance of exploring the person's responses and thinking more broadly for alternative options. Mr Smith agreed to a temporary placement within a care home until alternative accommodation became available. While it was clearly recognised that Mr Smith's medical needs were paramount and a care home was not the preferred option, it was the only option that he would consider and one where he could access medical care via district nursing services and also have his personal care needs met.

As this case illustrates, multi-disciplinary case conferences promote shared ownership of decision making and agreement that services can be made available even if they have to be delivered outwith conventional service areas. This more imaginative thinking in how we utilise services can result in better outcomes for the person, facilitating a more person-centred approach. Too often individuals have to fit into the service rather than services being organised to fit the person.

Conclusion

The different legal, policy and operational frameworks that inform adult safeguarding across the UK provide opportunities and challenges for effective multi-agency working. This Chapter has argued that successful implementation in practice of adult safeguarding law in theory is predicated on the provision of high-quality multi-disciplinary training. It further posits that adult protection legislation can offer protection to those who are at risk of harm and not able to be supported under other statutory measures. Such legislation reinforces the duty of all agencies to cooperate, report any concerns and share information. In Scotland, attendance at adult protection case conferences from all the partner agencies has improved as the ASPA has matured, and there are very good examples of joint working. This legislation has generated a wholesale shift towards effective partnership working by placing relevant duties on each organisation. While it may have initially been felt as putting 'additional demands on services', practitioners across frontline agencies are finding that better coordination and joint ownership of decision making prevents duplication and ultimately better outcomes for adults at risk of harm.

Implications for practice

> The successful implementation in practice of adult safeguarding law in theory is predicated on the provision of high-quality multi-disciplinary training.

➤ Partnership working is central to adult safeguarding in supporting people and professionals to make difficult decisions using a person-centred, outcomes-focused approach.

➤ Multi-agency case conferences, protection plans and core group meetings reinforce the shared responsibility of protecting adults at risk of harm.

➤ They can also facilitate imaginative thinking in how services may be utilised in safeguarding adults in complex situations where other legal measures cannot be used.

References

Braye, S., Orr, D. and Preston-Shoot, M. (2012) The governance of adult safeguarding: Findings from research. *Journal of Adult Protection*, 14(2): 55–72.

Braye, S., Orr, D. and Preston-Shoot, M. (2013) *A Scoping Study of Workforce Development for Self-Neglect Work*. Available at http://www.skillsforcare.org.uk/Document-library/NMDS-SC,-workforce-intelligence-and-innovation/Research/Self-Neglect-Final-Report-301013-FINAL.pdf [Accessed 17 June 2015].

Braye, S., Orr, D. and Preston-Shoot, M. (2015) Learning lessons about self-neglect? An analysis of serious case reviews. *Journal of Adult Protection*, 17(1): 3–18.

Braye, S. and Preston-Shoot, M. (2017) *Learning from SARs: A Report for the London Safeguarding Adults Board*. London: London ADASS.

Cornish, S. and Preston-Shoot, M. (2013) Governance of adult safeguarding in Scotland since implementation of the Adult Support and Protection (Scotland) Act 2007. *Journal of Adult Protection*, 15(5): 223–236.

Department of Health (DoH). (2016) *Care and Support Statutory Guidance: Issued Under the Care Act 2014*, London: Department of Health.

Dudau, A. I. and McAllister, L. (2010) Developing collaborative capabilities by fostering diversity in organisations. *Public Management Review*, 12(3): 385–402.

Flynn, M. (2011) *The Murder of Adult A (Michael Gilbert): A Serious Case Review*, Luton: Luton Local Safeguarding Adults Board.

Flynn, M. (2012) *Winterbourne View Hospital: A Serious Case Review*, Bristol: South Gloucestershire Safeguarding Adults Board.

France, A., Munro, E. R. and Waring, A. (2010) *The Evaluation of Arrangements for Effective Operation of the New Local Safeguarding Children Boards in England: Final Report*, London: Department for Education.

Jenness, V. and Grattet, R. (2005) The law-in-between: The effects of organizational perviousness on the policing of hate crime. *Social Problems*, 52(3): 337–359.

Klée, D. and Williams, C. (2013) *Making Safeguarding Personal: Summary*, London: Local Government Association.

LGA and ADASS. (2014) *Making Safeguarding Personal 2013/14 Report of Findings*, London: Local Government Association.

Preston-Shoot, M. (2014) *Making Good Decisions: Law for Social Work Practice*, Basingstoke: Palgrave Macmillan.

Preston-Shoot, M. and Cornish, S. (2014) Paternalism or proportionality? Experiences and outcomes of the Adult Support and Protection (Scotland) Act 2007. *Journal of Adult Protection*, 16(1): 5–16.

Preston-Shoot, M. and Pratt, M. (2014) 'Symbolic half measures? On local safeguarding children boards, their contributions and challenges', in Blyth, M. (ed.), *Moving on from Munro: Improving Children's Services* (pp. 159–182), Bristol: Policy Press.

Scottish Government. (2008) *Guidance for Adult Protection Committees*. Available at http://www.scotland.gov.uk/Resource/Doc/256411/0076139. pdf [Accessed 12 June 2015].

Shtukaturov v Russia, Application no 44009/05, (2008). Available at http://www. mdac.info/sites/mdac.info/files/English_Shtukaturov_V_Russia.pdf [Accessed 15 June 2015].

Social Work Services Inspectorate. (2004) *Report of the Inspection of Scottish Borders Council Social Work Services for People Affected by Learning Disabilities*. Available at http://www.gov.scot/Resource/Doc/25954/0025525.pdf [Accessed 15 September 2015].

Stevens, E. (2013) Safeguarding vulnerable adults: Exploring the challenges to best practice across multi-agency settings. *Journal of Adult Protection*, 15(2): 85–95.

PART 2

Safeguarding Adults: Practice Perspectives

6

Safeguarding Those Experiencing Mental Ill-Health

Jim Campbell, University College Dublin; Gavin Davidson, Queens University Belfast; Graham Morgan, Highland Users Group

There is considerable variation in UK laws and policies that seek to safeguard the rights of people with mental health problems. This Chapter will highlight a number of common issues and tensions. As a general principle, laws and policies designed to safeguard adults should normally be applied to the situation of those with mental health problems alongside more specialist mental health and capacity laws (Johns, 2011: 93–97); these will be discussed in the first part of this Chapter. We will then identify the policy drivers and legal requirements associated with capacity and mental health laws, in particular substitute and supported decision making in England and Wales (Brayne and Carr, 2010; Brown et al., 2009), and Scotland (Armstrong, 2008). Attention will also be paid to the particular situation in Northern Ireland where there are no distinct vulnerable adults laws but where practice is shaped by reference to common, criminal and civil law, a number of policy initiatives (Carter Anand et al., 2013) and the newly enacted Mental Capacity Act (Northern Ireland) 2016. The Chapter will then describe and analyse assessment processes, safeguards and oversight processes, mindful of some of the criticisms of policy and practice evidenced in the literature. In our discussions we are mindful of the views of those who are subject to these laws and policies. We will use the term service user to describe people in these circumstances, but are mindful of the contested nature of this concept (McLaughlin, 2009). Reference will then be made to studies of service user views, some carried out by peer researchers, about these processes, one of which forms a case study later in the Chapter. The Chapter concludes with a case study that illustrates the key themes brought together in the Chapter.

Policies and laws on safeguarding adults in the UK

A key to understanding safeguarding issues for people with mental health problems is to consider the interfaces between safeguarding policies, mental health and capacity laws. Graham et al. (2014) have traced the historical development of vulnerable adults, and later safeguarding adults policies in England, drawing some comparisons with other jurisdictions. Beginning with piecemeal responses to a number of inquiries into adult abuse in the 1980s and 1990s, UK policies tend to be more comprehensive, although variable across jurisdictions. Of particular note are the English Care Act 2014 and the Adult Support and Protection (Scotland) Act 2007. These place statutory duties on authorities to develop partnerships, structures of responsibility and guidelines to carry out necessary inquiries into allegations of abuse and neglect of adults. In Northern Ireland the main policy framework was set out by the Department of Health, Social Services and Public Safety (DHSSPS) in 2006 in *Safeguarding Vulnerable Adults: Regional Adult Protection Policy and Procedural Guidance*. This was revised and updated in cooperation with the Department of Justice (DoJ) and launched in 2015 as *Adult Safeguarding: Prevention and Protection in Partnership*. There are, however, a number of other relevant policies, including the *Protocol for the Joint Investigation of Alleged and Suspected Cases of Abuse of Vulnerable Adults* (2003), revised in 2009 by the Health and Social Care Board, Police Service of Northern Ireland and RQIA; Safeguarding *Vulnerable Adults: A Shared Responsibility* (Volunteer Now, 2010, revised 2013) which provides guidance for the voluntary and community organisations; *Adult Safeguarding in Northern Ireland* (DHSSPS, 2010b) which set up the Regional and Local Partnership arrangements; and *Achieving Best Evidence in Criminal Proceedings* (DoJ, 2012). What these myriad developments in policy in Northern Ireland have in common is a focus on establishing joint working protocols with an emphasis on shared responsibility and partnership working. A recent review of adult protection legislation across the UK, Ireland and internationally (Carter Anand et al., 2013), funded by the Commissioner for Older People in Northern Ireland, suggested that the argument either for or against specific adult protection legislation is not conclusive. It also asserted that:

> Legislative reform is neither required nor appropriate to address all issues raised by health professionals, services and older people, carers and families. Non legal solutions to the gaps and issues identified required a further review…The adoption of a human rights approach promotes greater service user involvement and recognition of the diverse cultural, social, political needs of older people in relation to informed policy and legislative reform.
>
> (Carter Anand et al., 2013: 6)

Compulsory mental health laws in the UK

Having set out key legislative and policy developments in relation to adult safeguarding across the UK, this section begins to consider how these might intersect with specialist laws that have been put in place to provide care and treatment to those experiencing mental distress. In particular, we consider two main areas of law: compulsory admission to hospital and the use of Community Treatment Orders (CTOs) by professionals in the UK. It should be noted that the term CTO as used in this Chapter relates only to community treatment orders and not to compulsory treatment orders as set out in the Mental Health (Care and Treatment) (Scotland) Act 2003. As in jurisdictions outside the UK (Davidson et al., 2016; Campbell et al., 2006), the State seeks to balance the coercive nature of these laws with a range of safeguards and systems of substitute and supportive decision making.

Before the 1980s nearly all forms of compulsory care and treatment took place within the confines of psychiatric institutions, and mental health laws reflected these forms of coercion. Typically, professionals use three broad threshold criteria when applying mental health laws: the existence of a mental disorder (that can include mental illness, learning disability and other impairments of mind); risk; and a judgement about the seriousness of the risk that justifies the use of compulsory powers. Admission to hospital under these circumstances does not automatically entail that treatment can be compulsorily used, except in particular, limited circumstances of immediate risk. A separate process is then followed to allow clinicians to detain for treatment. Depending on the jurisdiction, a number of safeguards are established in law, including access to mental health tribunals and the right to legal and peer advocacy services. Policy makers are increasingly interested in other safeguards such as advance directives (advance statements in Scotland), the right to independent advocacy and lasting powers of attorney (England and Wales)/ enduring power of Attorney (Northern Ireland). Service users and their carers should also expect to be the recipient of a coherent care planning process on discharge from hospital.

A great deal of literature on these laws has been generated that highlight strengths and limitations associated with a number of factors (Campbell, 2008). There seems little doubt that compulsory mental health laws are required when someone is so unwell that they may be in danger of harm to themselves or others. On the other hand, concerns have been expressed about how service user rights are sometimes compromised by processes and that professionals may not be sufficiently skilled to understand the negative impact of inpatient care and treatment (Evans et al., 2012).

While many of the measures and powers available within mental health law in the UK involve compulsion associated with removal from the community, a relatively newer option, that of CTOs or Outpatient Commitment (OPC as these forms of law are described in the USA and parts of Europe), are increasingly used by mental health professionals to manage situations of risk outside the hospital setting. They were introduced in Victoria, Australia, in the 1980s and are now commonplace across Australasia, some provinces in Canada and everywhere in the UK, including Northern Ireland where they have been included in the new Mental Capacity (Northern Ireland) Act 2016. CTOs permit approved professionals to compel patients to accept medication, attend facilities and live in designated residences. If some or all of these restrictions are not agreed or met by the service user, the result is often a return to hospital. Despite policy makers' intentions to restrict their use to targeted populations, there is almost always an upward trend in numbers of service users placed on these orders, and the evidence base for their effectiveness is contested (Burns et al., 2013, 2015; Churchill et al., 2007). The arguments for and against CTOs have been summarised by Castells-Aulet et al. (2013) as follows:

For:

➢ They have the potential to offer a less restrictive option for care and treatment by enabling the patient to remain in their own home.

➢ They may prevent relapse and the need for hospital admission, although further research is needed to provide robust evidence for this.

➢ They can lead to better access to community-based services and strengthen important social networks by allowing patients to maintain supportive relationships with family, friends, employers and other community members rather than disrupting these relationships.

Against:

➢ They may adversely affect the therapeutic relationship between the professional and service user as there is less likely to be ongoing opportunities for therapeutic interventions.

➢ They compromise the principle that people have a right to refuse treatment – refusal is likely to result in an admission to or recall to hospital.

➢ Some populations, particularly young men and those drawn from black and ethnic minority communities, are overrepresented in statistics, although this is also true of inpatient populations.

➢ They often lead to 'medication-only' regimens.

CA is underpinned by five principles that can be summarised
: (i) that capacity should always be presumed; (ii) the optimi-
the person's ability to make decisions; (iii) that patients are
o make 'unwise decisions'; (iv) decisions and actions made
e must be in their best interests; (v) and that such decisions
east restrictive in terms of rights and freedoms. Although this
ent to supporting decision making appears to be positive,
e substitute decision making continues to be the main type
ention when the MCA is used (Brown et al., 2009). The law
how a person may lack capacity, in terms of being unable to
d information relevant to the decision, retain this information,
information as part of the process of making the decision or
icate this decision.

scribed earlier in this Chapter, the process of substitute deci-
ing using the Mental Health Act 2007 in England is similar to
in other UK jurisdictions. Section 2 states the grounds: '(a)
fering from mental disorder of a nature or degree which war-
detention of the patient in a hospital for assessment (or for
nt followed by medical treatment) for at least a limited period;
he ought to be so detained in the interests of his own health
or with a view to the protection of other persons'. The 2007
g Act introduced compulsory community powers as outlined
rm of CTOs described above. It is important to note that in the
ental health law, whether in hospital or in the community, full
ations of capacity as described by the CRPD, was not a neces-
ria; thus the need for the interface between mental health and
laws.

MCA 2005 contains a number of important safeguards for peo-
. mental health problems, including the use of Best Interest
nts in which professionals support participation in the
-making process by service users who lack capacity. Such assess-
hould take into account past and present wishes, beliefs and
. Further safeguards are provided in the form of the Independent
Capacity Advocate Service (IMCAS), introduced after the 2007
se advocates can provide support and representation in impor-
ision-making situations (for example, in care or adult protection
substantial medical treatments, and where accommodation for
an 28 days in hospital or 8 weeks in a care home is being arranged
ged). A Court of Protection and Mental Health Tribunal also exist
ct the rights and interests of people with mental health problems
k capacity.

Capacity laws in the UK

Issues around capacity and incapacity and {
concepts were discussed in Chapter 4, hov
capacity and the ability to make decisions, pa
is also important for those working with indiv
distress. Decisions about capacity were allude
sionals traditionally used the types of mental l
and it is only in the last decade that the con
mental health and capacity have been made m
iation in these interfaces, across the UK. This l
of guidelines for professionals that are used ·
make decisions for themselves because of their
(often described as 'impaired capacity'). Wh
necessary, the professionals who use the law
decision makers'; but, importantly, they are als
portive decision making as an alternative.

International law and policy, notably the U
on the Rights of Persons with Disabilities (
Convention on Human Rights (ECHR), higl
professionals should follow in these circums
to assume capacity in the first instance; adh
option; support people to make their own de
about best interest and benefit; and ensure tha
vant family members, carers and professionals a
decision-making process. They are also expected
ments about the rights of the person whilst taki
of families and carers, and the wider public inter

Comparing and contrasting suppor decision making in UK

As we now discuss below, depending upon whe
UK and the range of services that are available,
substitute and supportive decision makers often ·

England and Wales

In England and Wales, the legal framework for
decision making is determined by two pieces o
Capacity Act 2005 (MCA) and Mental Health Act

The N
as follow
sation o
entitled
for peop
must be
commitr
in practi
of interv
describe:
understa
use this
commur

As de
sion mal
processe
he is su:
rants th
assessm
and (b)
or safety
amendii
in the fc
use of n
conside:
sary crit
capacity

The
ple witl
Assessm
decisior
ments :
attitude
Mental
Act. Th
tant de
reviews
more th
or char
to prote
who lac

Scotland

A different model of policy and law exists in Scotland where a 'pyramid' of legislation exists, including the Adults with Incapacity (Scotland) Act 2000 (AWIA), the Adult Support and Protection (Scotland) Act 2007 (ASPA) and the Mental Health (Care and Treatment) (Scotland) Act 2003 (MHCTA). The ASPA is often used as a piece of 'triage' legislation prior to the use of AWIA legislation (Stewart, 2012) where someone may not necessarily lack capacity but is considered to be at risk of harm according to a three-point test outlined in previous Chapters. This has provided the opportunity for previously hidden service users, including those whose capacity may be questionable, to receive assessment, support and protection at an early stage (Mackay, 2012).

For those experiencing mental distress, a range of compulsory measures are available including emergency detention certificates (EDCs), short-term detention certificates (STDCs), and compulsory treatment orders. Compulsory treatment orders can be community or hospital based. The different orders vary in terms of the powers offered and the level of compulsion permitted. They also vary in the extent to which treatment can be given and the level of compulsion involved. Alongside these orders there are a number of patient safeguards (although again these vary according to the order in question) as outlined in the previous section and in line with similar safeguards offered in other countries. These safeguards are discussed in more detail in Chapter 3.

In Scotland, the MHCTA introduced the concept of significantly impaired decision-making ability (SIDMA) as a criterion to compulsory mental health care and treatment (Shek et al., 2010). SIDMA is not the same as incapacity although it is a related concept that refers to the specific capacity of an individual to make decisions about medical treatment for mental disorder. According to the Scottish Government (2005: 45) SIDMA:

> occurs when a mental disorder affects the person's ability to believe, understand and retain information, and to make and communicate decisions. It is consequently a manifestation of a disorder of mind,

> arises out of mental disorder alone; 'incapacity' can also arise from disease of the brain or impaired cognition, and can include physical disability,

> is not the same as limited or poor communication, or disagreements with professional opinion.

It has been suggested that the vast majority of people with mental illnesses retain their ability to make decisions throughout the course of their illness. All adults are assumed to have a decision-making ability or capacity as a starting point. SIDMA is thought to occur for five broad reasons – lack of insight, cognitive impairment, presence of psychosis, severe depressive symptoms and learning disability – and it is argued that the threshold for SIDMA is thought to be lower than that for incapacity more generally (Shek et al., 2010). However, it has been argued that different professionals interpret SIDMA in various ways, thus presenting a complex picture of decision-making processes (Reilly and Atkinson, 2011).

Northern Ireland

In Northern Ireland the main legal framework for safeguarding those experiencing mental distress is the Mental Health (Northern Ireland) Order 1986 (the Order). The criteria for compulsory admission to hospital under the Order are that the person 'is suffering from mental disorder of a nature or degree which warrants his detention in a hospital…; and failure to so detain him would create a substantial likelihood of serious physical harm to himself or to other persons' (Article 4.2(a) and (b)). In Article 2(4) (a)(ii) it is clarified that the assessment of risk of harm to self may include 'that the patient's judgment is so affected that he is, or would soon be, unable to protect himself against serious physical harm'. The Order also provides some limited community-based powers (to reside, attend and allow access) in the form of guardianship which, if the mental disorder criterion is met, can be used if 'it is necessary in the interests of the welfare of the patient' (Article 18(2)(b)).

The Code of Practice for the Order specifies some broad principles which include that 'people suffering from mental disorder should:

> ➤ receive any necessary treatment or care with the least degree of control and segregation consistent with their safety and the safety of others; [and]

> ➤ be treated or cared for in such a way as to promote their self-determination and encourage personal responsibility to the greatest possible degree consistent with their needs, wishes and abilities.' (Department of Health and Social Services, 1992: para 1.8)

In addition to the requirement for medical and social work assessments to determine whether the criteria for intervention are met, there are other potential safeguards provided by the Order. For example, the person's nearest relative must be consulted, the person can appeal to the Mental Health Review Tribunal and the use of the Order is overseen by the Regulation and Quality Improvement Authority (RQIA). The Order also sets out offences in relation to the ill-treatment or wilful neglect of those subject to detention in hospital or guardianship and places a duty on providers to notify the Office of Care and Protection if someone is thought to be, because of their mental health problems, incapable of managing their financial affairs.

As explained earlier in the Chapter there are no separate laws addressing issues of mental capacity and/or adult safeguarding and these areas are covered by aspects of the common law, criminal law, civil law and policy. Instead a set of policies perform this function. In the absence of a capacity law, the Department of Health, Social Services and Public Safety has also issued guidance regarding deprivation of liberty which stated that 'If it is concluded that there is no way of providing appropriate care which does not amount to deprivation of liberty, then consideration will have to be given to using the formal powers of detention in the Mental Health (NI) Order 1986' (DHSSPS, 2010a: 5). The common law does allow substitute decision making based on the reasonable belief that the person lacks capacity and the proposed intervention is in their best interests. These policies explicitly include those experiencing mental distress within their scope and set out the procedures which should be followed to, if necessary, develop and implement a Care and Protection Plan. It should be noted that these plans do not introduce any additional or specific powers to care for and/or protect someone.

The views of service users

As we discussed at the beginning of this Chapter, it is important to highlight how service users experience such laws and policies. We now draw upon selected studies to explore this area. There have been attempts to identify service users' views of involuntary inpatient care, revealing concerns about approaches used by professionals and the application of coercive measures. Using a participatory approach, Gilburt et al. (2008) interviewed 19 service users who had had inpatient stays in psychiatric hospitals in London, some of whom had been subject to detention. They found that if their treatment in hospital was carried out with dignity and involved trust by professionals in a safe environment, then the experience was viewed to be beneficial. The study reinforced the importance of professionals developing positive styles of communication and a therapeutic milieu early in the relationship. This issue has also been highlighted in other contexts where legal coercion is used (Olofsson and

Jacobsson, 2001). A literature review by Coffey (2006), this time of users of forensic services, summarised the findings of studies that highlighted service users' concerns about experiences of caring and restrictions on their liberty as inpatients and as community residents. Whittington et al. (2009) surveyed the views of mental health service users and staff about the use of coercion in institutions, indicating contrasting views on the use of coercion. Evans et al. (2012) found that higher levels of coercion led to greater dissatisfaction amongst service users who had been admitted involuntarily. Their findings echo others by indicating that the experience of this type of coercion leads to high levels of dissatisfaction with levels of care and treatment.

There is some research into service users' experiences of being subject to CTOs, often reported in jurisdictions outside the UK where these legal powers have been in place for much longer. Gibbs et al. (2006) in their New Zealand study of service users, family members and mental health professionals experiences found that there were generally positive views about the purpose of CTOs but some concerns about their restrictive nature. Research by Light et al. (2014) reported the views of 11 service users, highlighting, in particular, a sense of distress and ambivalence about CTOs. The distress was associated with problems with living with mental ill-health and inadequate levels of service delivery. Similar study findings have been identified within the UK, for example, Newton-Howes (2012) used a factor analysis methodology to explore overlapping factors reported by services users subject to CTOs in England, including interpersonal difficulties, intra-psychic threats and feelings of insecurity and unhappiness.

There is also growing interest in the co-production of knowledge about the impact of involuntary care and treatment by teams of service users, academics and practitioners. Gillard et al. (2012) explored how these three groups constructed different analytical narratives and interpretations of secondary data on detained mental health patients. Kavanagh et al.'s (2012) Northern Irish study discussed the nature of a research partnership between academics, service users and carers, revealing the different approaches to understanding methods and results. In a larger Scottish study, Ridley and Hunter (2013) found that there was little evidence of service user participation and impact upon professional decision making, especially with regard to drug regimes. The authors argued for new practice paradigms that embrace therapeutic, holistic and recovery-focused support.

As a way of illustrating these points about the impact of these laws on service user communities, we now draw upon some findings from a recent study carried out by a mental health service user organisation based in Scotland (Highland Users Group). A total of 163 service users across a range of settings, many of whom had been detained under mental health legislation (HUG, 2015), were interviewed.

Case study A

Experiences of detention

A number of views were expressed about these experiences. Some service users felt that compulsory admission to hospital was often necessary to avoid harm and deal with ongoing mental health problems. When this happened, however, they felt that they should be treated with dignity by professionals. Others felt that hospital experiences were potentially damaging to their wellbeing. A number complained that the lack of community resources and support meant that compulsory powers were being overused. Overall, those interviewed felt strongly that they needed help and support to engage in and participate in their treatment willingly as far as possible and believed that greater participation promoted the chances of recovery. Yet on balance the majority recognised the need for compulsory detention when they were acutely unwell:

> Sectioning [detention] is justified. On one of those occasions if they hadn't sectioned me, I wouldn't be here now. They did it for my own safety. I was ill. We need care and protection at those times.

Views about capacity

Some service users were keen to make professionals aware that, even where they were experiencing impaired decision making, this was a fluid experience, and that this should be taken account of at the time and to recognise that:

> even when our decision making is impaired that we are not incapable of expressing our needs or making decisions in some areas of our lives – impaired decision making is a fluid thing and rarely impacts on every aspect of our lives.

Respondents also acknowledged that from time to time they may not be aware that they needed help, in which instances they felt it was important for professionals to respond to the concerns of friends and family.

Use of compulsory treatment orders

Mixed views were expressed about the use of compulsory treatment orders. A number of service users felt that these orders, if applied thoughtfully, helped them manage their mental health problems, but there were also worries that they could be restrictive of lifestyle and choice. Respondents also highlighted the need for preventative and crisis services that would respond to people's mental distress before compulsory measures became necessary. This might include looking out for warning signs that suggest a period of illness is imminent as well as the use of complementary and holistic services such as mindfulness training, massage and short breaks.

▶

◀

Safeguards

Some service users thought that the use of advance statements and advocacy services were important when issues of capacity arose. The use of a named person also helped protect rights. Respondents discussed the power differentials often present in the use of compulsory measures and felt that abiding by the Milan principles, which underpin the Mental Health (Care and Treatment) (Scotland) Act 2003, particularly the principle of participation was an important safeguard:

> If ultimately a decision is made to detain us, we need to feel sure that our friends, relatives and trusted other people are involved and as far as possible we are too.

Discussion: a unified approach to adult safeguarding and mental health?

As this Chapter has illustrated, in each jurisdiction of the UK a complex set of legal, policy and practice relationships are intertwined when we are considering principles of safeguarding the rights of people with mental ill-health. The way these relationships are configured may enhance the lives of service users, or, conversely, compromise such opportunities. Although there will always be a need for the use of compulsory measures in very specific circumstances, the literature implies accompanied measures to safeguard the interests of the individual.

A number of criticisms have been expressed about the overly complex nature of safeguarding processes, notably Best Interest Assessment and Deprivation of Liberty Safeguards in England (Lepping et al., 2010). On the other hand, as demonstrated above, where professionals take time and consideration in making decisions, positive outcomes are possible; in particular, building trusting relationships with service users and carers is crucial (Manthorpe et al., 2008). Others (Rapaport et al., 2009) suggest that a drift towards substitute decision making might be shaped by risk-averse rather than rights based approaches. There have been few studies of advocacy services in England and Wales, but one (Redley et al., 2011) that surveyed stakeholders during the first year of the operation of Independent Mental Capacity Advocacy services in a range of adult safeguarding contexts found some good practices, although there were sometimes inconsistencies in the way that individuals and organisations carried out assessments, as well as problems with inter-organisational working. In Scotland, the limited review of the MHCTA (Scottish Government, 2009) identified similar issues and in particular highlighted geographical variation in the provision of specialist advocacy services, despite this being a requirement of the Act. Strengthened measures to address some of these challenges are incorporated in the Mental Health (Scotland) Act 2015.

The complexities in making professional judgements in this area have been captured by Stewart (2012) who highlights the dilemmas faced by health and social care practitioners. A radical solution to deal with such dilemmas is to have a unified approach to adult safeguarding in the fields of mental health and capacity law making. In their influential paper on the English and Welsh arrangements, Dawson and Szmukler (2006) argued that the split between the Mental Health and Mental Capacity Acts led to the potential discrimination of services users with mental health problems. Thus service users may be compulsorily treated despite the fact that they may have capacity to refuse the intervention. The Mental Capacity (Northern Ireland) Act 2016 introduces such a legal framework for people with mental health problems. The Bamford Review on which it is based concluded that 'having one law for decisions about physical illness and another for mental illness is anomalous, confusing and unjust' and so 'the Review considers that Northern Ireland should take steps to avoid the discrimination, confusion and gaps created by separately devising two separate statutory approaches, but should rather look to creating a comprehensive legislative framework which would be truly principles-based and non-discriminatory' (Bamford Review, 2007: 49). The MCA 2016, provides the new legal framework for decision making for everyone who lacks the capacity to make a decision, regardless of whether this is due to mental distress or any other reason. It will therefore end the need for a separate mental health law and, it could be argued, prevent the need for a new, separate adult safeguarding law.

We will now illustrate this point using Figures 6.1 and 6.2. In these diagrams we have used proportions based on international estimates of impaired decision-making ability for treatment (Sessums et al., 2011) applied to the Northern Ireland context, the current numbers of compulsory admissions (DHSSPS, 2014) and vulnerable adults referrals in Northern Ireland (Carter Anand et al., 2013). There may be variation in the relative proportions across countries, but the diagrams are intended to provide some sense of the proportions. The capacity group may be an over-estimate as there may be some people with more than one cause of impairment who would be counted more than once. The numbers of compulsory admissions and vulnerable adults referrals may also be under-estimates of those who meet the relevant criteria but are not in contact with the relevant services.

The first diagram suggests that those whose decision-making ability is impaired are a much bigger group than those who are referred as part of vulnerable adults law and/or policy and those who are compulsorily admitted to hospital. It also reflects the current position that, even if someone retains decision-making ability, they may be subject to intervention under vulnerable adults law and/or policy and/or mental health law. Some studies have suggested these are relatively small populations (Davidson and Campbell, 2010; Owen et al., 2008).

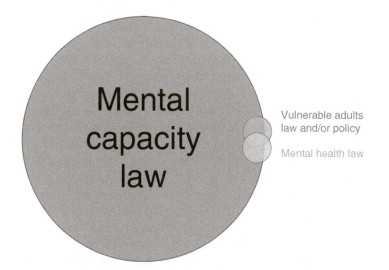

Figure 6.1   Relationships between conventional capacity laws, mental health laws and vulnerable adults policies

The new comprehensive capacity-based legislative framework for Northern Ireland provides a single law which facilitates decision making when there are concerns about a person's mental health and/or safety but on a compulsory basis only if the person's decision-making ability is sufficiently impaired. The Venn diagram in Figure 6.2 illustrates this framework.

This suggests that a much smaller proportion of people would be subject to compulsory measures using this new integrated approach. This may help to resolve concerns about discriminatory mental health law which allows compulsory interventions even when a person *retains the capacity to decide,* and about excessively paternalistic interventions to safeguard even when the person has the capacity to decide about the risks involved. On the other hand, it does raise some anxieties about how the risks involved in these relatively small numbers of cases will be managed. The following case study, based on the Northern Irish context, is now used as a way of considering these and other important issues of safeguarding.

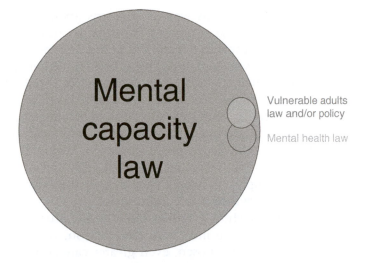

Mental
capacity
law

Vulnerable adults
law and/or policy

Mental health law

Figure 6.2   Relationships within a comprehensive legislative framework

---

Case study B

Billy is a 35-year-old, unemployed man who had a long history of mental health problems. When he was 18 he was given a diagnosis of schizophrenia and has been admitted, and often detained for treatment in psychiatric hospitals over the last two decades. For the last two years he has been living with a new partner, Rachel, in social housing, following a road traffic accident that left him with a partial brain injury, for which he received compensation of £150,000. For the last six months he has been placed under a CTO. The conditions of the order are that he attends outpatient appointments and receives a regular depot injection by a community psychiatric nurse. Billy also had occasional visits from a volunteer who worked with a local mental health community organisation. The volunteer was recently worried about some of the things that Billy had been saying. In particular the strange, intrusive thoughts that were now returning. He was fearful of going back into hospital and wanted to use his money to help avoid another period of detention. He mentioned that he believed that some people he had met in the pub could help him with advice, but they would require payment for this.

Discussion

Depending on the jurisdiction in which you live or work, it is important to be fully aware of the inter-relationships between law and policy, and the roles of professionals in making decisions about safeguarding in such situations. There are apparent issues of risk to Billy in terms of a possible relapse and return to hospital, as well as concerns about his ability to make judgements about his use of money. This Chapter has argued, however, that it is crucial that capacity is assumed in the first instance, until a full, multi-disciplinary, assessment indicates otherwise. When safeguarding laws are applied in such circumstances, best practice should prioritise supportive decision-making processes. Care should be taken in interviewing Billy, if need be working alongside specialist advocates. The views of Rachel, the volunteer and professionals involved in Billy's care and treatment should also be sought. This holistic approach, where Billy is enabled to express his fears about a possible detention in hospital, and which engages his broader support network, should seek the least restrictive option, for example by revising the conditions of the CTO or considering other legal avenues, such as guardianship. The literature in this field indicates that, even where the most restrictive option, that of compulsory admission to hospital, is chosen, even greater care should be taken in explaining these processes to Billy and Rachel, providing them with opportunity to contribute to multi-disciplinary decisions at the point of admission, during care and treatment in hospital and in discharge and care planning.

Conclusion

In concluding this Chapter, it is important to summarise the key issues that arise in these areas of law and policy. Historically, there was a tendency for mental health laws in the UK to be similar, a consequence of the unitary nature of the State. The move towards the devolution of powers to the four countries of the UK in the last decade has led to more heterogeneous laws with more variety of processes and safeguards. Another change has been an extension of the power of mental health professionals to apply forms of compulsorily care and treatment in the community. In each of the jurisdictions we described and discussed in this Chapter, attempts, some successful other less so, have been made to interpret and apply new principles associated with notions of capacity informed in particular by the CRPD.

Governments continually seek to make vulnerable adults policies, mental health and capacity law more coherent and transparent, and compensate loss of liberty with a range of safeguards. Nonetheless many problems remain. Service users routinely complain of a lack of confidence in professional judgement making and the overuse of coercive practices. It is often the case that professionals are faced with complex legal and ethical judgements and often lack resources to enable them to carry out mandated roles. The introduction of capacity laws has challenged traditional practices and professional attitudes towards service users' rights. We believe, however, that these challenges bring with them many opportunities to make decisions that enhance the liberties of service users experiencing mental health problems.

Implications for practice

➢ Practitioners need to have an understanding of the inter-relationship between law and policy and the roles of different professionals in making decisions about adult safeguarding.

➢ Decisions about capacity should be informed by a human rights–based approach that is enshrined in the United Nations Convention on the Rights of Persons with Disabilities.

➢ A more human rights–compliant approach involves introducing measures to support individuals to make their own decisions rather than resorting to substitute decision making.

References

Armstrong, J. (2008) 'The Scottish legislation: The way forward?', in Mantell, A. and Scragg, T. (eds), *Safeguarding Adults in Social Work*, Exeter: Learning Matters.

Bamford Review. (2007) *A Comprehensive Legislative Framework*, Belfast: Bamford Review.

Brayne, H. and Carr, H. (2010) *Law for Social Workers*, Oxford: Oxford University Press.

Brown, R., Barber, P. and Martin, D. (2009) *The Mental Health Capacity Act 2005: A Guide for Practice*, Exeter: Learning Matters.

Burns, T., Rugkåsa, J., Molodynski, A., Dawson, J., Yeeles, K., Vazquez-Montes, M., Voysey, M., Sinclair, J. and Priebe, S. (2013) Community treatment orders for patients with psychosis (OCTET): A randomised controlled trial. *The Lancet*, 381(9878): 1627–1633.

Burns, T., Yeeles, K., Koshiaris, C., Vazquez-Montes, M., Molodynski, A., Puntis, S., Vergunst, F., Forrest, A., Mitchell, A., Burns, K. and Rugkåsa, J. (2015) Effect of increased compulsion on readmission to hospital or disengagement from community services for patients with psychosis: Follow-up of a cohort from the OCTET trial. *Lancet Psychiatry* 2(10): 881–890.

Campbell, J., Brophy, L., Healy, B., and O'Brien, A. (2006) International perspectives on the use of community treatment orders: Implications for mental health social workers. *British Journal of Social Work,* 36(7): 1101–1118.

Campbell, J. (2008) Stakeholders views of legal and advice services for people admitted to psychiatric hospital. *Journal of Social Welfare and Family Law,* 30(3): 219–232.

Carter Anand, J., Taylor, B., Montgomery, L., Bakircioglu, O., Harper, C., Devaney, J., Lazenbatt, A., Pearson, K., Mackay, K. and Nejbir, D. (2013) *A Review of Elder Abuse in Northern Ireland and a Review of Adult Protection Legislation across the UK, Ireland and Internationally,* Belfast: Commissioner for Older People Northern Ireland.

Castells-Aulet, L., Hernandez-Viadel, M., Asensio-Pascual, P. Canete-Nicolas, C., Bellido-Rodriguez, C., Lera-Calatayud, G., and Calabuig-Crespo, R. (2013) Involuntary out-patient commitment: 2-year follow up. *The Psychiatrist,* 37: 60–64.

Churchill, R., Owen, G., Hotopf, M. and Singh, S. (2007) *International Experiences of Using Community Treatment Orders,* London: Institute of Psychiatry.

Coffey, M. (2006) Researching service user views in forensic mental health: A literature review. *The Journal of Forensic Psychiatry & Psychology,* 17(1): 73–107.

Davidson, G. and Campbell, J. (2010) An audit of assessment and reporting by Approved Social Workers (ASWs). *British Journal of Social Work,* 40(5): 1609–1627.

Davidson, G., Brophy, L., Campbell, J., Farrell, S. J., Gooding, P., and O'Brien, A. M. (2016) An international comparison of legal frameworks for supported and substitute decision-making in mental health services. *International Journal of Law and Psychiatry,* 44: 30–40.

Dawson, J. and Szmukler, G. (2006) Fusion of mental health and incapacity legislation. *British Journal of Psychiatry,* 188: 504–509.

Department of Health and Social Services. (1992) *Mental Health (Northern Ireland) Order 1986 Code of Practice,* London: HMSO.

Department of Health, Social Services and Public Safety (DHSSPS). (2006) *Safeguarding Vulnerable Adults: Regional Adult Protection Policy and Procedural Guidance,* Belfast: DHSSPS.

Department of Health, Social Services and Public Safety (DHSSPS). (2010a) *Deprivation of Liberty Safeguards (DoLS) – Interim Guidance,* Belfast: DHSSPS.

Department of Health, Social Services and Public Safety (DHSSPS). (2010b) *Adult Safeguarding in Northern Ireland – Regional and Local Partnership Arrangements,* Belfast: DHSSPS.

Department of Health, Social Service and Public Safety (DHSSPS). (2014) *Hospital Statistics for Mental Health and Learning Disability Report,* Belfast: DHSSPS.

Department of Health, Social Service and Public Safety and Department of Justice. (2015) *Adult Safeguarding: Prevention and Protection in Partnership,* Belfast: DHSSPS and DoJ.

Department of Justice (DoJ). (2012) *Achieving Best Evidence in Criminal Proceedings,* Belfast: DoJ.

Evans, J., Rose, D., Flach, C., Csipke, E., Glossop, H., Mccrone, P., Craig, T., and Wykes, T. (2012) VOICE: developing a new measure of service users' perceptions of inpatient care, using a participatory methodology. *Journal of Mental Health*, 21(1): 57–71.

Gibbs, A., Dawson, J., and Mullen, R. (2006) Community Treatment Orders for people with serious mental illness: A New Zealand Study. *British Journal of Social Work*, 36, 1085–1100.

Gilburt, H., Rose, D. and Slade, M. (2008) The importance of relationships in mental health care: A qualitative study of service users' experiences of psychiatric hospital admission in the UK. *BMC Health Services Research*, 8(1): 92.

Gillard, S., Simons, L., Turner, K., Lucock, M., and Edwards, C. (2012) Patient and public involvement in the coproduction of knowledge reflection on the analysis of qualitative data in a mental health study. *Qualitative Health Research, 22*, 1126–1137.

Graham, K., Norrie, C., Stevens, M., Moriarty, J., Manthorpe, J. and Hussein, S. (2014) Models of adult safeguarding in England: A review of the literature. *Journal of Social Work*, doi:10.1177/1468017314556205.

Health and Social Care Board, Police Service of Northern Ireland and Regulation and Quality Improvement Authority. (2009) *Protocol for the Joint Investigation of Alleged and Suspected Cases of Abuse of Vulnerable Adults,* Belfast: Health and Social Care Board.

Highland User Group (HUG). (2015) *Detention under the Mental Health Act: The Views and Experiences of 163 Ppeople,* Inverness: Highland User Group.

Johns, R. (2011) *Using the Law in Social Work*, Exeter: Learning Matters.

Kavanagh, D., Daly, M., Harper, M., Davidson, G., and Campbell, J. (2012) 'Mental health service users and carers as researchers: reflections on a qualitative study of citizens' experiences of compulsory mental health laws', in Goodson, L. and Phillimore, J. (eds), *Community Research: From Theory to Method* (pp. 234–252), Bristol: Policy.

Lepping, P., Singh Sambhi, R., and Williams-Jones, K. (2010) Deprivation of liberty standards: How prepared are we? *Journal of Medical Ethics,* 36(3): 170–3.

Light, E. M., Robertson, M. D., Boyce, P., Carney, T., Rosen, A., Cleary, M., Hunt, G. E., O'Connor, N., Ryan, C. and Kerridge, I. H. (2014) The lived experience of involuntary community treatment: A qualitative study of mental health consumers and carers. *Australasian Psychiatry*, 22(4): 345–351.

Mackay, K. (2012) A parting of the ways? The diverging nature of mental health social work in the light of the new Acts in Scotland, and in England and Wales. *Journal of Social Work*, 12(2): 179–193.

Manthorpe, J., Rapaport, J., and Stanley, N. (2008) Expertise and experience: People with experiences of using services and carers' views of the Mental Capacity Act 2005. *British Journal of Social Work*, 39(5): 884–900.

McLaughlin, H. (2009) What's in a name: 'Client', 'patient', 'customer', 'consumer', 'expert by experience', 'service user' – what's next? *British Journal of Social Work*, 39(6): 1101–1117.

Newton-Howes, G. (2012) A factor analysis of patients' views of compulsory community treatment orders: The factors associated with detention. *Psychiatry, Psychology and Law,* 20(4): 519–526.

Olofsson, B. and Jacobsson, L. (2001) A plea for respect: Involuntarily hospitalized psychiatric patients' narratives about being subjected to coercion. *Journal of Psychiatric and Mental Health Nursing,* 8(4): 357–366.

Owen, G. S., Richardson, G., David, A. S., Szmukler, G., Hayward, P. and Hotopf, M. (2008) Mental capacity to make decisions on treatment in people admitted to psychiatric hospitals: Cross sectional study. *British Medical Journal,* 337(7660): 40–42. doi:10.1136/bmj.39580.546597.BE.

Rapaport, J., Manthorpe, J. and Stanley N. (2009) Mental health and mental capacity law: Some mutual concerns for social work. *Practice,* 21(2): 91–105.

Redley, M., Clare, I., Dunn, M., Platten, M., and Holland, A. (2011) Introducing the Mental Capacity Advocate (IMCA) Service and the Reform of Adult Safeguarding Procedures. *British Journal of Social Work,* 41(6): 1058–1069.

Reilly, J. and Atkinson, J. (2011) The use of capacity criteria in mental health law in the UK. *History and Philosophy of Psychology,* 13(1): 52–56.

Ridley, J. and Hunter, S. (2013) Subjective experiences of compulsory treatment from a qualitative study of early implementation of the Mental Health (Care & Treatment) (Scotland) Act 2003. *Health and Social Care in the Community,* 21(5): 509–518.

Scottish Government. (2005) *Approved Medical Practitioners: Mental Health (Care and Treatment) (Scotland) Act 2003, Training Manual,* Edinburgh: Scottish Government.

Scottish Government. (2009) *Limited Review of the Mental Health Care and Treatment (Scotland) Act, 2003,* Edinburgh: Scottish Government.

Sessums, L. L., Zembrzuska, H. and Jackson, J. L. (2011) Does this patient have medical decision-making capacity? *Journal of the American Medical Association,* 306(4): 420–427.

Shek, E., Lyons, D. and Taylor, M. (2010) Understanding 'significant impaired decision making ability' with regard to treatment for mental disorder: Empirical analysis. *Psychiatrist,* 34(6): 239–242.

Stewart, A. (2012) *Supporting Vulnerable Adults: Citizenship, Capacity, Choice,* Edinburgh: Dunedin Academic Press.

Volunteer Now. (2013) *Safeguarding Vulnerable Adults: A Shared Responsibility,* Belfast: Volunteer Now.

Whittington, R., Psychol, C., Bowers, L., Nolan, P., Simpson, A. and Neil, L. (2009) Approval ratings of inpatient coercive interventions in a national sample of mental health service users and staff in England. *Psychiatric Services,* 60(6): 792–798.

7

Safeguarding Older Adults: Carers' Perspectives

Claire Pearson, South Lanarkshire Council; Martin Kettle, Glasgow Caledonian University

This Chapter explores the issue of safeguarding older adults, with a particular focus upon the perspective of carers of older adults. Older adults (as well as other adults with care needs) are more likely to experience abuse or neglect than the general population and are less likely to report this abuse (Penhale and Iborra, 2014). This Chapter therefore draws on the views and experiences of carers in order to understand some of the key issues that must be considered in relation to safeguarding this particular group. Beginning with a review of the literature, including an overview of the position in the different jurisdictions of the United Kingdom, this Chapter will go on to draw upon a small-scale piece of research conducted with carers of older adults who, although they had no direct involvement in formal safeguarding processes, were able to offer some useful insights and observations about harm to older adults and when caring for a vulnerable adult has the potential to become harmful. As a counterpoint to that, we will then go on to explore the story of one carer, whose experience of the safeguarding process of a relative was unfortunately negative. Whilst it is not claimed that this represents the experience of all carers, it does provide a reminder of the importance of information being delivered in a timely manner by professionals and of recognising the importance of taking a broader view of safeguarding adults – one that goes beyond a technical interpretation and application of the law. It should also be highlighted that preparation for the writing of this Chapter did not involve direct work with older adults, and this is highlighted as an area for further research. The Chapter concludes with a discussion of the implications for practice. Within the context of this discussion, carers are defined as those who provide unpaid care to a family member, friend or neighbour. Written from a Scottish perspective, the issues raised nonetheless have broader implications for current under-standings of safeguarding as it relates to carers and older people.

Safeguarding adults across the United Kingdom

Recognising that this has been covered in more detail in other Chapters within this volume, this section briefly outlines the different legislative and policy contexts for safeguarding older adults across the UK.

Scotland

In Scotland, the concept of 'harm' provides the basis for all safeguarding interventions, although defining the types of harm and thresholds of harm remains problematic, as does balancing an adult's right to self-determination with that of the duty of care (Ash, 2013; Stewart and Atkinson, 2012). The Adult Support and Protection (Scotland) Act 2007 (ASPA), was implemented from October 2008 prior to the review of Wales' statutory adult safeguarding guidance *In Safe Hands* (Magill et al., 2010) and England's *No Secrets* (DoH, 2000) guidance. Against the backdrop of these reviews, older adult abuse remained in the public eye through investigations into individual cases of abuse. These include the case of Steven Hoskin, a man with learning disabil-ities who was murdered after being targeted because of his learning disability (Flynn, 2007), and Miss X, a woman with learning disabilities who suffered serious sexual abuse over a 30-year period (Mental Welfare Commission and the Social Work Services Inspectorate, 2004). These individual cases sit alongside cases of collective, institutional harm, such as the case of Fiona Pilkington who killed herself and her daughter after the systematic failure of the police to identify the family as vulnerable and provide them with assis-tance despite repeated requests for help (Independent Police Complaints Commission, 2009).

The ASPA was implemented in 2008. The statute is based on a clear set of principles including that any intervention must provide benefit to the adult and that the benefit cannot be reasonably achieved without intervention. Further, any intervention being considered needs to be the least restrictive option to safeguard the adult's wellbeing. The ASPA places a duty on a range of agencies to investigate suspected harm and for local authorities and their partners to work together in doing so. It introduces powers to carry out assessments, to remove an adult to a place of safety and, as a last resort, to invoke a banning order and force entry into an adult's home. None of the powers can be exercised without the consent of the adult. However, consent can be overridden if the adult is believed to be experiencing undue pressure.

England

No Secrets (DoH, 2000) set out a clear policy framework for adult protection in England underpinned by the development of local policies and procedures as well as joint protocols. As in Scotland, Social Services Departments are the lead agency. The consultation on the Review of *No Secrets* (DoH, 2009) highlighted that 68% of respondents were in favour of introducing a legislative framework for adult safeguarding, following Scotland's example. Most recently, the Care Act 2014 created a legal framework for adult safeguarding in England for the first time. This included introducing a responsibility to ensure enquiries are made in relation to abuse and neglect, enshrining in legislation Safeguarding Adults Boards (SAB) and legislating for information sharing in relation to adult safeguarding (Local Government Association, 2014).

Wales

Wales' statutory guidance, *In Safe Hands,* was reviewed, with a number of recommendations made from reviewing the term 'vulnerable' to ensuring there is a greater focus on care and support (Stewart and Atkinson, 2012). As a result of this review (Magill et al., 2010), the Social Services and Well-being (Wales) Act was passed in May 2014. The new Act, which has been heralded as encompassing the most significant legal change in Wales since devolution, requires local authorities to investigate when they suspect an adult with care and support needs is at risk of neglect or abuse. It also introduces adult support orders to provide Local Authority officers with the authority to enter premises to investigate if they suspect an adult to be at risk of harm. The Act has also established a national adult safeguarding board which will provide advice and support to newly established local safeguarding boards.

Northern Ireland

Northern Ireland's *Safeguarding Vulnerable Adults: Regional Adult Protection Policy and Procedural Guidelines* has also been subject to a recent review (DHSSPS, 2009) resulting in the establishment of a new national Northern Ireland Adult Safeguarding Partnership and five local Adult Safeguarding Partnerships and publication of the *Northern Ireland Adult Safeguarding Policy* (Department of Health, Social Services and Public Safety, 2015). The aim of the policy is to improve safeguarding procedures for adults at risk of harm, with a key focus on preventing harm from occurring. It sets out partnership arrangements across government departments, voluntary agencies and individuals as well as setting out clear guidance for the reporting of concerns and how these will be responded to. The policy emphasises a consent driven approach whereby any intervention will take place only with the consent of the adult in question, where possible.

A review of the literature

Analysing adult safeguarding for any service user group is characterised by definitional challenges, which include differentiating between types of harm and threshold judgements, for example when being insulted or sworn at becomes harmful (Fulmer et al., 2014). Further, there are issues of age categorisation, including different points at which an adult becomes 'older' (Davies et al., 2011). There have been expressions of caution in relation to definitions of abuse with calls being made for further clarification and elucidation (Dixon et al., 2010).

Prevalence

The most recent UK prevalence study of 'elder' abuse carried out in 2006 (Biggs et al., 2009) found that 2.6% of the 2,111 respondents aged 65 and over reported mistreatment by family members, close friends or care workers. Women were more likely to experience abuse than men. Neglect was the most common type of abuse reported at 1.1%, followed by financial abuse at 0.7%. Sexual abuse was the least reported type at 0.2%. The prevalence of psychological and physical abuse was just slightly higher at 0.4%. A more recent study completed in America (Fulmer et al., 2014) of 142 older people living in the community found that older adults reporting verbal abuse also reported higher levels of depression and an overall poorer quality of life than older adults reporting no verbal abuse.

A systematic review of prevalence studies carried out in the UK by Cooper et al. (2008) found that older people who were *reliant on others for care* were at higher risk of experiencing abuse, and of those at higher risk, one in four had been subject to psychological abuse. Action on Elder Abuse (2015) also found that women over the age of 70 who live alone and are frail and dependent are more likely to be victims of abuse; this abuse takes multiple forms and the perpetrators are often in positions of trust (e.g. a friend).

Cooper et al.'s (2008) systematic review of 49 studies of elder abuse found that 6% of older people had reported significant abuse in the last month and that 5% of older couples reported physical violence in their relationships. McGarry et al. (2011) state that older women's experiences of domestic abuse (now included as a classification of harm within the ASPA) are markedly different to younger women's but that domestic abuse in older age is relatively under-researched and is difficult to measure because of barriers to reporting, and due to professionals failing to recognise its prevalence in older age.

The spectrum of abuse

Complicated social relationships and family dynamics arguably cloud the discourse in relation to elder abuse, as do varying definitions of harm. Though research has shown 'caring' to be satisfying (McKee et al., 2009) it remains challenging and stressful for many carers (Chadwick et al., 2013; Askham et al., 2007). In reviewing the literature in relation to adult safeguarding and harm it appears that for professionals, service users and carers there is a *spectrum* of harm and though UK policy and legislation provides a framework from which to work, there is still a strong element of subjectivity around what constitutes harm and abuse. In their study of family carers, Askham et al. (2007) refer to the balancing act of providing care and highlight the extremes of the perceived harm spectrum (e.g. from a husband placing his hand over his wife's mouth to stop her shouting out to the often unintended erosion of identity as a result of the way in which some older people with dementia are treated by family members). However, this spectrum needs to be considered within the context of the pressures family carers can face. Individual ability and resources to develop coping mechanisms for supporting people with a range of psychosocial impairments, including learning disability and dementia, also have to be considered. Research has indicated that carers adopt strategies to avoid harming the cared-for person, such as physically removing themselves from a stressful situation, and recognises the value placed on resources such as respite or short breaks in reducing stressors, and therefore reducing the likelihood of vulnerable adults being harmed (Perera and Standen, 2014).

Johnson (2011) places the issue of harm in a broader context and questions the extent to which society reinforces harmful behaviour through cultural norms, such as placing an older person in a nursing home rather than dealing with the perpetrator of harm or the broader structural causes of harm. Through looking at adult support and protection prior to the implementation of the ASPA she found that professionals' views in relation to harm varied and that responses to harm were inconsistent. Wider societal issues were discussed in her research with a lack of formal supports identified as contributory factors to harmful practice.

Dixon et al. (2010) explored definitions of older adult abuse. They found that the older adults interviewed cited age-related poor health, mental frailty and loneliness as factors increasing their vulnerability, with some respondents choosing to remain in abusive relationships rather than face the alternative of being alone. The basis for the study was 'harm perpetrated in a relationship created with an expectation of trust' (Dixon et al., 2010: 405); similarly, it found varying definitions of harm, with some respondents attributing a perceived lack of formal services as a key barrier to accessing help.

Impact of broader policy development on adult safeguarding

The development of adult safeguarding policies has been shaped and influenced by a range of other social care and health policies. In particular, the UK-wide personalisation/self-directed support agenda, which, whilst ostensibly aimed at increasing service user independence, carries with it a perceived risk of financial harm. Preston-Shoot and Cornish (2014) confirmed that in the majority of cases reviewed in their Scottish study, harm was taking place within the family home, which is the setting for most personalised care. Analysis of feedback from professionals found, however, that proportionality was embedded in practice (Preston-Shoot and Cornish, 2014: 9) with practitioners making considerable efforts to stop financial or physical harm prior to applying for the use of protection orders. Manthorpe and Samsi (2013) explored the views of 15 Adult Safeguarding Coordinators in England in relation to the uptake in direct payments and the associated risks of people with dementia being subject to financial abuse. They concluded that the potential risks from individual budgets could be minimised, but that practitioners need to be more alert to the signs of financial harm as well as more aware of potential risks, highlighting the important role of reviews and monitoring. They also found that perceived risks did not necessarily relate to an increase in safeguarding referrals and that practitioners felt that risks could be minimised if managed well – for example, through the provisions of extra support in relation to money management. Reviewing and monitoring was cited as important but so too was risk enablement, suggesting the need for a delicate balancing act. The study also suggested caution in placing an onerous role on carers who may not wish to take on more responsibility in supporting older people. Davies et al. (2011) note that the living circumstances of older people may increase their risk of financial abuse, with living with a son or daughter seen as more risky than living in residential care.

The experiences of professionals, older adults and their carers

Although the policy intention is that older people should be viewed as an asset to society, for example, *A New Vision for Older Workers: Retain, Retrain, Recruit* (Department for Work and Pensions, 2015) and *Reshaping Care for Older People* (Scottish Government, 2011), age discrimination remains a reality. Ash (2013) argues that ageism in society is still very much in existence as evidenced by the provision of substandard services, and that there is a complex interplay of factors that contribute to poor practice with older people, and by default an underlying acceptance of harm. She states there is a 'cognitive mask', which narrows vision so as to exclude the social, cultural and political factors that impact on how older people are seen in society. Ash (2013) highlights the contested nature of professionals' response to abuse and questions to what extent professionals adjust their thresholds when dealing with harm. She found in the Welsh local authority, where she completed her research, that 'sheer exhaustion [on the part of carers] and a pre-existing poor relationship [between the carer and cared-for person] could lead to fragile care situations collapsing' (Ash, 2013: 108).

Mackay et al. (2011) interviewed 29 practitioners and 6 service users in Scotland. They found a tension between balancing service users' rights to self-determination with statutory safeguarding duties. The research concluded that practitioners often had to address their own anxieties and sometimes needed to accept that adults may choose to remain in what could be considered a harmful environment. They also found that despite the existence of a clear legislative framework, professional judgement remained central to the safeguarding process. In their study into people's experience of ASPA, Preston-Shoot and Cornish found that service users were more trusting of adult support and protection processes and that their lives felt 'safer' (2014: 9) but their research also highlighted the ambiguity of adult safeguarding in that some service users were deemed to have mental capacity but could not identify that they were being harmed. One example cited a woman's choice to have her long-term partner move back in with her even though he was her abuser, highlighting the tension between autonomy and protection. A further case study illustrates challenges in implementing Scottish legislation using the example of an older woman being abused by her son who was her primary carer. Dealing with the abuse potentially increased her isolation and undermined a relationship that she valued. However, the authors conclude that the Act had achieved a delicate balance between autonomy and protection, as illustrated by the relative lack of compulsory intervention (Preston-Shoot and Cornish, 2013). Arguably, the unique interplay of social work values and ethics contribute towards this, in that intervention respects people's rights, narratives and perspectives.

Carer stress

Carer stress remains a significant factor in harm to vulnerable older people. One research report, *Rest Assured* (Shared Care Scotland, 2012), found that 57% of carers had not accessed a short break despite being known to carers' centres. Studies such as this suggest that the quality of the relationship between the carer and the cared-for person impacts on the quality of the care-giving, but also needs to be placed within the context of that relationship.

Addressing concerns that the current body of safeguarding research under-represents the views of older adults in relation to harm/abuse, Anand et al. (2013) sought to re-dress the balance through their study comprising eight focus groups with older people across Ireland. This study categorised abuse as an older person 'no longer having the personal agency or power to resist pressure within the interaction' (Anand et al., 2013: 285). Older people themselves were able to identify the grey area of what constitutes harm contextualised within 'normal family interactions' such as shouting at one another.

The issue of older people's experiences of elder abuse being largely missing from the discourse was also identified by Morbey (2002) who highlighted 'carer stress' as a contributory feature to the harm of older adults, with respondents voicing concerns that carer stress can be exacerbated by lack of support, social isolation and no 'time out'.

The literature review highlights a number of issues. Firstly, further research is needed into the experiences of service users, carers and professionals in relation to adult safeguarding, particularly as it relates to older adults (Perera and Standen, 2014; Preston-Shoot and Cornish, 2014). In particular, it is reasonable to conclude that it would be useful to gain the perspectives of family carers, including those who are struggling to cope. Given that the financial value of carers is £87 billion a year (Carers Trust, 2015), the role they play should be respected whilst balancing this with offering support and protection as the ASPA aims to do. It is also clear that 'grey areas' exist and that when older people themselves think of harm, they widely conceptualise it as loss of dignity, control, choice and rights (Anand et al., 2013). Related to this, there is also a need for clearer definitions of what constitutes elder abuse as highlighted by Dixon et al. (2010) in relation to cases of mistreatment without age-related factors (e.g. long-standing domestic abuse or interpersonal abuse). It is with these issues in mind that the focus of this Chapter now turns to the views of carers supporting older adults and to service users themselves.

The views of carers

The discussion that follows, based on the views of carers who took part in a single focus group, informs the writing of this Chapter. The focus group comprised five carers, all of whom were supporting an older person. Some of the group members had supported people at home who had subsequently moved into residential or nursing home care, while others continued to support a person in the community. They were recruited through contact with two carers' groups in the West of Scotland. The carers taking part provided care to a range of people such as a parent, spouse, parent-in-law and/or a family member/friend. Some of the carers had experience of providing care to more than one person. One carer was not familiar with ASPA, although the other four were. All carers were in touch with carers' support organisations, and some were legally responsible for managing the cared-for person's affairs (for example, through power of attorney). Questions were used to stimulate conversation and to explore key areas, for example in relation to taking decisions for the cared-for person against their expressed wishes, but emphasis was placed on encouraging a free-flowing discussion. Despite guarantees of confidentiality, the group did not wish to have the discussion audio recorded because of the likelihood of sensitive topics being discussed, and thus field notes were taken by both facilitators.

Context

There are two interesting points in relation to extrapolating from a small-scale focus group discussion. Firstly, this was a group of carers who were in touch with carers' organisations, and it could reasonably be expected that they would have a greater awareness of issues affecting carers, including adult safeguarding. Although it would have been more difficult to gain access, it would have been helpful to have the opportunity to engage with carers who were not in touch with carers' organisations to elicit whether issues for them were the same or different or to involve carers who had direct experience of ASPA involvement, but issues of confidentiality and access worked against this.

The second issue in relation to context was that, despite the best efforts of the facilitators, the discussion often moved away from issues relating to safeguarding older adults to broader issues for carers, necessitating gentle redirection back to the main theme. Under the circumstances, it is perhaps not surprising that this was the case as this is a reflection of the reality of the lives of someone who is acting, or who has acted, as a full-time carer with all the implications in relation to their identity. For example, one carer spoke of the label of 'carer' and of professionals pointing him in the direction of support and 'getting me out of the door', by which he meant establishing an identity beyond the caring role. All carers spoke of getting good support from the carers' organisations they are in touch with, and this reinforces the above point about the need to explore perceptions of carers who are not in contact with support organisations.

Need for support and its relationship to adult protection

Despite the limitations identified, carers were very able to engage in a discussion of the issues around adult safeguarding. In terms of seeing adult safeguarding in context, this group of carers identified and explored the need for preventative support and its importance in ensuring that any potential risk of harm is minimised. Whilst carers clearly benefited from getting support for themselves and the person for whom they were caring, they were also able to articulate feelings of guilt about accessing support. Further, they expressed the need for information, support and greater awareness of their rights. They discussed planning ahead and the difficulties of planning for when a person may pass away. One carer spoke of the feelings of placing a family member in a care home but stated that on reflection he would have done this earlier given the pressures he was under as a result of his caring role. One carer said, 'You need the strength to go forward to know you need the help'. Another carer spoke of her reluctance to share her husband's behaviour with her daughters and that she kept this from them although he was aggressive and physically harming her.

The group were also able to identify with refusing support as an issue that could actually exacerbate risk to vulnerable adults, and they gave examples of older people refusing respite or support at home. There was an acute awareness of not being able to 'force' the issue, but this was counterbalanced by a need to look after themselves, both in relation to their own needs and in respect of their ability to meet the longer-term needs of the person for whom they were caring. This led into a broader exploration of the Scottish legislation, and there was recognition amongst several carers that, whilst they viewed the legislation as welcome, they had some concerns about it potentially being something of a blunt instrument and being rather prescriptive, with complex procedures that were difficult to understand.

Carers' understanding of harm and of reporting it

One of the criticisms of adult support and protection legislation in Scotland is the very broad definition of harm that sometimes makes it difficult to make sense of and put into practice (Sherwood-Johnson, 2012). This lack of clarity was raised by the group, who had some difficulty in pinning down what was meant by harm and how a broad range of behaviours could potentially be regarded as being harmful. At first, carers expressed their thoughts of harm as being physical and emotional stating it is 'something that causes distress'. They spoke of financial abuse, of people being shouted at or threatened. Perceptions were there that 'financial abuse is rife' and anecdotally stories were shared of Department for Work and Pensions' monies being misspent and of families holding back money from older people. One of the factors that carers thought was important in differentiating between whether behaviour should be deemed as harmful or not was the motivation of the behaviour of the person delivering the care, in particular whether it was possible to discern whether there was any ill-intent or malice involved. Although they lacked detailed knowledge of the legislation, the carers in the group all agreed they would report harm, with some saying they would directly challenge a person thought to be causing harm. They also spoke of reporting it to the police, depending upon the nature and severity of the harm that was being caused.

During the discussion, carers were well able to differentiate between harm potentially being caused by informal carers and people who were being paid to provide care. In this latter respect, carers raised the issue of collective harm and a culture of abuse that they perceived as being portrayed in the media, with one carer expressing a strongly held opinion that abuse in care homes was often under-reported. Mirroring findings reported in Chapter 10 of this volume, the group suggested that arrangements to deliver care could inadvertently end up being harmful. In some instances, for example, the high numbers of people involved in providing care to one person could be viewed as harmful because they could not reasonably be expected to have a close knowledge of the individual's needs and preferences.

Carers spoke of care home residents being assaulted by other care home residents but raised very strong concerns that 'The level of staffing does not allow for good support'. One carer cited abusive behaviour she had witnessed at the hospital when an older gentleman was being shouted at by NHS staff, which she challenged. She stated that 'Services we are providing are abusive because we can't meet the needs'. However, it was also recognised that there were a number of barriers that prevented carers feeling confident in raising the issue in a care home setting, not least the anxiety that they could not be there 24 hours a day, and that raising concerns might potentially make things worse for the person who was receiving care.

Whilst at the same time as expressing a view that multiple carers could, by their very nature, be seen as harmful, there was a recognition that care needed to be provided, and that there were potentially greater risks associated with not providing care. This was one of a number of areas where carers recognised that there were balances to be struck, some of which were potentially very delicate indeed.

Carers also recognised that the potential for harm that existed in the relationship between the carer and the person they cared for stemmed in large part from the unequal and dependent nature of the relationship. That relationship, of itself, set up the potential for harm to occur, and it was broadly recognised that the stress of providing care for a relative whose behaviour could be challenging could very easily lead to harm occurring. This was also seen as an area that required a delicate balance between behaviour that could be deemed as harmful and behaviour that was an appropriate response to a stressful set of circumstances. Carers also emphasized the importance of understanding the needs of carers, which were not always acknowledged by agencies who, in the eyes of carers at least, were seen as being judgemental about the ability of carers to care.

A number of examples were given of how the dynamic of the caring relationship helped set up the potential for harm. One carer acknowledged that she sometimes shouted at her husband who had a disability. She acknowledged that she had questioned whether she would address her husband in such a way if he did not have a disability, and she expressed the view that there would be times when she shouted at him in the normal course of their relationship – that joking and shouting at each other formed part of their loving relationship.

Another example was of carers putting pressure on the person they cared for to make decisions, particularly in relation to the acceptance of respite care. It was recognised that the views of the person they cared for needed to be taken into account, and that the potential existed for pressure to accept care to blur into being coercive, especially when there was a felt need for a break that, in the short term, would allow the carer to recharge their batteries. This underscored the importance of recognising the complexity of human relationships and how caring provides an added dimension. The issue of the potential for financial harm was discussed in some detail, especially when power of attorney was in place, and carers stressed how important it was for their own peace of mind to have a clear trail of expenditure in the event of there being any element of scrutiny.

The 'grey area' of 'harm' and applying 'common sense'

The group discussed applying 'common sense' in response to 'grey areas' particularly in relation to supporting people with dementia and how the potential existed for people with dementia (as well as others) to make statements that may, at least on the surface, be viewed as allegations of 'harm', but that when explored turned out to not be accurate. This opened up a discussion about the vulnerability of carers and their need for protection in such situations. It was stated that there was a need for enquiries into potential harm to be conducted sensitively and that sensible, 'common sense' approaches needed to be applied.

Suggestions for good practice

The focus group had a number of useful recommendations for good practice. Firstly, that there is a need for more information in relation to adult protection legislation. This group of carers acknowledged that they were 'in the know' as one of them put it and that to some extent they were in a privileged position. It was suggested that GP surgeries are one of the best points of contact in identifying carers and following through with information on ASPA, and this could possibly reduce some of the stigma and isolation carers can face. Social work practice was discussed from both ends of the spectrum, from having received excellent support through therapeutic engagement to being on the receiving end of poor practice. Whilst this group acknowledged respecting service users' rights, they also requested that carers are sensitively supported.

Case Study – One carer's story

Gaining access to carers who had involvement with formal safeguarding procedures was very difficult, but we did find one carer who was prepared to share their story. As identified above, it is not claimed that this is representative, rather it is illustrative of some of the challenges faced by those in a caring role, and the importance of keeping people informed as the process unfolds.

I felt I got stopped at the bottom rung of the ladder.

We spoke to an older male carer who supports his sister. She has a learning disability and he is now her legal guardian as determined by the AWIA (2000) in Scotland. The carer was concerned about financial abuse, alleging that his sister's savings had disappeared and that benefits were being inappropriately claimed by other family members on her behalf. He reported his concerns to his sister's allocated social worker.

The allocated worker said he needed to get advice from his manager, but I was told that I couldn't go down the Adult Support and Protection route because I didn't have guardianship

▶

◀ at that point and by this time my sister was 'safe' as she moved to live with us. I now know this was wrong. I contacted the Social Work Department to make enquiries about Adult Support and Protection, and I downloaded the Council's procedures to find out for myself. I also contacted the Adult Support and Protection Committee to make enquiries about the Act, and I was reassured this would be looked into. But I had to keep pushing for my concerns to be taken up under Adult Protection. I even got onto my Councillor. I kept being told by those I spoke to, 'I need to take advice'. I feel let down and that my concerns should have been referred to someone who was totally clued up on this Act. I was told my sister didn't meet the three-point criteria for the Act. But I Googled this and I felt I knew as much as them [the professionals]. We had a planning meeting under ASPA with my sister present. Because the financial abuse is historical, it feels like they want me to go away. The meeting was to discuss how to take things forward, but now I've asked for a copy of my sister's file because the Social Work Department hold the evidence they need. I just feel I've not been listened to. I'd like social workers or students reading this to think about the timeframes under ASPA (this has just dragged on for me), to take concerns seriously, to refer onto those with specialist knowledge of the Act to be sure of the procedures and to keep those raising an ASPA inquiry informed and up-to-date. In my experience there seems to be a lack of knowledge around the Act and how to implement it. Personally, I've lost all confidence in the system.

This case brings together a number of the key points raised earlier in the Chapter. In this case, an older adult was potentially being exploited financially by another family member – something that is relatively common in relation to older adults at risk of harm. The experience of the carer in question suggests that his views were not always taken seriously and that he didn't feel listened to or communicated with at key points during the process. This highlights the importance of providing accessible information in a timely fashion and ensuring all of those involved are treated with respect. This carer may have benefited from a referral to an independent advocacy organisation who could have supported him to raise his concern. It also highlights the need for effective joint working in order to ensure that people in receipt of care and their families have access to professionals with appropriate expertise and to avoid unnecessary duplication and delays.

Conclusion

As stated, this small-scale study is not representative of carers' perceptions and experiences of adult support and protection, but it does highlight some interesting and concerning issues that echo the findings from the existing literature outlined above. The protection of vulnerable adults is a complex area not least because the population of adults discussed, the different forms of harm or abuse likely to be experienced, and those likely to be perpetrators of such acts are not well defined. The legal and policy responses across the four countries of the UK have focused on early intervention and prevention, inter-agency working and working with the consent of the adult involved. This requires the provision of appropriate and accessible information for older adults and their carers, as well as appreciating the stressful context within which many caring relationships take place. The evidence from the literature review, as well as our discussion with carers, would suggest that sound assessment of the situation at the initial inquiry stage as well as good therapeutic engagement are essential to the delivery of safeguarding for older adults.

Implications for practice

> Practitioners need to consider safeguarding of older adults within its broader social context, and any assessment should highlight both the needs of the person being cared for and their carer.

> Accessible information needs to be provided in a timely manner to older people and their families so they can have a clear understanding of the safeguarding process and any supports that might be available.

> Ongoing training and improved multi-disciplinary working is required for all those involved in the safeguarding of older access to ensure families have access to professionals with appropriate expertise, avoiding unnecessary delays.

References

Action on Elder Abuse. (2015) Home. Available at http://www.elderabuse.org.uk/ [Accessed 10 January 2015].

Anand, J., Begley, E., O'Brien, M., Taylor, B. and Killick, C. (2013) Conceptualising elder abuse across local and global contexts: Implications for policy and professional practice on the island of Ireland. *The Journal of Adult Protection*, 15(6): 280–289.

Ash, A. (2013) A cognitive mask? Camouflaging dilemmas in street-level policy implementation to safeguard older people from abuse. *British Journal of Social Work*, 43: 99–115.

Askham, J., Briggs, K., Norman, I. and Redfern, S. (2007) Care at home for people with dementia: As in a total institution? *Aging and Society*, 27: 3–24.

Biggs, S., Manthorpe, J., Tinker, A., Doyle, M. and Erens, B. (2009) Mistreatment of older people in the United Kingdom: Findings from the first national prevalence study. *Journal of Elder Abuse and Neglect*, 21(1): 1–14.

Carers Trust. (2015) *Carers Save the UK Economy £87 Billion a Year*. Available at http://www.carers.org/news/carers-save-uk-economy-%C2%A387-billion-year [Accessed 10 January 2015].

Chadwick, D. D., Mannan, H., Iriarte, E. G., McConkey, R., O'Brien, P. Finlay, F., Lawlor, A. and Harrington, G. (2013) Family voices: Life for family carers of people with intellectual disabilities in Ireland. *Journal of Applied Research in Intellectual Disabilities*, 26: 119–123.

Cooper, C., Selwood, A. and Livingston, G. (2008) The prevalence of elder abuse and neglect: A systematic review. *Age and Ageing*, 37(2): 51–160.

Davies, M., Harries, P., Gilhooly, K. and Gilhooly, M. (2011) *Financial Elder Abuse: A Review of the Literature*, Middlesex: Brunel Institute for Ageing Studies.

Department for Work and Pensions. (2015) *A New Vision for Older Workers: Retain, Retrain, Recruit*, London: HMSO.

Department of Health (DoH). (2000) *No Secrets Guidance: The Protection of Vulnerable Adults – Guidance on the Development and Implementation of Multi-agency Policies and Procedures*, London: HMSO.

Department of Health (DoH). (2009) *Safeguarding Adults: Report on the Consultation on the Review of No Secrets*, London: HMSO.

Department of Health, Social Services and Public Safety (DHSSPS). (2009) *Reforming Northern Ireland's Adult Protection Infrastructure*, Belfast: DHSSPS.

Department of Health, Social Services and Public Safety (DHSSPS). (2015) *Adult Safeguarding: Prevention and Protection in Partnership*, Belfast: DHSSPS.

Dixon, J., Manthorpe, J., Biggs, S., Mowlam, A., Tennant, R., Tinker, A. and McCreadie, C. (2010) Defining elder mistreatment: Reflections on the United Kingdom study of abuse and neglect of older people. *Aging and Society*, 30: 403–420.

Flynn, M. C. (2007) *The Murder of Steven Hoskin – A Serious Case Review: Executive Summary*, Cornwall: Cornwall County Council.

Fulmer, T., Rodgers, R. F. and Pelger, A. (2014) Verbal mistreatment of the elderly. *Journal of Elder Abuse and Neglect*, 26(4): 351–364.

Independent Police Complaints Commission. (2009) *IPCC Report into the Contact between Fiona Pilkington and Leicestershire Constabulary 2004–2007*.

Johnson, F. (2011) Problems with the term and concept of 'abuse': Critical reflections on the Scottish adult support and protection study. *British Journal of Social Work*, 42(5): 833–850.

Local Government Association. (2014) *Get in on the Act: The Care Act, 2014*, London: Local Government Association.

Mackay, K., McLaughlan, C., Rossi, S., McNicholl, J., Notman, M. and Fraser, D. (2011) *Exploring How Practitioners Support and Protect Adults at Risk of Harm in the Light of the Adult Support and Protection (Scotland) Act 2007*, Stirling: University of Stirling.

Magill, J., Yeates, V. and Longley, M. (2010) *Review of in Safe Hands: A Review of the Welsh Assembly Government's Guidance on the Protection of Vulnerable Adults in Wales*, Welsh Institute for Health and Social Care, Glamorgan: University of Glamorgan.

Manthorpe, J. and Samsi, K. (2013) 'Inherently risky?': Personal budgets for people with dementia and the risks of financial abuse: Findings from an interview-based study with Adult Safeguarding Coordinators. *British Journal of Social Work,* 43: 889–903.

McGarry, J., Simpson, C. and Hinchliff-Smith, K. (2011) The impact of domestic abuse for older women: A review of the literature. *Health and Social Care in the Community,* 19(1): 3–14.

McKee, K., Spazzafumo, L., Nolan, M., Wojszel, B., Lamura, G. and Bien, B. (2009) Components of the difficulties, satisfactions and management strategies of carers of older people: A principal component analysis of CADI-CASI-CAMI. *Aging and Mental Health,* 13(2): 255–264.

Mental Welfare Commission and the Social Work Services Inspectorate. (2004) *Investigations into Scottish Borders Council and NHS Borders Services for People with Learning Disabilities,* Edinburgh: Scottish Executive.

Morbey, H. (2002) Older women's understanding of elder abuse: Quality relationships and the 'Stresses of Caregiving'. *The Journal of Adult Protection,* 4(3): 4–13.

Mowlam, A., Tennant, R., Dixon, J. and McCreadie, C. (2007) *UK Study of Abuse and Neglect of Older People: Qualitative Findings,* London: Comic Relief.

Penhale, B., and Iborra, I. (2014) 'The epidemiology of elder abuse,' in *Oxford Textbook of Violence Prevention: Epidemiology, Evidence, and Policy,* Oxford: Oxford University Press.

Perera, B. D. and Standen, P. J. (2014) Exploring the coping strategies of carers looking after people with intellectual disabilities and dementia. *Advances in Mental Health and Intellectual Disabilities,* 8(5): 292–301.

Preston-Shoot, M. and Cornish, S. (2013) Governance in adult safeguarding in Scotland since the implementation of the Adult Support and Protection (Scotland) Act 2007. *The Journal of Adult Protection,* 15(5): 223–236.

Preston-Shoot, M. and Cornish, S. (2014) Paternalism or proportionality? Experiences and outcomes of the Adult Support and Protection (Scotland) Act 2007. *The Journal of Adult Protection,* 16(1): 5–16.

Scottish Government. (2011) *Reshaping Care for Older People: A Programme for Change 2011–2021.* Available at http://www.scotland.gov.uk/Topics/Health/Support-Social-Care/Support/Older-People/ReshapingCare [Accessed 8 January 2015].

Shared Care Scotland. (2012) *Rest Assured? A Study of Unpaid Carers' Experiences of Short Breaks,* Glasgow: IRISS.

Sherwood-Johnson, F. (2012) Problems with the term and concept of 'abuse': Critical reflections on the Scottish Adult Support and Protection study. *British Journal of Social Work,* 42: 833–850.

Stewart, A. and Atkinson, J. (2012) Citizenship and adult protection in the UK: An exploration of the conceptual links. *The Journal of Adult Protection,* 14(4): 163–175.

8

Safeguarding Adults with Learning Disabilities

Robert Jenkins, University of Glamorgan; Alan Middleton, Glasgow Caledonian University

This Chapter will critically explore current issues facing professionals working in health and social care settings in regards to safeguarding adults with learning disabilities. Particular attention will be paid to the rights of people with learning disabilities in their encounters with health and social care professionals. Current limitations in practice will be identified, including gaps in knowledge, skills and understanding in assessing capacity and in ensuring the legal rights of adults are upheld. To that effect the Chapter will critically examine practice examples which highlight the blurred nature of the boundaries between informal and legally mandated care. Practice examples will be drawn from two contexts. The first will examine the issues of adults with learning disabilities accessing secondary health care services such as general hospitals. The second will consider the experiences of adults with learning disabilities using sexual health services within a primary health care setting. The practice examples will draw attention to the importance of health and social care professionals adopting effective partnership working approaches with individuals, carers, family members and where appropriate the wider community. They will also explore the professional's role in considering the question of capacity and informed consent, and establishing the legal basis for family members' and carers' decision making in relation to health care.

Vulnerability and people with learning disabilities

The term 'learning disability' is difficult to define precisely because it is a contested notion and means different things to different people (Gates, 2007). Indeed, there is some evidence to suggest that some service users prefer the term learning difficulties rather than being referred to as having a learning disability (Jones et al., 2004). Arguably, the most widely accepted definition is provided by the Department of Health (DoH, 2001) which uses the term learning disability and provides some explanation of what this constitutes by stating that the individual must satisfy the following three factors:

➤ Impaired intelligence (a significantly reduced ability to understand new or complex information, to learn new skills); with

➤ Impaired social functioning (a reduced ability to cope independently); and

➤ These conditions must have started before adulthood and have a lasting effect on development.

There are also four degrees of learning disabilities based partly on Intelligent Quotient's (IQ) criteria and these include 'mild' (IQ 50–69), 'moderate' (IQ 35–49), 'severe' (IQ 20–34) and finally 'profound' (IQ less than 19) (WHO, 1992). These categories attempt to provide a relatively clear understanding of the types of abilities and skills of individuals, albeit this conceptualisation primarily locates disability at the level of the individual paying little attention to its socially constructed nature (Emerson and Heslop., 2010). Within the IQ approach, people who are classed as having a 'profound' learning disability would usually have severe limitations in areas such as mobility, communication, self-care and continence. At the other end of the scale, a 'mild' learning disability classification can indicate that the individual has the potential to be able to work, maintain relationships, communicate verbally and contribute to society. However, these categories or clinical descriptions may be viewed as being a rather crude measure of the individual's true abilities as there are no clear boundaries between each degree of learning disability. Therefore, it is a matter of clinical judgement as to the degree of learning disability a person may possess. These measures may also serve to further stigmatise those individuals labelled as having severe and profound learning disabilities by focusing more on what the individual cannot do rather than what they can do and their worth as a human being.

In regards to the above definition, it is perhaps easy to see why people with learning disabilities would be viewed as belonging to a 'vulnerable' or 'at risk' group of people (for further discussion of these terms see Chapter 2). Impaired intelligence and social functioning may affect the ability of the individual to safeguard their own interests due to being overly reliant on the support of others. However, people with learning disabilities are not a homogeneous group, and there is great variation in the abilities and disabilities between individuals (Gates, 2007). For example, some individuals will have capacity to make life-changing decisions and live independently while others will lack capacity in certain aspects of decision making and require best interest decisions to be made on their behalf. Furthermore, other individuals may just need appropriate support and the opportunity to make their own decisions (via supported decision-making processes). Therefore, it cannot be assumed that because the label 'learning disability' has been applied to an individual they will inevitably be vulnerable or at increased risk and in need of safeguarding. Jenkins and Davies (2011) highlight that certain risk factors may heighten an individual's vulnerability and these factors are not limited to physical conditions or medical problems but encompass a range of psychological and sociological issues such as poverty, frailty, communication difficulties, homelessness, sensory impairment, disability and dependency on others. Vulnerability can also be increased by the culture within organisations which allow abuse to flourish giving rise to institutional abuse (Northway and Jenkins, 2013). As Chapter 10 indicates, the Winterbourne View Hospital scandal in 2011 highlighted management failures which allowed inhumane practices to flourish, resulting in residents being physically and emotionally abused and neglected, restraint being used inappropriately with a general lack of respect and dignity shown towards people with learning disabilities (DoH, 2012). However, it must be remembered that such factors and abuses may fluctuate over time, and some individuals can develop personal strategies to help protect themselves from harm.

Safeguarding people with learning disabilities

People with learning disabilities are at greater risk of abuse when compared to the general population, particularly in relation to physical and sexual abuse (Beadle-Brown et al., 2010). There is also evidence that hate crime is a particular problem for people with learning disabilities with many being, for example, assaulted, shouted and spat at on a daily basis (Gravell, 2012; Stephenson, 2009; Perry, 2004). The Department of Health (2009a) policy document *Valuing People Now* that applied in England and Wales placed great emphasis on addressing hate crime and argued for improvements in accessing the police and justice system as well as ensuring justice for the victims of disability hate crime, as does the *Keys to Life* (Scottish Government, 2013) learning disability strategy in Scotland. To date, much of the research undertaken into the abuse of people with learning disabilities has used quantitative methods of inquiry, which have failed to capture the views regarding abuse of people with learning disabilities. However, Northway et al. (2013) undertook a participatory study which included researchers who had a learning disability that explored people with learning disabilities' views of what help and support they needed to keep safe and if they experienced abuse. A key message coming from this pioneering research was that people with learning disabilities needed someone they could trust and who, most importantly, would not only believe what they communicated but also act on it. 'Circles of support' were also felt to be helpful with both prevention and post-abuse support. Essentially a circle of support is a group of people that form a bond or community around an individual with disabilities or significant needs in order to support them in achieving personal goals. This is more in keeping with the central tenets of safeguarding, which has empowerment as a key principle as well as proportionality, accountability, protection, prevention and partnership working (DoH, 2011). Adult protection in the past was felt to be too reactive whereas safeguarding places much more emphasis on proactive approaches which focus on enabling vulnerable adults to take more control and to be less passive (Northway and Jenkins, 2013) – for example, by improving knowledge and developing assertiveness skills, so that people with learning disabilities will be more likely to speak out or raise concerns if they felt they were being abused. One of the areas which is often overlooked in terms of safeguarding people with learning disabilities is having their health needs met (Jenkins and Davies, 2006).

Meeting the health needs of people with learning disabilities

McClimens and Richardson (2010) argue that services for people with a learning disability in the UK have sought to move from a mainly institutionalised medical model of care through to a social model of care within the community. This aspiration has been helped by growing research into the views and narratives of people with learning disabilities who have had to endure much oppression in their lives. There is strong evidence that people with learning disabilities do not want to live in hospitals, preferring less restrictive environments such as group homes or living independently in their own home (McClimens and Richardson, 2010). Historically, the use of the medical model resulted in people with learning disabilities being viewed as 'ill' and as such unable to take control of their lives due to their impairment. Their unmet health needs would also be assumed to have stemmed from their learning disability. In contrast, the social model of disability argues that society itself imposes barriers that exclude people with disabilities from participation (Thomas, 2014). There is little doubt that people with learning disabilities have greater health needs compared to the general population. Evidence from numerous research studies and reports (Heslop et al., 2013; Scottish Government, 2013; Emerson et al., 2012; Mencap, 2012, 2007, 2004; Backer et al., 2009; Michaels, 2008; DRC, 2006) highlight that not only do people with learning disabilities have greater health needs compared to the general population, they also have greater difficulties in accessing appropriate health care due to a number of barriers. These include institutional discrimination, ignorance, indifference and negative attitudes by health care professionals as well as limited understanding and poor communication skills. People with learning disabilities may not have the capacity to articulate their health needs or be aware of what is available to them unless supported to identify the available options. Health promotion materials may also be too vague or complicated and not in accessible formats for people with learning disabilities to understand. People with mobility and sensory problems can have great difficulty in accessing buildings and rooms due to poor environmental design. As a result, thousands of people with learning disabilities have experienced additional ill health and/or died prematurely due to delays in or not receiving appropriate health care (Mencap, 2012, 2007, 2004; Michaels, 2008). The recent Confidential Inquiry into the premature deaths of people with learning disabilities (Heslop et al., 2013) provides sound evidence that, on average, men with learning disabilities died 13 years and women 20 years earlier when compared to men and women in the general population.

In spite of the overwhelming evidence indicated above, very few health care professionals or organisations have been held fully accountable for such abuses and, as such, people with learning disabilities have often not received justice. This is partly because key inquiries and reports have not made recommendations calling for specific health care organisations or health care professionals to be held accountable or prosecuted for alleged abuses. In addition, people with learning disabilities may lack confidence to speak out, have little understanding of complaints procedures and may be more accepting of abuses due to previous negative experiences of health care services (DoH, 2009a). Interestingly, such instances are often not viewed within the NHS as abuse, but as poor practice and dealt with internally rather than being referred to local authority safeguarding teams (Pinkney et al., 2008). Jenkins and Davies (2006) argue that in seeking to improve safeguarding, such practices must be classified as neglect and nurses (within the parameters of this discussion) and other professionals should be held accountable by their professional body. This is reinforced by the definition of abuse provided by Brüggemann et al. (2011: 130) who argue that:

> Abuse in health care is defined from patients' subjective experiences of encounters with the healthcare system, characterised by events that lack care, where patients suffer and feel they lose their value as human beings.

The events are most often unintentional and nurtured and legitimized by the structural and cultural contexts in which the encounter takes place. The outcomes of abuse in health care are negative for patients and presumably for staff and the health care system as well.

This definition places much more focus on the patient's perceptions of whether their experiences are abusive or not as well as structural and cultural influences which may lead to institutional abuse. If this definition of abuse was widely adopted within the NHS, it might go some way to reducing the difficulties that people with learning disabilities face in accessing appropriate health care. The previous wide-ranging definition of abuse used in both Wales (National Assembly for Wales [NAfW], 2000) and England (DoH, 2000) – 'a violation of an individual's human and civil rights by another person or persons' – was perhaps too wide ranging and difficult to operationalise (Magill et al., 2010; DoH, 2009b). The recently introduced English Care Act 2014 and the Welsh Government's Social Services and Well-being (Wales) Act 2014 do not specifically define abuse. Instead both Acts between them describe different types of abuse and neglect such as physical, psychological, exploitation, emotional, sexual, financial, institutional and discrimination (although such categorisations were also present within the previous guidance outlined above). The guidance offered by the Department of Health (2014) for the Care Act 2014 is that 'local authorities should not be constrained in their view of what constitutes abuse and neglect, and should always consider the circumstances of the individual case' (DoH, 2014: 193).

The range of issues explored in this discussion will now be contextualised in a series of case studies. The first case study provides an example of the difficulties that people with learning disabilities may face when accessing appropriate health care and the implications for health and social care professionals. The second explores the need to adopt effective relationships with service users, carers and the wider community. The third considers the role of parent/carer supports in health care decisions, and the fourth and final case study discusses health and social care providers' roles and responsibilities in addressing sexual health needs.

Case study A

Daniel Baker is a 24-year-old adult with 'severe' learning disabilities who lacks capacity to make major decisions in his life. He resides in a community house in England with two other tenants and communicates with others by means of grunting

▶

and 'shouting' very loudly, which at times verges on screaming. He has visited his local GP several times regarding abdominal pains and was eventually admitted to his local hospital for investigation. During this time the hospital asked for his social care support worker to attend as the hospital staff found it difficult to manage his challenging behaviour, particularly his screaming. He spent approximately two weeks in a side room and ate and drank very little and was eventually discharged with a diagnosis of severe constipation. During his time in hospital he developed grade two pressure sores and his family were not happy with this or the diagnosis, as they felt that something more serious was wrong with Daniel due to his increased screaming. They made a formal complaint to the local health care provider and the response dismissed these concerns and also suggested that the social care staff were partly to blame for the pressure sores as they supported him for most of his stay.

In this example, it can be seen that several visits to the GP were necessary in order for Daniel to be referred for a suitable investigation. This is not an unusual occurrence for people with learning disabilities, as has been highlighted in many of the aforementioned inquiries and reports that have investigated inadequate treatment in the NHS (Heslop et al., 2013; Michaels, 2008; Mencap, 2004). Importantly, these reports also underscored the struggles of families to get health professionals to recognise that their relatives had serious health issues and gave examples of where delays in treatment proved fatal.

In terms of Daniel's treatment while in hospital, there are a number of concerns. All patients are owed a duty of care by the local health board and the health staff they employ. They were responsible for making reasonable adjustments under the Equality Act (2010) to ensure that needs arising from his disability were met, hence promoting equality of access. For example, the Trust could have employed specialist health liaison nurses trained in meeting the needs of people with learning disabilities, who could have supported him through the whole process of hospital admittance and treatment. This type of approach is advocated by the Michaels' report (2008), which also highlighted other good practices in the NHS related to caring for people with learning disabilities.

The issue of social care support staff undertaking nursing care duties can also be problematic. This may often be embarked on with good intentions and the belief that it is in the best interests of the person with a learning disability, providing continuity of care and familiarity with the care they receive outwith the hospital setting. Lines of responsibility can become blurred, however, as in this case in relation to the development of pressure sores. Ultimately, however, the duty of care always lies with the hospital and its staff and not social care staff.

The development of pressure sores would indicate that Daniel's care needs may have been neglected. This should have been reported to the local safeguarding team but appears to have been kept in-house and the blame apportioned to social care staff. This reflects similar findings in the Mid Staffordshire NHS Foundation Trust public inquiry (Francis Report, 2013), which highlighted evidence of 'a defensive institutional instinct to attack those who criticise it, however honestly and reasonably those criticisms are made'.

Case study B

Mary is a 45-year-old woman with 'mild' learning disabilities living in Wales who has been assessed as having capacity in relation to the treatment of her epilepsy and has been refusing to take anticonvulsive medication. She has lived independently for the last 20 years after moving away from her mother, whom she felt was too 'controlling'. Previously her epilepsy was well controlled but she did not like the side effects of the medication, which she feels result in excessive weight gain, increased facial hair and gingivitis. Mary believed this was the main reason she could not get a boyfriend. Her increased epilepsy may have resulted in a fire at her accommodation, as it appears she may have left a candle burning during a seizure. Mary also inadvertently caused a road traffic accident after having a seizure while crossing the road. Her support worker and neighbours, particularly those living in the flat above hers, have tried to persuade her to take her medication and are fearful for her and their own safety if she keeps having uncontrolled seizures. Her mother wants her to move back in with her as she feels she cannot cope on her own.

Mary's situation captures the difficulties faced by health and social care professionals in not only safeguarding the individual and protecting his or her rights, but also potential risks to others in the community. On the one hand Mary has capacity to decide whether to take medication or not, while on the other hand this potentially has major implications for those living in her community when her seizures are not controlled. There are also serious risks to Mary's own health and wellbeing. Both incidents could have resulted in fatalities. The Mental Capacity Act 2005 is clear in England and Wales people are entitled to make decisions that others think are unwise provided they have the capacity to do so. As indicated previously, however, the Care Act 2014 and the Social Services and Well-being (Wales) Act 2014 do not specifically define abuse. This is also the case in Scotland and Northern Ireland. The nurse professional code (NMC, 2015) reinforces this viewpoint by stating that registered nurses must respect a person's right to accept or refuse treatment. However, it also states that registered nurses must ensure that public safety is protected. Social workers are required to work to a similar principle in that they must respect the right of individuals to self-determination provided it does not threaten the safety of others (BASW, 2013).

The definition and principles of safeguarding highlighted earlier in this Chapter stressed the importance of empowering the individual in the safeguarding process. To Mary it seems that finding a partner is more important that having seizures, and making this decision may seem very empowering to her in the face of opposing views, particularly from her mother who has been a dominant person in her life. There is evidence that people with learning disabilities believe that too much focus is placed on their learning disability rather than what they can do, leading to many restrictions being made in their lives (Towers, 2013). The approach for professionals should be to work with all key stakeholders to try and reach a reasonable solution which safeguards both the individual and wider community. Possible ways forward in Mary's case include seeking ways to support her wish for a relationship, framing this as a positive incentive for the better management of her medication. Given the level of risk involved to Mary and to others, an adult safeguarding plan would appear necessary. However, it would be of central importance to engage in a genuine partnership with Mary in developing such a plan, particularly given her experience of having decisions taken by others, including her mother. The plan could include clear guidance on what steps to take should Mary present at risk of harm. Together with regular safeguarding meetings, it could help to engage Mary in making changes that are important to her, whilst also enabling her to remain safe and managing the vulnerability professionals often feel when there is no easy answer to a safeguarding concern. It would also provide a formal forum for decision making and recording decisions and outcomes.

Case study C

Erin is a 34-year-old woman with 'mild' learning disabilities who lives in Scotland. She attended a sexual health clinic with her mother. Erin's mother wanted her to have a long-acting contraceptive prescribed and for the treatment intervention to take place immediately. Erin's mother was adamant that she did not want her daughter getting pregnant now that she has a boyfriend. Erin can communicate verbally although she can become anxious in unfamiliar situations. She has been living in her own rented flat close to her mother for the past two years and she receives two hours' support to assist with household tasks each day. Her mother continues to visit on a daily basis to check on her. Erin was asked in front of her mother whether she wanted a contraceptive prescribed and she responded saying that she did. The nurse prescribed Depo-Provera and administered the first dose as she understood this was an effective contraception for people with learning disability where compliance may be an issue.

In this case study, the views of Erin and her mother should have been considered independently as part of the consultation process. There can, on occasion, be an assumption by health care staff that because the individual has a learning disability that the parent or carer will be acting in the best interests of the individual without considering whether or not they have the legal authority to do so. The nurse should therefore try to establish whether the mother has in fact the legal powers to make decisions in areas of sexual wellbeing that are considered to be in the best interests of her daughter (Scottish Government Health Department, 2000). There may be a need to see Erin and her mother separately in order to explore the issues from both perspectives. This can be a challenge for health care staff, where a parent may wish to be present at every step of the consultation process. In this situation, health care staff would need to acknowledge that Erin's mother is naturally worried about her daughter having a boyfriend and getting pregnant. From Erin's perspective there is a need to explore what she wants and understands. It becomes necessary, therefore, to establish with Erin whether she is currently in a sexual relationship and who this is with, what she understands about sexual and reproductive health matters, pregnancy and in particular contraception. This is necessary to inform assessment of her capacity to consent to the proposed treatment and make an informed decision. For example, Erin may say that she wants to have a baby, but it would be important to ascertain whether she fully understands the consequences of such a decision. Further consideration must be given to the legal and ethical aspects of this decision, at the same time acknowledging that women with a learning disability have the same rights as any other woman when making choices around pregnancy. Therefore, unless it has been legally established that she lacks capacity to make an informed decision, Erin has the right to choose to have a baby and crucially can also change her mind in the future, to have a termination or indeed to consent to having her baby adopted. As such, Erin should be offered the necessary guidance, support and time to assist her to make her decisions without undue influence and importantly in a format that she understands (Glasgow City Council Social Work Services and NHS Greater Glasgow & Clyde, 2012).

A factor to consider as part of the process is who Erin's boyfriend is, and whether he also has a learning disability. This may be particularly significant if there is a possibility of a safeguarding issue arising due to a power imbalance and whether the relationship is one that respects Erin's rights or is coercive and/or unlawful. This can be challenging for health care staff, particularly if there are issues with communication, understanding and establishing a rapport in which to gain trust. Specific issues that need to be considered by the practitioner when interviewing Erin are in relation to suggestibility, acquiescence and confabulation which can make communicating with an individual and interpreting responses more difficult (Gudjonsson and Clare, 1995).

Acquiescence is when an individual has the tendency to say 'yes' to a question regardless of the question's content. Reasons for this include social desirability and impaired cognitive development, and this can be more common when the question is not understood or when the respondent does not know how to answer it. Confabulation arises from problems in memory processing, where people replace gaps in their memory with imaginary experiences that they believe to be true or desire to give what they think are appropriate answers to questions. This is more common when the question or how to answer it is not understood; indeed, the individual may not know what is expected of them in the situation. Suggestibility is where individuals, often in a heightened state of anxiety, will give in to leading questions and side with the questioner. This may lead to confabulation as they process the new information. This may also be due to memory and cognitive difficulties, a lack of assertiveness or indeed anxiety and mistrust in others (Gudjonsson and Clare, 1995).

Putting the person at ease can help minimise the effects of confabulation, suggestibility and acquiescence, facilitated with a relaxed informal approach. Giving simple and clear explanations and checking the individual's understanding as the discussion unfolds are also important. The use of anchor events to establish time, such as TV programmes or seasonal occasions, may also be helpful. In addition, being creative with questioning techniques can help address communication blocks, which includes seeking the views of others who know the adult (whilst not assuming their versions to be the correct or only approaches to take) and employing a variety of strategies, such as pictures or actual items (e.g. condoms), to support the discussion. NHS Health Scotland (2007) published tip cards, which are a quick, easy-to-use resource to help staff know what to do to support people with disabilities which include a section on people with learning disabilities. This resource suggests that when addressing the needs of people who have a learning disability it is important to consider the following points:

> Talk directly to the service user rather than to a carer, personal assistant or advocate.

> Explain what is going to happen to help reassure and calm.

> Avoid the use of jargon. Use plain language with familiar words and short sentences.

> Check that you have understood what the person is saying to you and that they understand you.

> Make sure any further information is available in an appropriate and understandable format, such as 'easy-read'.

> Provide time and opportunities for questions.

Best practice in Erin's case would indicate that health care staff should not allow themselves to be pressured into making a rash decision if there are wider aspects to consider, information to be sought and facts to establish (Glasgow City Council Social Work Services and NHS Greater Glasgow & Clyde, 2012). There may be a need for subsequent visits, utilising suitable health and social care resources for people with learning disabilities, as well as the need to consult with others, which in this example might include Erin's general practitioner or Adult Learning Disability Team/Service. Health care staff will also have to consider the additional and unmet health needs of people with learning disabilities and explore these within the context of sexual health services (NHS Health Scotland, 2004). For example, with the incidence of mental health issues and epilepsy being higher than the general population, there is a need to establish current medications and possible interactions between them (NHS Health Scotland, 2004).

In following the correct pathway for care and treatment, as explored above, this should ensure that Erin receives the most appropriate service and that health care staff work in accordance with the appropriate safeguarding legal framework.

Case study D

James is a 54-year-old man with learning disabilities living in Scotland. He attended the sexual health clinic with a social care support worker. When called to see the nurse, the support worker who came into the room with James suggested that James needed a sexual health check as he has been having sex with other men in public toilets and they were worried that he has contracted a sexually transmitted infection (STI). James lives in a group home with five other people with learning disabilities. There are always social care staff available to support him if required, but he does not receive any specific one-to-one time. He can travel independently and spends a lot of time in the town's shopping center or at the local park. He has been cautioned by the police on at least two previous occasions when found loitering in and around public toilets and been returned by police to his home. When James is asked by the support staff if he is gay he firmly states that he is not.

This final case study illustrates the difficulties faced by health and social care professionals when an individual with a learning disability places themselves in vulnerable and potentially high-risk or dangerous situations. Once again, sexual health staff are faced with establishing who has the authority and power to make decisions about James's life, bearing in mind that adults should be assumed to have capacity to make their own decisions unless it is known otherwise.

Within this case study there is a particular need to explore whether James is indeed making an informed decision about the type of sex he is engaging in and where this is taking place. The number of men with learning disabilities who have sexual relations with other men is difficult to estimate, as many men do not openly disclose this type of sexual behaviour due to the influence of negative stereotyping (Abbott and Howarth, 2005). Individuals may, therefore, keep this aspect of their lives hidden from those who support them. The additional risks to men with learning disability who have sex with other men can be attributed to increased difficulties negotiating and practising safe sex, as the sexual encounters often take place in public places or risky situations often leading to experiences that are both physically and emotionally painful (Cambridge, 1996, 1994; Thomson, 1994). This can be challenging for support staff if it is indeed established that, despite the risks to sexual health and other aspects of physical wellbeing, an individual continues to choose to take sexual risks. However, concerns with 'risk' and 'harm' must be considered against the views of many men, including those with a learning disability, who consider having sex in public environments as a valid choice, and one impeded by discriminatory legislation and the opinions of others (Withers et al., 2001). Relatedly, there may be a need to explore gaps in knowledge of sexual health of staff in working with people with a learning disability and to consider when it is appropriate to seek help either to work in partnership with learning disability services or indeed to raise and escalate concerns. As previously highlighted, the health needs of people with learning disabilities are different from the general population (NHS Health Scotland, 2004), and there are specific challenges to accessing health services that address individual needs (Brown et al., 2010). Consequently, it is helpful to consider what may be required in order to improve access. The individual's confidentiality and choice should be respected at all times, unless there are specific concerns for their safety. The issues should be raised respectfully and agreement sought from the adult to engage in any discussion with others. It is important to establish the type of relationship the individual is in and the type of sex, if any, that they are practicing and to avoid jumping to any conclusions. Based on this discussion, clarity of the health education information required and in which format can be established (e.g. utilising condoms for safer penetrative sex and the use of a condom demonstrator in a practical educational session). It should be remembered, however, that the adult may not hold the same views on what is an acceptable risk to take and may choose to continue in what others perceive to be high-risk sexual behaviour. Although all professionals working with people with a learning disability have a role to play in offering advice, it is also important to recognise when additional input is required from more specialised health or social care professionals (Glasgow City Council Social Work Services and NHS Greater Glasgow & Clyde, 2012).

Conclusion

This chapter has considered safeguarding in relation to adults with learning disabilities, set against UK-wide legal and policy contexts and drawing upon a range of evidence to explore contemporary issues and dilemmas. There has been a particular focus on the rights of people with learning disabilities in their encounters with health care professionals. Current limitations in practice have been explored, and gaps in knowledge, skills and understanding have been identified, particularly in assessing capacity and in ensuring the legal rights of adults are upheld.

Through critical examination of practice examples, the blurred nature of the boundaries between informal and legally mandated care have been highlighted, with a particular emphasis on ways in which people can be empowered and supported to make their own decisions. Crucially, the chapter has identified the need for health and social care staff to be aware of their duty of care in safeguarding adults, as it applies in this context, and their responsibilities in knowing when to escalate and raise concerns. The examples from practice, across secondary and primary care contexts, have examined in detail some of the difficult day-to-day ethical issues that arise for adults with learning disabilities, their carers and the professionals responsible for facilitating their independence and safeguarding them from harm. In acknowledging the – albeit contested – issues of reduced IQ and social functioning, along with additional factors such as sensory deficits, the importance of effective communication has been made clear (e.g. avoiding acquiescence, suggestibility and confabulation) (Gudjonsson and Clare, 1995).

Particular focus has been given to the experiences of adults with learning disabilities using sexual health services, and attention paid to the importance of health and social care professionals adopting effective partnership working approaches with individuals, carers, family members and, where appropriate, the wider community. A further theme arising from this chapter is the need to raise awareness of the additional support needs of people with learning disabilities among health care providers, which in many instances will necessitate further training for health care staff. Relatedly, there is also a need to establish local referral pathways to services that can offer additional supports to people with learning disabilities, towards realising the dual aims of upholding their rights and offering adequate and proportionate protection from harm.

Implications for practice

> ➢ Adults with learning disability are more likely to be at risk of harm than other adults in relation to having their health needs met. A multi-disciplinary approach is required to ensure people have adequate access to services.

> ➢ Practitioners need to balance the duty to safeguard people and protect them from harm while at the same time empowering them to make their own decisions via supported decision making.

> ➢ Involving people in the decision-making process can help to reduce the risk of further harm taking place.

References

Abbott, D. and Howarth, J. (2005) *Secret Loves, Hidden Lives? Exploring Issues for People with Learning Difficulties Who Are Gay, Lesbian or Bisexual*, Bristol: Policy Press.

Backer, C., Chapman, M. and Mitchell, D. (2009) Access to secondary healthcare for people with intellectual disabilities: A review of the literature. *Journal of Applied Research in Intellectual Disabilities,* 22(6): 514–525.

Beadle-Brown, J., Mansell, J., Cambridge, P., Milne, A. and Whelton, B. (2010) Adult protection of people with intellectual disabilities: Incidence, nature and responses. *Journal of Applied Research in Intellectual Disabilities*, 23(6): 573–584.

British Association of Social Workers (BASW). (2013) *The Code of Ethics for Social Work Statement of Principles,* Birmingham: British Association of Social Workers.

Brown, M., MacArthur, J., McKechanie, A., Hayes, M. and Fletcher, J. (2010) Equality and access to general health care for people with learning disabilities: Reality or rhetoric? *Journal of Research in Nursing,* 15(4): 351–361.

Brüggemann, A. J., Wijma, B. and Swahnberg, K. (2011) Abuse in health care: A concept analysis. *Scandinavian Journal of Caring Sciences,* 26(1): 123–132 (March).

Cambridge, P. (1994) A practice and policy agenda for HIV and learning difficulties. *British Journal of Learning Disabilities*, 22: 134–139.

Cambridge, P. (1996) Men with learning disabilities who have sex with men in public places: Mapping the needs of services and service users in South East London. *Journal of Intellectual Disability Research*, 40(3): 241–251.

Care Act. (2014) England Chapter 23. Available at http://www.legislation.gov.uk/ukpga/2014/23/pdfs/ukpga_20140023_en.pdf [Accessed 24 May 2015].

Department of Health (DoH). (2000) *No Secrets: Guidance on Developing and Implementing Multi-agency Policies and Procedures to Protect Vulnerable Adults from Abuse*, London: The Stationery Office.

Department of Health (DoH). (2001) *Valuing People: A New Strategy for Learning Disability for the 21st Century*, London: Department of Health.

Department of Health (DoH). (2009a) *Valuing People Now: A New Three-Year Strategy for People with Learning Disabilities*, London: Department of Health.

Department of Health (DoH). (2009b) *Safeguarding Adults: Report on the Consultation on the Review of No Secrets*, London: Department of Health.

Department of Health (DoH). (2011) *Safeguarding Adults: The Role of Health Service Practitioners*, London: Department of Health.

Department of Health (DoH). (2012) *Transforming Care: A National Response to Winterbourne View Hospital*, London: Department of Health. Available at https://www.gov.uk/government/uploads/system/uploads/attachment_data/file/213215/final-report.pdf [Accessed 2 October 2017].

Department of Health (DoH). (2014) *Care and Support Statutory Guidance*, London: Department of Health. Available at https://www.gov.uk/government/uploads/system/uploads/attachment_data/file/315993/Care-Act-Guidance.pdf [Accessed 2 October 2017].

Disability Rights Commission (DRC). (2006) *Part 1. Equal Treatment: Closing the Gap. A Formal Investigation into the Physical Health Inequalities Experienced by People with Learning Disabilities and/or Mental Health Problems*, London: Disability Rights Commission.

Emerson, E., Baines, S., Allerton, L., and Welch, V. (2012). Health inequalities & people with learning disabilities in the UK: 2012. Available at: https://www.improvinghealthandlives.org.uk/securefiles/141020_1442//IHAL%202012-11%20Health%20Inequalities_r1.pdf

Emerson, E. and Heslop, P. (2010) *A Working Definition of Learning Disability*, IHAL. https://www.researchgate.net/publication/265306674_A_working_definition_of_Learning_Disabilities [Accessed 02 October 2017].

Emerson, E., Baines, S., Allerton, L. and Welch, V. (2012) Health inequalities & people with learning disabilities in the UK: 2012. Available at https://www.improvinghealthandlives.org.uk/securefiles/141020_1442//IHAL%202012-11%20Health%20Inequalities_r1.pdf

Equality Act. (2010) London: The Stationery Office. Available at http://www.legislation.gov.uk/ukpga/2010/15/contents [Accessed 2 October 2017].

Francis, R. (2013) *Report of the Mid Staffordshire NHS Foundation Trust Public Inquiry*. Available at https://www.gov.uk/government/publications/

report-of-the-mid-staffordshire-nhs-foundation-trust-public-inquiry [Accessed 2 October 2017].

Gates, B. (2007) 'Understanding learning disability', in Gates, B. (ed.), *Learning Disabilities* (pp. 3–19), Edinburgh: Churchill Livingstone.

Glasgow City Council Social Work Services and NHS Greater Glasgow & Clyde. (2012) *Relationships & Sexual Wellbeing: A Policy and Practice Guidelines for those Who Work with People with Learning Disabilities,* Glasgow: Author.

Gravell, C. (2012) *Loneliness + Cruelty: People with Learning Disabilities and their Experience of Harassment, Abuse, and Related Crime in the Community,* London: Lemos and Crane.

Gudjonsson, G. H. and Clare, I. C. H. (1995) The relationship between confabulation and intellectual disability, memory, interrogative suggestibility and acquiescence. *Personality and Individual Differences,* 19(3): 333–338.

Heslop, P. Blair, P. Fleming, P., Hoghton, M., Marriott, A. and Russ, L. (2013) *Confidential Inquiry into Premature Deaths of People with Learning Disabilities,* Bristol: Norah Fry Research Centre, University of Bristol.

Jenkins, R. and Davies, R., (2006) Neglect of people with intellectual disabilities: A failure to act? *Journal of Intellectual Disabilities,* 10(1): 35–45.

Jenkins, R. and Davies, R. (2011) Safeguarding people with learning disabilities. *Learning Disability Practice,* 14(1): 32–39.

Jones, V., Davies, R. and Jenkins, R. (2004) Self-harm by people with learning difficulties: Something to be expected or investigated? *Disability & Society,* 19(5): 487–500.

Magill, J., Yeates, V. and Longley, M. (2010) *Review of In Safe Hands: A Review of the Welsh Assembly Government's Guidance on the Protection of Vulnerable Adults,* Welsh Institute for Health and Social Care, Pontypridd.

McClimens, A. and Richardson, M. (2010) 'Social construction and social models: Disability explained?', in Grant, G., Ramcharan, P., Flynn, M. and Richardson, M. (eds), *Learning Disability: A Life Cycle Approach* (2nd edition) (pp. 19–32), Maidenhead: McGraw-Hill/Open University Press.

Mencap. (2004) *Treat me Right: Better Healthcare for People with a Learning Disability,* London: Mencap.

Mencap. (2007) *Death by Indifference: Following up the Treat Me Right Report,* London: Mencap.

Mencap. (2012) *Death by Indifference: 74 Deaths and Counting. A Progress Report 5 Years On,* London: Mencap.

Michaels, J. (2008) *Report of the Independent Inquiry into Access to Healthcare for People with Learning Disabilities.* Available at http://webarchive. nationalarchives.gov.uk/20130105064756/http://www.dh.gov.uk/ prod_consum_dh/groups/dh_digitalassets/@dh/@en/documents/digitalasset/ dh_106126.pdf [Accessed 2 October 2017].

National Assembly for Wales (NAfW). (2000) *In Safe Hands: Protection of Vulnerable Adults in Wales,* Cardiff: NAfW.

NHS Health Scotland. (2007) *Tip Cards*. Available at http://www.healthscotland.
    com/uploads/documents/5809-Updated%20Tip%20Cards%20-%2031.01.08.
    pdf [Accessed 2 October 2017].
NHS Health Scotland. (2004) *Health Needs Assessment Report,* Glasgow: Clifton
    House.
Northway, R., Bennett, D., Melsome, M., Flood, S., Howarth, J. and Jones, R.
    (2013) Keeping safe and providing support: A participatory survey about
    abuse and people with intellectual disabilities. *Journal of Policy and Practice in
    Intellectual Disabilities,* 10(3): 236–244.
Northway, R. and Jenkins, R. (2013) *Safeguarding Adults in Nursing Practice,*
    London: SAGE.
Nursing & Midwifery Council (NMC). (2015) *The Code. Professional Standards of
    Practice and Behaviour for Nurses and Midwives,* London: NMC.
Perry, J. (2004) Hate crime against people with learning difficulties: The role of
    the Crime and Disorder Act and No Secrets in identification and prevention.
    Journal of Adult Protection, 6(1): 27–34.
Pinkney, L., Penhale, B., Manthorpe, J., Perkins, N., Reid, D. and Hussein, S.
    (2008) Voices from the frontline: Social work practitioners' perceptions of
    multi-agency working in adult protection in England and Wales. *The Journal
    of Adult Protection,* 10(4): 12–24.
Scottish Government Health Department. (2000) Adults with Incapacity
    (Scotland) Act 2000. Available at http://www.legislation.gov.uk/asp/2000/4/
    contents [Accessed 2 October 2017].
Scottish Government Health Department. (2003) Mental Health (Care and
    Treatment) (Scotland) Act 2003. Available at http://www.legislation.gov.uk/
    asp/2003/13/contents
Scottish Government Health Department. (2007) Adult Support and Protection
    (Scotland) Act 2007. Available at http://www.legislation.gov.uk/asp/2007/10/
    contents
Scottish Government (2013) The Keys to Life, available at https://keystolife.
    info/, accessed on 2nd October 2017.
Stephenson, P. (2009) Tackling hate crime in Barnsley. *Learning Disability
    Practice,* 12(7): 20–23.
Thomas, C. (2014) 'Disability and impairment', in Swain, J., French, S.,
    Barnes, C. and Thomas, C. (eds), *Disabling Barriers-Enabling Environments,*
    London: SAGE.
Thomson, D. (1994) Sexual experience and sexual identity for men
    with learning disabilities who have sex with men. *Changes,* 12(4):
    245–263.
Towers, C. (2013) *Thinking Ahead: Improving Support for People with Learning
    Disabilities and their Families to Plan for the Future,* London: Foundation for
    People with Learning Disabilities. Available at https://www.mentalhealth.
    org.uk/learning-disabilities/publications/thinking-ahead-report [Accessed
    2 October 2017].

Welsh Government (WG). (2014) *Social Services and Well-being (Wales) Act,* Cardiff: Welsh Government. Available at http://www.legislation.gov.uk/anaw/2014/4/pdfs/anaw_20140004_en.pdf [Accessed 2 October 2017].

Withers, P., Ensum, I., Howarth, D., Krall, P., Thomas, D., Weekes, D., Winter, C., Mullholland, A., Dindjer, T. and Hall, J. (2001) A psychoeducational group for men with intellectual disabilities who have sex with men. *Journal of Applied Research in Intellectual Disabilities*, 14: 327–339.

World Health Organization (WHO). (1992) *International Classification of Mental and Behavioural Disorders ICD-10*, Geneva: WHO.

9

Self-Harm and Suicide

Pearse McCusker, Glasgow Caledonian University; Jackie Jackson, Renfrewshire Council

Self-harm and suicide are poorly understood in the general population (Royal College of Psychiatrists, 2010) and research indicates that people who self-harm and attempt suicide are often subject to stigma and hostility, even from professionals who regularly work with them, including doctors, nurses, the police and social workers (Scottish Association for Mental Health, 2012; Saunders et al., 2011; Royal College of Psychiatrists, 2010). Self-harm and suicide are, however, major public health concerns making it essential for professionals across a range of sectors to have the requisite skills and knowledge to provide effective interventions (Scowcroft, 2016; Timson et al., 2012). This Chapter considers these issues further in the context of adult safeguarding to explore current challenges and good practice. It begins by defining self-harm and suicide, and argues that they should be conceived as safeguarding concerns across the UK. Current prevalence and policy are explored, along with emerging themes drawn from adult protection and safeguarding committee reports and discussions with health and social care practitioners. This highlights working with people who frequently present with self-harming and suicidal behaviours as a key challenge. A case study is then used to identify approaches for providing holistic, humane and effective responses to protect this group of adults from harm.

Defining self-harm and suicide

Self-harm is defined as an act of self-injury with a non-fatal outcome (Madge et al., 2008). It is an intentional act that takes numerous forms, including self-cutting, poisoning and burning (Scottish Government, 2013). Self-harm additionally includes suicide attempts, as well as acts where little or no suicidal intent is involved, for example when people harm themselves to reduce internal tension, distract themselves from intolerable situations or punish themselves. Self-harm may result in short- or long-term damage to a person's physical or emotional health. In contrast, suicide is defined as someone purposely taking their own life (Office of National Statistics, 2011). Here, emphasis is placed on 'intentionality' and having a set of circumstances and evidence that allow it to be established. However, as suicide can be difficult to prove, the official definition used by UK statistical bodies includes deaths where suicide cannot be confirmed but is thought to be the cause, giving rise to the term 'probable suicides' defined as 'deaths which are the result of intentional self-harm or events of undetermined intent' (National Records of Scotland, 2015). Notwithstanding these definitional distinctions, it is important to note that people who repeatedly self-harm are at much higher risk of completing suicide due to increased probability of accidental suicide and/or the gradual process of normalising self-injurious behaviours (Timson et al., 2012).

Prevalence

Self-harm and suicide are acknowledged as major national and international public health issues (Scottish Government, 2013; WHO, 2013; Timson et al., 2012).

Self-harm is one of the top five causes of acute medical admission in the UK (Department of Health, 2012). The UK has also had one of the highest rates of adult self-harm in Europe (Horrocks and House, 2002). In England and Wales there are an estimated 140,000 presentations each year for self-poisoning and self-injury, although this is likely to be a significant under-estimate due to differences in hospital admission policies and data collection methods (Hawton et al., 2007). Self-harm predominates in younger age groups, starting on average at around 12 years old (Fox and Hawton, 2004) and becoming more common after the age of 16 (Timson et al., 2012). *Truth Hurts,* the report of the UK National Inquiry into self-harm among young people, cites a figure of approximately 1 in every 15 young people having self-harmed (Camelot Foundation and Mental Health Foundation, 2006). It highlights increasing pressures facing young people, ranging from academic achievement at school, bullying, family breakdown, isolation, sexuality, poor body image and economic uncertainty, and indicates that self-harming behaviour can sometimes be the only way the young person feels able to express his or her distress.

The World Health Organization cites suicide as the cause of almost one million deaths annually (WHO, 2013), but official figures for suicide are believed to reflect significant under-reporting (Scowcroft, 2016). In the UK, for 2014, 6122 people are registered as having completed suicide. Men between the ages of 45–49 had the highest rate, with 26.5 per 100,000. Across the UK, rates of suicide for men are consistently higher than for women (Scowcroft, 2016). The highest suicide rates for men and women are in Scotland and Northern Ireland (Scowcroft, 2016).

Policy

Despite its prevalence, self-harm is recognised as having been significantly neglected in national policy and in need of a coordinated strategy (Royal College of Psychiatrists, 2010). The *Truth Hurts* inquiry found evidence of approximately two children/young people self-harming in every classroom and yet widespread misunderstanding about the issue among the professionals who are often their first port of call for help:

> Over and over again, the young people we heard from told us that their experience of asking for help often made their situation worse. Many of them have met with ridicule or hostility from the professionals they have turned to.
>
> (Camelot Foundation and Mental Health Foundation, 2006: 3)

In Scotland, the government responded to the *Truth Hurts* inquiry's findings by acknowledging that policy initiatives to reduce self-harm were inadequate and establishing the National Self-Harm Working Group in 2009. It reported similar findings, including poor levels of understanding, knowledge and inadequate responses among professionals, and it helped to inform the government's plan, *Responding to Self-Harm in Scotland* (Scottish Government, 2011a). Its objectives included increasing the rate of identification of people who are self-harming, developing services to support people to reduce the frequency and severity of self-harming behaviour (harm reduction), addressing the underlying causes of self-harming and improving people's experience of health and social services.

In contrast, suicide awareness and prevention have been the focus of major public health and wellbeing policy initiatives across the UK over the past two decades. In 2012, *Preventing Suicide in England: A Cross-Government Outcomes Strategy to Save Lives* was launched, with one objective being to re-dress poor media representations and further reduce stigma surrounding mental health (Her Majesty's Government, 2012). Similarly, in Wales, the Assembly introduced its five-year action plan, *Talk to Me* in 2009 (Welsh Assembly Government, 2009) and in Northern Ireland, the *Protect a Life* strategy was updated in 2012

(DHSSPS, 2012). North of the border, *Choose Life: A National Strategy and Action Plan to Prevent Suicide in Scotland*, was launched in 2002 (Scottish Government, 2013). It sought to reduce the suicide rate by taking a 'whole systems' approach in order to raise national awareness; engage in community-based work; train professionals in health, social care and other sectors; and develop research to inform interventions. A key objective was to reduce suicide by 20% between 2002 and 2013, where the actual reduction achieved was 17% (Scottish Government, 2013). These initiatives have contributed to significant progress across the UK in reducing suicide, however, since around 2007 there has been a general increase, particularly among females (Scowcroft, 2016).

Are self-harm and suicide adult safeguarding concerns?

Self-harm and suicide arise from a complex range of factors that may include unemployment, marital status, relationship breakdown, social isolation, early life trauma, life stage adjustment, sexual orientation, bereavement, bullying, substance misuse and physical health problems, among others (Milner et al., 2014; Scottish Government, 2013; Camelot Foundation and Mental Health Foundation, 2006). They can be variously defined as rational responses to difficult life circumstances or medical conditions, or a combination or both. As such, the intersection with civil liberties is complex and gives rise to questions about illness, capacity and the right to self-determination. Consequently, their status in terms of adult safeguarding and deciding when to intervene to protect, in some cases against the adult's will, is not easy to determine.

For the purposes of this discussion we take the view that interventions under adult safeguarding should always be considered when an adult is contemplating suicide. This position is premised on the view that the State has a responsibility to provide people with appropriate supports to address their difficulties in ways other than completing suicide. In extremis, this may include the use of compulsory intervention, where the person is experiencing mental distress and relevant legal criteria are met, and the intervention is required to ensure their safety for a limited period of time.

The position with self-harm is, however, less clear, as the motivation to self-harm can be to cope with overwhelming emotional distress, with no intent to cause significant harm or end life (Camelot Foundation and Mental Health Foundation, 2006). People who self-harm do so for a wide range of reasons and with substantial variations in severity. It is therefore important to understand the reasons for the self-harming behaviour, the degree of harm and the risk this poses to the individual (Camelot Foundation and Mental Health Foundation, 2006). In Scotland, self-harm is a specified category of harm under the Adult Support and Protection (Scotland) Act 2007 (ASPA), however this is not the position in the rest of the UK. In principle, and in accordance with the Scottish legal position, we take the view that self-harming behaviours are adult safeguarding concerns, but that professionals' responses must be informed by the adult's circumstances, their capacity to make decisions and the potential benefits the 'harmful' behaviours are serving.

In summary, this Chapter advocates a rights-based, empowering, person-centred and consent-driven approach to working with people with self-harming and suicidal behaviours; one that upholds individuals' rights to self-determination but is also willing to make proportionate use of safeguarding legislation to protect people from harm.

Emerging trends and themes in safeguarding relating to self-harm and suicide

Local Safeguarding Adult Boards in England, Area Adult Protection Committees in Wales, Local Adult Safeguarding Partnerships in Northern Ireland and Adult Protection Committees (APCs) in Scotland comprise local authorities, health boards and other public bodies. They are required to coordinate the protection of adults from harm as outlined in Chapter 5 of this volume. Differences in recording, however, make it difficult to compare issues across the jurisdictions. APCs in Scotland are unique in recording self-harm as a specific category and therefore, in the main, their reports have been used to explore emerging trends and themes in relation to self-harm and suicide.

Prevalence in Scotland

The Scottish figures indicate that self-harm is one of the principal reasons for adult protection referrals. In the period 2008–2010 it accounted for 21.23% of adult support and protection referrals across Scotland, with attempted suicide making up 2.85% (Scottish Government, 2011b). The prevalence rate varies geographically and across age ranges. For example, in Glasgow, in the period April 2011–March 2012, self-harm accounted for 24.5% of all referrals however, the rate was considerably higher for the group aged 20 and under, representing almost 30% of the total (Glasgow City Council Adult Protection Committee, 2012). Individual local APC reports for the period 2012–14 indicate that self-harm remains a significant issue: in one area accounting for 32.9% of adult protection referrals in the period April 2013–March 2014 (South Lanarkshire Adult Protection Committee, 2014) and 37% in another (East Dunbartonshire Adult Protection Committee, 2014).

Accident and emergency

APC reports have identified problems with how accident and emergency (A&E) sites respond to people who present with self-harming behaviours, which correlates with research findings (Friedman et al., 2006) and appears to be related to a range of factors. People with self-harming behaviours who present at A&E are often under the influence of alcohol or drugs (South Lanarkshire Adult Protection Committee, 2014). This compounds difficulties in accurately assessing and treating them in working environments that may already be under significant resource strain. Staff attitudes towards self-harming patients have also been identified as adversely influencing the quality of care. Friedman et al. (2006) found that staff lacked knowledge and skills in relation to self-harm and had received little training on the subject. They also found a correlation between those without training who had been employed for longer at A&E departments with higher levels of anger towards people presenting with self-harm and a tendency not to see them as having a mental health problem. Staff attitudes are recognised as having a major effect on the quality of professional care (Di Caccavo and Reid, 1998), that together with inadequate training, may explain high levels of dissatisfaction for this group of patients attending A&E (Kuisma et al., 2003) and inaccurate assessments of their needs (Hickey et al., 2001). APC reports suggest that while many people who present at A&E with self-harming/suicidal behaviours may have their immediate health needs met, they often do not receive appropriate follow-up care, potentially leading to repeated visits to hospital (South Lanarkshire Adult Protection Committee, 2014).

Accordingly, processes and practices within A&E settings have received increasing focus across the UK in line with the policy drive to reduce self-harm. In Scotland, in 2012, adult support and protection (ASP) within A&E settings was identified as one of five national priority areas, arising from a lack of knowledge about how well ASP was working in these settings and a perceived lack of engagement by the NHS in adult protection in general (Carr, 2014). A working group was established to deliver on a range of objectives, including an audit of knowledge and understanding of ASP among A&E and ambulance staff. In addition, the project sought to facilitate the development of training and good practice initiatives using three test sites, with the overall aim of enabling the NHS to meet its legal obligations in relation to ASP and to improve practice and processes across the country. The findings illustrate some success in achieving the objectives, including improved knowledge and understanding among A&E and ambulance staff, a significant increase in the number of appropriate ASP referrals made from A&E sites and improved engagement with police and social work departments (Scottish Government, 2014). The project's recommendation included mandatory training for A&E and ambulance staff to use existing incident reporting systems to prompt staff to record and refer ASP concerns and to introduce governance arrangements for ASP that mirror those for child protection (Scottish Government, 2014). The test site findings are not, however, reflected uniformly across the country. While some areas report a marked increase in the number of safeguarding referrals coming from A&E settings (South Lanarkshire Adult Protection Committee, 2014), others recorded only a very marginal increase (City of Dundee Adult Support and Protection Committee, 2014) and the overall national picture reflects a consistently low number (Care Inspectorate, 2014).

'Frequent attenders'

People who frequently present in crisis with self-harming and suicidal behaviours pose particular challenges for agencies in terms of sharing information and providing coordinated responses. Many areas across the UK have developed protocols to provide more integrated approaches. In England, the 'Cornwall Trigger Protocol' enables local agencies to agree on responses to safeguarding presentations, with 'frequent attenders' triggering specific actions, such as safeguarding alerts, which may include multi-agency responses (e.g. more than five calls per month to the ambulance service triggers liaison with GP and partner agencies) (Cornwall and Isles of Scilly Safeguarding Adults and Children Boards, 2012). Similarly, in Edinburgh, a multi-disciplinary monthly 'frequent attenders' meeting is held to monitor progress and enhance the range of supports provided. The trigger is more than five contacts within a three-month period or ten times within a year, leading to a review of the case, a letter being sent to the individual's GP and consideration given to revising the care plan and putting an alert on the patient information system. The importance of finding more effective and compassionate ways of responding to 'frequent attenders' is illustrated in a recent significant case review, which identified that people who go on to complete suicide have often repeatedly presented at A&E departments beforehand (City of Edinburgh Council, 2014).

The experience 'on the ground'

In addition to exploring national trends emerging from safeguarding reports, this Chapter sought to reflect practitioners' experiences of working with self-harm and suicide in order to gain additional insights into issues, challenges and opportunities for developing informed safeguarding practice. To achieve this, a multi-disciplinary discussion group was arranged, comprising social workers, a social work assistant, an adult support and protection police officer, a community psychiatric nurse and a third-sector mental health service manager in a community mental health setting in one Scottish local authority area. The group was not intended to represent all of the professionals involved in adult safeguarding for people experiencing self-harm or suicidal behaviours, nor was it designed to evaluate practice in a particular geographical area. Rather, the aim was to explore effective approaches and barriers to working with people with self-harming and suicidal behaviours, including the role of multi-disciplinary working and other issues that might help inform practice more widely.

In effect, the overwhelming focus of the discussion was on people who repeatedly engage in self-harming and/or suicidal behaviours and who frequently present at A&E settings. A consensus emerged of a relatively small number of service users with complex health and social circumstances who had become entangled in cycles of self-harm or threats to self-harm. Personality disorder, either suspected or formally diagnosed, was considered to be a key factor in this dynamic, and this practice view is supported by evidence of high rates of suicidal and/or self-harming behaviours for people with this diagnosis (National Health and Medical Research Council, 2014).

The discussion group identified stigma as a significant barrier to 'frequent attenders' receiving an effective service, noting treatment by A&E professionals as often perfunctory and sometimes punitive. Better training for A&E staff was therefore viewed as essential, particularly in relation to understanding personality disorder and its relationship to self-harm. The suitability of A&E settings for treating people with self-harm and suicidal behaviours was questioned, and consideration was given to potentially more appropriate alternatives, including acute psychiatric wards and out-of-hours 'crisis flats'. The latter was felt to be a much more effective preventative measure and one that might provide a genuine 'place of safety' until the crisis had lessened. However, it was acknowledged that such resources are not routinely available, despite calls from survivors of psychiatry for the provision of less medical, more therapeutic places of safety (Webb, 2015). In addition, this type of resource was seen as an important correction to the 'nine-to-five' model used by many health and social care services. As an alternative to hospital, it was also seen to provide opportunities to work with service users from a social perspective towards addressing the underlying needs precipitating their behaviours, rather than attending only to narrowly defined forms of 'medical treatment'. The more familiar care pathway (whereby a service user is brought by police or ambulance to A&E, treated and then discharged) was considered to be ineffective, and a poor example of inter-professional working.

Despite the many systemic and attitudinal challenges of working with people who frequently present with self-harming and suicidal behaviour, the group identified approaches considered to be more likely to effect longer-term positive change. In this regard, adult support and protection legislation was seen as offering a helpful framework, both for providing support to the service user and coordinating inter-professional care. A significant benefit of the legislation in Scotland was the requirement to use protection plans for people who had been repeatedly referred. Based on a detailed assessment of need and stipulating the type and frequency of support the person should receive, protection plans were seen to enable professionals to build more effective relationships and provide consistent levels of support. Participants gave detailed examples of service users feeling more valued by this approach, noting how the legal framework led to greater reliability, clearer expectations and boundaries, all of which underpin effective practice with people with personality disorders (Roth and Pilling, 2013).

Protection plans were also reported to support better inter-professional working, providing greater role clarity and a framework for shared decision making. Discussion indicated that some service users had requested staying on protection plans, having benefited from the levels of support they provided, including increased frequency and consistency in relation to contact with relevant agencies. In addition, it noted a positive impact for service users of reading their protection plans, which for some was felt to lead to a 'wake-up' call about the consequences for their health and wellbeing. Throughout the discussion, effective relationship-building by professionals with service users and close multi-disciplinary working were identified as essential to achieving positive outcomes, leading to greater role clarity and reducing the potential for professional disputes to occur.

Assessing and supporting adults who are believed to be suicidal or have or are threatening to self-harm

Assessing adults who have self-harmed, threatened self-harm and/or are suicidal is ethically complex. There are hazards and disadvantages to both over-estimating and under-estimating risk. For example, over-sensitivity to risk can result in inappropriate and unhelpful admissions to hospital, as well as civil rights intrusion in the form of unwarranted compulsory treatment and detention under mental health legislation. Conversely, under-estimating suicidality can jeopardise a person's safety and have fatal consequences. Health, social care and other professionals may be held liable if an under-estimation of suicidality is a result of a partial or poor assessment. Even with careful assessment, predicting risk is inherently difficult and prone to false positives (Callaghan and Ryan, 2014). A lack of knowledge, skills or confidence to make clear assessments may result in interventions that 'err on the side of caution'. Moreover, alcohol misuse is strongly associated with self-harm and suicide, in part due to its disinhibiting effects on behaviour (Mental Health Foundation, 2006). The presence of alcohol also further complicates any risk assessment. Frequently adults under the influence of alcohol will not be assessed as being suitable for hospital admission. Currently there are few safe alternatives to hospital, often resulting in adults being taken into police custody.

This Chapter argues that the appropriate use of safeguarding frameworks which support a multi-disciplinary approach to assessment, care and treatment, may offer a means of counteracting knowledge gaps for professionals in working with people who self-harm and present with suicidal behaviours. The exchange of knowledge and expertise with other professionals, the adults at risk themselves and their families, supports good risk-management practice and includes sharing responsibility. Further, safeguarding legislation provides the authority to breach professional confidentiality when an adult is thought to be at risk of serious harm. This can therefore help to counter problems with information sharing between different professional groups, which is a noted contributory factor in failures to protect adults from harm (Hull Safeguarding Adults Partnership Board, 2014).

In most instances it is the role of health professionals to assess adults presenting with self-harming thoughts or episodes of self-harm, usually at a GP surgery, A&E setting, community mental health team (CMHT), crisis team or acute psychiatric unit. As indicated, this can often be a complex assessment, particularly for adults who have long-standing and intractable problems and frequent episodes of self-harm. Hospital admission may not be helpful and may even cause longer-term harm and dependency. Health professionals need to carefully assess risk and be satisfied that hospital admission is going to benefit the adult and also that resources are used appropriately. Other professionals and the wider public, however, have important roles in identifying adults at risk of harm and making appropriate, timely referrals to relevant agencies and services. Offering advice and support following an episode of self-harm is also crucial as frequently adults have a range of underlying difficulties including debt, unemployment, work/school exam stress, relationship problems, trauma and abuse, as well as other diagnosed and undiagnosed mental health problems.

Case study A

The following case study addresses some of the key themes raised thus far and high-lights the advantages of using an adult safeguarding framework with a woman who repeatedly presents with self-harming and suicidal behaviours. It is a composite case study, derived from a range of practice examples explored in the discussion group that informed this chapter. It is underpinned by the Adult Support and Protection (Scotland) Act 2007, but the approach taken is designed to be illustrative of best practice and consequently to be applicable across the UK.

Adult protection referral/safeguarding concerns

June is a 35-year-old woman who has been referred to local authority A, under ASPA procedures by the police on three occasions. The first followed an incident when she was intoxicated and called the police to report thoughts of suicide. The police escorted her to A&E where she was assessed by liaison psychiatry and discharged. Two days later a member of the public called the police when they noticed a woman (June) climb-ing onto the safety barriers of a motorway bridge. She was heavily under the influence of alcohol and told the police she wanted to kill herself. The police managed to remove June safely from the bridge and took her to A&E, where she was discharged following psychiatric assessment. Later that day June's neighbours called emergency services when they found her unconscious outside her front door.

Adult protection inquiry

The duty social worker who received the referrals conducted an inquiry. June was not known to local authority A as she had recently relocated there. The social worker contacted June's GP to request relevant med-ical information, which in Scotland is legally mandated under Section 5 (ASPA). June's GP reported a long history of self-harm and suicide attempts, resulting in multiple admissions to psychiatric units in different parts of the UK. She was diagnosed with emotionally unstable personal-ity disorder, but had never managed to engage with community mental health or substance misuse services due to a chaotic and transient lifestyle.

The main aim of the inquiry was to establish if June was at risk of harm and to respond accordingly. It was evident from the inquiry that June lacked the ability to safeguard herself. However, the information gathered indicated that she presented with problematic alcohol use and was intoxicated on each of the occasions she came to harm. Problematic alcohol use would not in itself result in an individual being defined as an 'adult at risk' (ASPA); however, in June's case there was clear evidence of self-harming and possible suicidal behaviours and she was diagnosed with emotionally unstable personality disorder. The inquiry process also revealed a long history of failed attempts by professionals and services to support June. It identified a clear and ongoing risk of harm, and a need for multi-agency working and cooperation to maximise the assistance that could be provided.

In summary, the information gathered suggested that June was an adult at risk of harm and that intervention in her affairs under ASPA was necessary to protect her. Having established this, the outcome was to progress to an adult protection investigation.

Adult protection investigation

The investigation was led by social work staff. The investigating officers visited June, however, she remembered little of the incidents that lead to the adult protection referrals and the workers shared details of police concerns with her. They highlighted risks to her safety, in particular, the risk of accidental death due to intoxication while in dangerous environments. As a temporary measure, they provided crisis numbers for emotional support and advice when thoughts of self-harm and suicide might occur. A comprehensive risk assessment and multi-disciplinary case conference were recommended to protect June from further harm. A chronology of significant events gathered for the risk assessment displayed a pattern of alcohol misuse followed by incidents of self-harm and suicide attempts; on two such occasions June was very fortunate to survive. Clear patterns and triggers emerged. June experienced a very traumatic childhood, having been sexually abused by her father for as long as she could remember and witnessed repeated domestic abuse. Social services' attempts at intervening were largely unsuccessful as the family continually moved to different locations throughout the UK. She began self-harming aged 11 and had twelve admissions to psychiatric hospital following suicide attempts between the ages of 14 to 18. June felt safe in hospital and enjoyed the company of the other patients. A period of stability followed in her 20s, which coincided with meeting her partner. Subsequently, however, a violent sexual assault precipitated deterioration in her mental health, characterised by suicidal thoughts and suicide attempts and heavy drinking, leading to several admissions to psychiatric hospital and separation from her partner. At this point she was diagnosed with emotionally unstable personality disorder. June had moved around the country since then, frequently having contact with police, health and social services in relation to self-harm and suicide attempts, all whilst under the influence of alcohol. She sustained significant physical injuries as a result of jumping or falling from heights. Her physical health was also at significant risk due to the frequency of overdoses of both prescribed and over-the-counter medication.

June was well known to the local police due to members of the public, or more frequently, June herself, repeatedly calling them during episodes when she was distressed, intoxicated and threatening suicide. At such times the police escorted her to A&E to be medically assessed, consistent with their duty of care to members of the public in need of protection. This was, however, very time consuming and to some extent frustrating for police officers, as on most occasions June did not require medical treatment and was discharged, while her behaviour had also been very challenging. June had been referred to alcohol and CMHT services on numerous occasions but frequently missed appointments and disengaged. As indicated, she had a diagnosis of emotionally unstable personality disorder but during the adult protection investigation it transpired that she was unaware of this. She had been assessed as being unsuitable for psychological services due to a chaotic lifestyle and problematic alcohol use.

Adult Protection Case conference

A multi-disciplinary Adult Protection Case conference was convened to consider the investigation's conclusions and to agree a way forward. June attended the conference with the support of an advocacy worker which was important for enabling her to participate meaningfully in the meeting and to have her views heard. The assessment found that she was at risk of harm of accidental or intentional suicide, further trauma, further deterioration to physical health, exploitation and exclusion from services. The chronology illustrated the impact of multiple traumas on her life and led to discussion of factors that contribute to the development of personality disorders (Roth and Pilling, 2013). This was believed to have helped the professionals involved to begin changing their perceptions of June as a 'problem' towards a more informed and empathic understanding of her situation. This mirrored the beginnings of a shift in how June viewed herself, through reframing her difficulties as understandable responses to traumatic events and recognising the possibility of changing her behaviours with support. The case conference concluded that an 'Adult Protection Plan' was required to protect June; this was supplemented by a community care assessment aimed at supporting June to access appropriate services.

Outcome

Support from a woman's service assisted June in keeping appointments and developing a more consistent pattern of engagement. She began to develop trusting relationships with the allocated social worker and support workers. The protection plan encouraged a proactive, assertive outreach approach by the agencies involved, which June required due to her lack of trust in services and professionals. She had weekly contact with the allocated social worker and together they developed a 'Wellness Recovery Action Plan'. This level of contact and consistency was key to enabling her to make sense of her traumatic experiences and begin to change how she responded to distressing thoughts. June also benefited from education around the diagnosis of emotionally unstable personality disorder. This allowed her to make connections between childhood and adult trauma and her current emotional problems. June was also working towards being stable enough to benefit from psychology services to help further alleviate her emotional problems.

The assessment and implementation of June's protection plan was facilitated by multi-disciplinary adult protection meetings, involving June, her advocacy worker, the police, social work, addiction and mental health services on a four-weekly basis to discuss progress and address any difficulties that arose. This coordinated and focused multi-agency approach assisted in sharing information, supporting each professional involved as well as in identifying and managing risk.

In sum, June was made subject to an adult safeguarding investigation due to the number of times she was referred to the police and A&E, and perceived risks to her health and safety. The adult safeguarding procedures triggered a social work assessment, including an assessment of risk and need. The subsequent case conference supported a multi-disciplinary approach towards identifying needs, risks and protective factors. The risk assessment, particularly the chronology of significant events, assisted decision making by ensuring all relevant information was gathered, collated and shared. Gathering information was particularly relevant and helpful in June's situation, as she had experienced serious trauma over an extended period of time. Following assessment, the multi-disciplinary team and June agreed that she met the criteria for adult protection and that she would benefit from having a formal adult protection plan, which was aimed at educating her and the professionals about her situation and needs. The adult protection plan did not stop all adult protection referrals. June and members of the public continued to call the police when she was distressed and threatening suicide, however, their number reduced. The allocated social worker was able to discuss all of the referrals with June and help her reflect on what she could have done differently to cope with the emotional distress and prevent crisis situations from recurring.

Conclusion

Self-harm and suicide remain significant social and public health concerns. Suicide in particular has been the focus of major awareness-raising campaigns in the UK over the past decade, resulting in some positive outcomes, including a notable reduction in suicide rates. Considerable challenges remain in reducing the prevalence of self-harm and suicide, not least in the current economic climate, with unemployment and poverty being strong contributory factors (Milner et al., 2014). Other challenges include professionals' understanding, skills and attitudes, together with organisations' ability to provide and coordinate support for people with complex health and social circumstances who frequently present with self-harming and/or suicidal behaviours. The use of adult safeguarding legislation in this area is ethically difficult and striking a balance between protection and infringement of human rights takes skilled professional judgement. This chapter has drawn on evidence from adult protection committee reports, research and practitioner experience which point to a need for more humane and effective responses to suicide and self-harm. In particular, there is a need for coordinated and structured interventions that stand a greater degree of success in addressing repeated patterns of self-harming and suicidal behaviour. The case example demonstrates how a legal safeguarding framework can enable professionals from a wide range of services to work collaboratively to support and protect an adult with an extensive history of trauma and self-harm. It illustrates the importance of understanding the adult's situation, particularly the origins of personality disorder and the importance of having consistent and compassionate multi-professional responses. In addition, a formal safeguarding approach allows information to be accessed quickly, sidestepping potential issues with confidentiality. The case study also illustrates how safeguarding approaches can provide a structure for working with people who struggle to engage, and thus help begin to change entrenched cycles of harmful behaviour.

Implications for practice

➤ Formal adult safeguarding processes can facilitate effective responses to people with self-harming and suicidal behaviours.

➤ They also have the potential to significantly increase understanding of underlying issues and improve inter-professional working.

➤ The inclusion of risk of self-harm and suicide as criteria within formal adult safeguarding legislation is recommended across the UK.

➤ Improved training is required to meet the particular needs of people who frequently present with self-harming and suicidal behaviours, and there are examples of innovative practice across the UK.

References

Callaghan, S. M. and Ryan, C. (2014) Is there a future for involuntary treatment in rights-based mental health law? *Psychiatry, Psychology and Law*, 21(5): 747–766. Available at http://dx.doi.org./10.1080/13218719.2014.949606.

Camelot Foundation and Mental Health Foundation. (2006) *Truth Hurts: Report of the National Inquiry into Self-harm among Young People*. Available at http://www.mentalhealth.org.uk/content/assets/PDF/publications/truth_hurts.pdf [Accessed 8 September 2015].

Care Inspectorate. (2014) *A Report on the Effectiveness of Adult Protection Arrangements across Scotland*. Available at http://www.careinspectorate.com/images/documents/1059/Adult%20protection%20arrangements%20across%20Scotland.pdf [Accessed 10 September 2015].

Carr, S. (2014) *National Adult Support & Protection in NHS Accident & Emergency Settings Project, Scottish Government*. Available at http://www.scotland.gov.uk/Resource/0045/00453795.pdf [Accessed 20 September 2015].

City of Dundee Adult Support and Protection Committee. (2014) *Independent Convenor's Biennial Report to the Scottish Government*. Available at http://www.dundeeprotectsadults.co.uk/sites/default/files/Biennial%20Report%202014_2.pdf [Accessed 20 September 2015].

City of Edinburgh Council. (2014) *Edinburgh Adult Support and Protection Committee Biennial Report 2012–2014*. Available at http://www.edinburgh.gov.uk/meetings/meeting/3538/health_social_care_and_housing_committee [Accessed 20 September 2015].

Cornwall and Isles of Scilly Safeguarding Adults and Children Boards. (2012) *Multiagency Protocol for Single and Multiagency 'Triggers' to Share Information*. Available at http://www.cornwall.gov.uk/media/3630678/CIOS-SAB-Safeguarding-Adults-Triggers-Protocol-July-2012.pdf [Accessed 22 September 2015].

Department of Health. (2012) *Improving Outcomes and Supporting Transparency. Part 2: Summary Technical Specifications of Public Health Indicators.* Available at https://www.gov.uk/government/uploads/system/uploads/attachment_data/file/382115/PHOF_Part_2_Technical_Specifications_Autumn_2014_refresh_02.12.2014_FINAL.pdf [Accessed 23 September 2015].

Department of Health, Social Services and Public Safety (DHSSPS). (2012) *Protect a Life, A Shared Vision: The Northern Ireland Suicide Prevention Strategy 2012 – March 2014.* Available at http://www.dhsspsni.gov.uk/suicide_strategy.pdf [Accessed 30 September 2015].

Di Caccavo, A. and Reid, F. (1998) The influence of attitudes toward male and female patients on treatment decisions in general practice. *Sex Roles*, 38(7–8): 613–629.

East Dunbartonshire Adult Protection Committee. (2014) *Adult Protection Committee Biennial Report 2012–14.* Available at http://www.eastdunbarton.gov.uk/pdf/SW%20Planning%20Dev/SW-ACC%20ED%20Biennial%20Report%202014.pdf [Accessed 23 September 2015].

Fox, C. and Hawton, K. (2004) *Deliberate Self-harm in Adolescence*, London: Jessica Kingsley Publishers.

Friedman, T., Newton, C., Coggan, G., Hooley, S., Patel, R., Pickard, M. and Mitchell, A. (2006) Predictors of A&E staff attitudes to self-harm patients who use self-laceration: Influence of previous training and experience. *Journal of Psychosomatic Research*, 60(3): 273–277. http://doi:10.1016/j.jpsychores.2005.07.007.

Glasgow City Council Adult Protection Committee. (2012) *Biennial Report, 2012.* Available at http://www.gov.scot/Resource/0041/00417644.pdf [Accessed 23 September 2015].

Hawton, K., Bergen, H., Casey, D., Simkin S., Palmer, B., Cooper, J., Kapur, N., Horrocks, J., House, A., Lilley, R., Noble, R. and Owens, D. (2007) Self-harm in England: A tale of three cities, Multicentre study of self-harm. *Social Psychiatry Psychiatric Epidemiology*, 42: 513–521. http://doi 10.1007/s00127-007-0199-7.

Her Majesty's Government. (2012) *Preventing Suicide in England: A Cross-Government Outcomes Strategy to Save Lives.* Available at https://www.gov.uk/government/uploads/system/uploads/attachment_data/file/216928/Preventing-Suicide-in-England-A-cross-government-outcomes-strategy-to-save-lives.pdf [Accessed 23 September 2015].

Hickey, L., Hawton, K., Fagg, J. and Weitzel, H. (2001) Deliberate self-harm patients who leave the accident and emergency department without a psychiatric assessment: A neglected population at risk of suicide. *Journal of Psychosomatic Research*, 50(2): 87–93.

Horrocks, J. and House, A. (2002) Self-poisoning and self-injury in adults. *Clinical Medicine JRCPL*, 2: 509–512. Available at http://www.clinmed.rcpjournal.org/content/2/6/509.full.pdf+html [Accessed 14 September 2015].

Hull Safeguarding Adults Partnership Board. (2014) *A Decade of Serious Case Reviews.* Available at http://www.adass.org.uk/uploadedFiles/adass_content/policy_networks/safeguarding_adults/key_documents/A%20Decade%20 of%20Serious%20Case%20Reviews%20-%20August%202014.pdf [Accessed 23 September 2015].

Kuisma, M., Maatta, T., Hakala, T., Sivula, T. and Nousila-Wiik, M. (2003) Customer satisfaction measurement in emergency medical services. *Academic Emergency Medicine*, 10(7): 812–815.

Madge, N., Hewitt, A., Hawton, K., Jan de Wilde, E., Corcoran, P., Fekete, S., van Heeringen, K., De Leo, D. and Ystgaard, M. (2008) Deliberate self-harm within an international community sample of young people: Comparative findings from the Child & Adolescent Self-harm in Europe (CASE) Study. *Journal of Child Psychology and Psychiatry*, 49(6): 667–677. http://doi:10.111 1/j.1469-7610.2008.01879

Mental Health Foundation. (2006) *Cheers? Understanding the Relationship between Alcohol and Mental Health*. Available at http://www.mentalhealth.org.uk/ content/assets/PDF/publications/cheers_report.pdf?view=Standard [Accessed 30 September 2015].

Milner A., Morrell S. and La Montagne, A. (2014) Economically inactive, unemployed and employed suicides in Australia by age and sex over a 10-year period: What was the impact of the 2007 economic recession? *International Journal of Epidemiology*, 43(5):1500–1507.

National Health and Medical Research Council. (2014) *Clinical Practice Guideline for the Management of Borderline Personality Disorder*. Available at https://www. nhmrc.gov.au/_files_nhmrc/publications/attachments/mh25_borderline_ personality_guideline.pdf [Accessed 12 September 2015].

National Records of Scotland. (2015) *Probable Suicides: Deaths Which are the Result of Intentional Self-harm or Events of Undetermined Intent*. Available at http://www.gro-scotland.gov.uk/statistics-and-data/statistics/ statistics-by-theme/vital-events/deaths/suicides [Accessed 3 September 2015].

Office of National Statistics. (2011) Suicide definition. Available at http://www. ons.gov.uk/ons/rel/subnational-health4/suicides-in-the-united-kingdom/2011/ stb-suicide-bulletin.html#tab-Suicide-definition [Accessed 1 September 2015].

Roth, A. D. and Pilling, S. (2013) A competence framework for psychological interventions with people with personality disorder. Available at http://www.ucl.ac.uk/clinical-psychology/CORE/Docs/Personality%20 disorder%20background%20document%20web%20version.pdf [Accessed 16 September 2015].

Royal College of Psychiatrists. (2010) *Self-harm, Suicide and Risk: College Report CR158 June 2010*. Available at http://www.rcpsych.ac.uk/files/pdfversion/ CR158xx.pdf [Accessed 30 September 2015].

Saunders, K., Hawton, K., Fortune, S. and Farrell, S. (2011) Attitudes and knowledge of clinical staff regarding people who self-harm: A systematic review. *Journal of Affective Disorders*, 139(3): 205–216.

Scottish Association for Mental Health. (2012) *Beyond Appearances: Experiences of Self-Harm, Glasgow*. Available at http://www.samh.org.uk/media/277482/ beyond_appearances_full_report_final.pdf [Accessed 30 September 2015].

Scottish Government. (2011a) *Responding to Self-Harm in Scotland, Final Report.* Available at http://www.gov.scot/Resource/Doc/346117/0115190.pdf [Accessed 30 September 2015].

Scottish Government. (2011b) *Adult Protection Committee Biennial Reports 2008–2010 Summary Report.* Available at http://www.scotland.gov.uk/Resource/0039/00399027.pdf [Accessed 7 September 2015].

Scottish Government. (2013) *Engagement Paper on the Prevention of Suicide and Self-Harm.* Available at http://www.scotland.gov.uk/Topics/Health/Services/Mental-Health/Suicide-Self-Harm/Working-Group/EngagementPaper [Accessed 7 September 2015].

Scottish Government. (2014) *National Adult Support & Protection in NHS Accident & Emergency Settings Project: Project Review and Closure Report.* Available at http://www.scotland.gov.uk/Resource/0045/00458759.pdf [Accessed 13 September 2015].

Scowcroft, E. (2016) *Suicide Statistics Report 2016: Including Data for 2012–2014, Samaritans.* Available at https://www.samaritans.org/sites/default/files/kcfinder/files/Samaritans%20suicide%20statistics%20report%202016.pdf [Accessed 12 December 2016].

South Lanarkshire Council. (2014) *Adult Protection Committee, 2014, Biennial Report, October 2014.* Available at http://www.gov.scot/Topics/Health/Support-Social-Care/Adult-Support-Protection/Committees/APC [Accessed 8 September 2015].

Timson, D., Priest, H. and Clark-Carter, D. (2012) Adolescents who self-harm: Professional staff knowledge, attitudes and training needs. *Journal of Adolescence*, 35: 1307–1314.

Webb, D. (2015) 'The social model of disability and suicide prevention', in Spandler, H., Anderson, J. and Sapey, B. (eds), *Madness, Distress and the Politics of Disablement*, Bristol: Policy Press.

Welsh Assembly Government. (2009) *Talk to Me: The National Action Plan to Reduce Suicide and Self-Harm in Wales 2009–2014.* Available at http://gov.wales/docs/phhs/publications/talktome/091102talktomeen.pdf [Accessed 13 September 2015].

World Health Organization (WHO). (2013) *Suicide Prevention, WHO.* Available at http://www.who.int/mental_health/prevention/en/ [Accessed 3 September 2015].

10

Safeguarding within Institutions

Andrew Molondynski, Oxford Health NHS Foundation Trust;
Frank Reilly, The Scottish Recovery Network

The phrase 'adult safeguarding' has become commonly used since the influential publication *No Secrets* in 2000 by the United Kingdom Department of Health (DoH, 2000). The support, empowerment and protection of vulnerable members of society have been debated for centuries, however, with numerous early accounts of conditions for the 'mentally ill' (as they were then often described) in the earliest 'mad houses' and asylums as well as outside of them (Prins, 1987). Safeguarding of adults who are or may be vulnerable is now a core element of practice across health and social care with well-defined procedures for preventing abuses and for reporting them if this fails (HIS, 2014; DoH, 2012, 2000). The most vulnerable adults are almost certainly those with mental health problems or learning disabilities whose difficulties are severe and/or complex enough to necessitate them residing in some sort of institution. In closed institutions in particular there may be limited autonomy for individuals and limited or no opportunities to raise concerns regarding potential abuse. Even when concerns are raised in such settings, we have a proven track record of not always taking them seriously such as with Kerr–Haslam, Winterbourne View and Mid Staffordshire (Francis, 2013a; DoH, 2012; HM Government, 2005). We will come back to these later to look at what lessons can be learned from them.

Historical development of services

Prior to the middle of the last century the societal response to people with mental health problems was to build facilities of increasing size and capacity in which to accommodate them outside 'the community'. Initially this was in privately run so-called 'mad houses' such as the notorious one run by Thomas Warburton at Bethnal Green, which took any 'pauper lunatic' paid for by local parishes regardless of the individual's problems or issues of space. Such establishments were ruthlessly exposed in the Parliament select committee reports of 1815 (Rogers, 1815) and 1816 (Select Committee Report, 1816).

The rise of psychiatry led to large asylums being built across many Western industrialised nations to care for and house the mentally ill. Prior to the introduction of effective treatments such as antipsychotic and anti-depressant medications and ECT in the middle of the last century, they primarily aimed to provide material support, care and 'asylum' from society at large. They also, explicitly or implicitly, aimed to 'protect society' from those who were different.

By 1950, there were approximately 150,000 people with mental health problems or learning disabilities living in hospitals in England and Wales (Turner et al., 2015). Around this time the momentum began to shift with a progressive reduction in numbers of those in institutions and (in the UK at least) a parallel rise in community care services (Killapsy, 2007). The reasons for this 'move into the community' were complex but included such important factors as the introduction of the welfare state in 1948, the first 'modern' Mental Health Act in 1959 and the discovery of effective treatments such as chlorpromazine and amitryptiline (Turner et al., 2015). Also crucially important were concerns regarding levels of abuse and poor standards of care in large institutions as highlighted by Erving Goffman's seminal book 'On Asylums' (Goffman, 1961) and a number of high-profile failures of safeguarding. Politicians also realised that asylums, with their enormous infrastructure, land mass, and staff bodies were expensive and the famous water tower speech by Enoch Powell (then Conservative health minister) in 1961 marked a sea change in national policy regarding the care of the mentally ill.

Over the last 50 years bed provision has steadily reduced in the UK, and a 2012 census reported an average number of occupied mental health beds within the NHS of 18,924 (HSCIC, 2013). It is impossible however to ascertain the exact numbers of people who are residing in 24-hour staffed care homes and private hospitals that provide similar levels of support.

Although Goffman's book was not the first to describe poor conditions and what we would now call 'safeguarding issues', it was extremely influential due to the power of his writing and observation and its timing. Since its publication over 50 years ago there have been a number of descriptions of poor conditions. The term 'institutionalisation' was introduced by Wing in his influential report of 1960 that provided evidence that large institutions could be disempowering, reduce autonomy and worsen individual patient outcome (Wing and Brown, 1970). As a result of these concepts, ongoing concerns regarding the quality and safety of care, the availability of a welfare state and effective treatments, and political imperative, hospitals continued to close. Ironically these reductions have led in part to a situation where some senior clinicians are describing the shortage of NHS mental health beds as a serious safeguarding issue.

Current types of accommodation

Care homes and supported accommodation

Care homes are defined under Chapter 14, Section 3 of the Care Standards Act 2000 (HM Government, 2000) in England and Wales and under the Regulation of Care Act 2001 in Scotland (Scottish Executive, 2001). The Act defines a care home as any home that provides accommodation together with nursing or personal care for any person who is or has been ill. They commonly house people with mental health problems, physical health problems, learning disability, substance misuse or a combination of these. As might be expected, there is substantial variation in care homes in a number of respects: size, staffing mix, ability to manage certain types of disability or behaviour, physical environment and geographical location. Available evidence suggests that over recent years there has been a gradual increase in overall size of care homes and the proportion of care home beds provided within the private sector.

In mental health, care provision for adults of working age can be enormously variable and a large proportion of privately run care homes aim for low numbers of residents and a homely feel.

Acute adult mental health units

> The purpose of an adult acute psychiatric inpatient service is to provide a high standard of humane treatment and care in a safe and therapeutic setting for service users in the most acute and vulnerable stage of their illness. It should be for the benefit of those service users whose circumstances or acute care needs are such that they cannot at that time be treated and supported appropriately at home or in an alternative, less restrictive residential setting.
>
> (DoH, 2002a)

This is the initial statement of the Department of Health 2002 Policy Implementation Guide (DoH, 2002a). The guide is detailed and comprehensive and utilises feedback from service users and staff alongside evidence and policy already in existence. It gives ideas and guidance on such matters as regular meaningful activity, the physical environment, physical health care, and staff training and deployment levels. It does not (in contrast with the more specific guidance regarding specialist units described below) give detailed descriptions of what 'a ward' should be like. The majority of adult acute wards have between 15 and 25 beds and are now either single sex accommodation or have well-defined separate areas by gender. The majority of inpatients have their own room and this is ubiquitous in new builds. The move to single sex and largely en-suite accommodation has been almost entirely in response to safeguarding issues, particularly those affecting vulnerable female patients. Safeguarding has also played a very significant role in the recent 'evolution' of inpatient psychiatry as a sub-specialty for staff of all disciplines (but especially nurses and doctors) (Bowers et al., 2005).

Intensive care units

Psychiatric intensive care units (PICUs) should be reserved for those detained under the appropriate legislation and who are in an acutely disturbed phase of illness and pose risks that cannot be contained in an acute open ward. Care must be multi-disciplinary, intensive and rapidly responsive to need in critical situations. While length of stay is dependent on clinical need, the Department of Health Guidance (DoH, 2002b) states that it 'would not normally exceed eight weeks'. The DoH guidance gives detailed advice and recommendations for all areas of practice, including staffing levels, training, audit, management meetings and service user involvement. In general terms these units will have locked doors and windows to prevent absconding, as risk-free an internal environment as possible, and higher staff-to-patient ratios than on acute open wards. Although physically large, with wide corridors, high ceilings and private en-suite rooms, the numbers of patients are low, with the guidance suggesting a maximum of 15. These units typically will include areas for de-escalation and seclusion – key safeguarding issues with this population as levels of distress, agitation and acting out can be high.

Low secure and locked rehabilitation units

Low secure units are generally used for patients who have ongoing behavioural difficulties in the context of a severe mental illness and require the ongoing provision of security. The DoH guidance (DoH, 2002a) states 'patients will be detained under the Mental Health Act and need rehabilitation for up to two years'. In practice, a substantial proportion will stay longer, some indefinitely. It is arguably even more important in these units that there is careful consideration of the individual's experiences and their environment with good quality accommodation, unobtrusive observation and access to pleasant outside areas for fresh air. These units less frequently have seclusion areas, and staffing levels are often only minimally higher than on acute open units and generally significantly less than on PICU. The long-term deprivation of liberty within a legal framework raises particular safeguarding issues that will be returned to later. Robust systems to monitor practice, quality and outcome are needed.

Medium or high secure hospitals

NHS England (NHS England, 2013) state that there are approximately 680 patients in high secure beds and 2800 in medium secure beds in England. This represents a population prevalence of 1.3 and 5.3 respectively per 100,000 of the overall population. The figures in Scotland are 144 and 191 (2.8 and 3.82 per 100,000) (Scottish Government, 2008). As can be seen, the ratio differs significantly between the two largest countries in the UK.

The stated aim of secure services is to 'provide a therapeutic psychiatry service for individuals with a mental disorder...who present a significant risk of harm to others' (NHS England, 2013). The same document states that recovery should be supported and that a wide range of evidence-based interventions should be available, such as sex offender treatment programmes. The aim of treatment should be 'for the individual to safely return to the community or prison or transfer out of secure services'. It is emphasised in the contracting documents that there should be therapeutic use of the minimum levels of physical, procedural and relational measures necessary to provide a safe and recovery focused environment. The contract then goes on to describe in some detail measures such as audit, staff training, service user involvement and external scrutiny that may reduce unnecessary coercion. There is relatively little description of the role of family and visitors, and one of the difficulties for those in secure care is often geographical dislocation. This is particularly problematic in high secure care as there are few locations where this is provided.

Safeguarding issues

A number of key safeguarding areas have repeatedly been identified by public enquiries. *No Secrets* (DoH, 2000) was influential in the development of safeguarding policy and practice in England and Wales and the Miss X case (Mental Welfare Commission/Social Work Services Inspectorate, 2004) was highly influential in Scotland. The Miss X case identified significant failings in health and social work responses to the repeated physical abuse of Miss X over more than a decade, including a lack of communication between relevant agencies, poor recording and overworked staff.

While institutional care environments differ enormously, what they have in common is more important: a principle of reciprocity that requires them to 'look after' those entrusted to their care. Institutions are by their very nature complex systems of care that require routines to enable them to work efficiently. Such efficiency can be a challenge to personalised care. For example, admission to a hospital or similar institutional care (even for a short period) requires the individual to give up freedoms we routinely take for granted. Today, before reading this book, you will no doubt have risen, eaten, travelled and socialised as you wish (within the parameters allowed by family and work perhaps!). Within institutional settings we relinquish some of these liberties in order to receive care. There is a reciprocal responsibility on the authority providing our care to maintain our safety and take into account our wishes. These things cannot be taken for granted however. Research and repeated investigations (McNicholl, 2013; Kalaga and Kingston, 2007; DoH, 2006; Wardhaugh and Wilding, 1993) have identified the following main areas of concern:

Psychological or emotional abuse

This may include actions taken to bully or harass a person, such as denying access to personal items, humiliating the person in private and/or in public or denying their right to personal choices. There were clear examples of this at Winterbourne View Hospital (HM Government, 2005), which exposed the physical and psychological abuse of people with learning disabilities, including staff repeatedly assaulting and restraining people in chairs, and ultimately led to criminal convictions for the carers involved.

Sexual abuse, including grooming

This consists of preparing and making a person susceptible to inappropriate sexual acts or performing those acts without their consent. In this context it is clearly an abuse of position or trust. Older people, particularly those with dementia, can be at particular risk (Burgess et al., 2002; Dergal and de Nobrega, 2000; Ramsey-Klawsnik, 1996, 1993) and this may not receive the attention it merits.

Physical abuse

This involves direct assaults or contact intended to cause physical harm to the person. This would include, for example, lifting a person using inappropriate techniques or equipment. Again, many of these were documented in the Winterbourne Review (HM Government, 2005).

Financial abuse

This involves misusing a person's financial resources or property or conditioning/coercing them to use their financial resources to the benefit of an abuser. This is most commonly documented in residential care for older people (Harris, 1999; Harris and Benson, 1999; Halamandaris, 1983) but does occur in other care groups.

Neglect and incompetent care

This is where a person has responsibility for taking care of another but fails to look after their basic needs either deliberately or as a result of not fully understanding what that person's care needs are. The recent Princess of Wales Hospital review (Andrews and Butler, 2014) documented examples of neglect leading to the development of bed sores. This is also discussed in more detail in Chapter 8 in relation to adults with learning disabilities.

Discrimination

Discrimination involves treating patients or service users differently as a result of their racial characteristics, sexual orientation, gender or age. On an individual level this can take the form of direct verbal abuse or similar behaviour. On a systems level it can be such things as the absence of culturally appropriate services for some groups or a lack of access to particular services.

Infringement of privacy and right to family life

Infringing someone's right to privacy and a family life (as enshrined for example in the United Nations Convention on the Rights of Persons with Disabilities) might include discussing confidential information in a public area or unjustly restricting visits from family and friends as highlighted in the 2012 *Time to Listen* report (CQC, 2012a, 2012b).

Restricted budgets or recruitment problems can lead to inadequate staffing structures in both publically and privately funded settings. These may then lead to dehumanising and poor-quality care. High-profile examples have been identified recently in the Mid Staffordshire hospital (Francis, 2013a) and historically in the investigation into the routine use of face-down restraint – referred to as pin down – in children's homes (Wardhaugh and Wilding, 1993). Winterbourne View and similar tragedies suggested that there were inadequate safeguards for the operation of caring environments (BBC, 2014). It has been suggested that responses to incidents focus all too readily on 'bad apples' rather than the systems that allow them to thrive, and that there is often a failure of systems and procedures to support whistle-blowers (Whistleblowing Commission, 2013).

Regardless of the type of safeguarding, the same key issues in behaviour and systems recur:

➢ Inadequate or improper supervision by managers (Mental Welfare Commission/Social Work Services Inspectorate, 2004).

➢ Systems of control which reduce professional autonomy (Preston-Shoot et al., 2010).

➢ Professionally isolated workers (Wardhaugh and Wilding, 1993).

➢ Actions driven by financial rather than care imperatives which further reduce the autonomy of frontline workers (Andrews and Butler, 2014).

These elements are all represented in the following three examples – failures of care which have fundamentally changed health and social care in the United Kingdom.

'Failures' of safeguarding

Winterbourne View

The two words above are no doubt familiar to the vast majority of readers. In May 2011 persistent high-level emotional and physical abuse was revealed in a small independent hospital near Bristol. There were several outcomes:

➢ A number of staff were successfully prosecuted and some were jailed

➢ Winterbourne View was closed

➤ A wide ranging review both of Winterbourne View itself and the wider issues in the care of people with learning disabilities was commissioned.

The review (DoH, 2012) concluded that there had been 150 separate incidents that 'could and should have raised the alarm'. These included such things as A&E attendances, police attendance at the unit, and safeguarding concerns raised with the local council. It was concluded that a closed and punitive culture had been allowed to develop amongst a group of junior staff in a closed unit with very restricted visiting and ineffective management and training. Patients stayed far too long and were often many miles from home. Recommendations were made for a substantial reduction in such placements, that the institutions themselves should be more tightly regulated and held to account, and that training and supervision of staff should be improved with explicit codes of conduct.

Kerr–Haslam

William Kerr and Michael Haslam were both psychiatrists working at a hospital in York. A 2005 inquiry (HM Government, 2005) told in detail how, over a period of more than two decades, they had been serially sexually abusing female patients, despite a number of patients being brave enough to raise the alarm. A number of failings contributed to a lack of action and ongoing abuse. The report concluded that patients were either not taken seriously or dropped their complaints after a less-than-sympathetic reception. A dedicated member of nursing staff who attempted to ensure scrutiny ended up being on 'the wrong end' of disciplinary proceedings. The detailed and lengthy report made a number of practical and grounded interventions that could work to reduce the likelihood of such abuse: three references including the current employer being required to provide clinical supervision for consultants, guidance for behaviour of staff, an obligation on staff to report suspected abuse, anonymous helplines to report concerns, and more detailed research into the nature and prevalence of sexualised behaviour among mental health practitioners. The majority of these recommendations have been introduced into practice. but practical arrangements for things such as consultant supervision remain variable and poorly articulated. There has, over recent years, been a sea change in the reporting of suspected abuse and protections for those who do, and this is likely to be due at least in part to Kerr–Haslam.

Mid Staffordshire Hospital

Between 2005 and 2008 conditions of appalling care were able to flourish in the main hospital serving the people of Stafford and its surrounding area. During this period the hospital was managed by a Board which succeeded in leading its Trust (the Mid Staffordshire General Hospital NHS Trust) to Foundation Trust (FT) status. The Board was one which had largely replaced its predecessor because of concerns about the then NHS Trust's performance. In preparation for its application for FT status, the Trust had been scrutinised by the local Strategic Health Authority (SHA) and the Department of Health. Monitor (the independent regulator of NHS foundation trusts) had also subjected it to assessment. It appeared largely compliant with the then applicable standards regulated by the Healthcare Commission (HCC). It had been rated acceptable by the NHS Litigation Authority (NHSLA) for its risk management. Local scrutiny committees and public involvement groups detected no systemic failings. In the end, the truth was uncovered in part by attention being paid to the true implications of its mortality rates, but mainly because of the persistent complaints made by a very determined group of patients and those close to them.

The Francis Inquiry was established in 2012 to examine the causes of the failings in care in the Mid Staffordshire NHS Foundation Trust between 2005 and 2009. The first paragraph of the final executive summary of the Francis report states:

> Harrowing and persistent neglect and abuse had not been detected by a number of processes intended to do so. This included people being left in their own faeces or urine for prolonged periods, inadequate or absent nutrition, excess falls and injuries, and uncaring staff attitudes.
>
> (Francis, 2013b)

The systemic failures of the hospital and the equally serious systemic failures that allowed it to go unnoticed and unmediated led to a public outcry and a re-evaluation of the whole basis of care. Francis (2013a) concluded that that the core problem was 'a culture focused on doing the system's business – not that of the patients'. The first and most important recommendation was a brutally simple one: 'Foster a common culture shared by all in the service of putting the patient first' (Francis, 2013a).

Potential ways forward

A number of changes in legislation and scrutiny have, over the last decade, aimed to safeguard people in institutional settings. A number of systems established in the United Kingdom (DoH, 2006, Scottish

Government, 2007a) seek to prevent workers with a history of offending or abuse from working in caring environments. Legislation and guidance supports early intervention and can compel services to prevent any reported harm from worsening (Scottish Government, 2007b). Legislation in isolation is, however, insufficient. The mechanisms below have been identified as being 'best practice' and if used properly have the potential to minimise risk.

Advocacy

Independent advocates in the UK support vulnerable people to understand care decisions and ensure that their wishes are considered fully. They have a key role in institutions and are typically independent from the host service, as suggested by the statement below from the Scottish Independent Advocacy Alliance:

> Independent advocacy is structurally, financially and psychologically separate from service providers and other services. Such independence helps to ensure that there is no possibility of any conflict of interest arising in relation to any other services accessed by the individual or group.
>
> (Scottish Independent Advocacy Alliance, 2016)

In England and Wales, Independent Mental Capacity Advocates (IMCAs) have powers under the Mental Capacity Act (DoH, 2005) to support those who lack capacity to make important decisions about their future or their care. They should be involved in decisions about providing, stopping or withholding significant medical treatment except where there is an 'urgent' need for it. IMCAs have been available since 2007. Other legislation also outlines a requirement to provide advocacy for those subject to measures under various legislation. In Scotland, for example, Independent Advocacy Services have been in existence since 2000 (Scottish Executive, 2000) and Mental Health Officers have a duty to inform patients subject to compulsory measures under the Mental Health (Care and Treatment) (Scotland) Act 2003 of their right to independent advocacy.

Multi-disciplinary working

There is an increasingly strong body of opinion that individuals working within their speciality without the support, information and perspective of other disciplines are less likely to deliver high-quality care and may increase risk (ADASS, 2011; White et al., 2002; Herman et al.,

2001; Wardhaugh and Wilding, 1993). Repeated investigations (Kalaga and Kingston, 2007; Mental Welfare Commission/Social Work Services Inspectorate, 2004; White et al., 2002) have highlighted poor communication between different professionals involved in a person's care network – and assumptions about whose responsibility it was to act – as key factors in the failure to act on information regarding risk. Multi-disciplinary teams (MDTs) increase opportunities for communication – particularly if they are physically co-located – and improve the coordination of care and intervention (ADASS,2011). These principles apply to multi-disciplinary teams in the community and within institutions and enable safeguarding to become a team rather than an individual pursuit, reducing variability (Wardhaugh and Wilding, 1993). The challenge for MDT working is to ensure that members of all disciplines are able and encouraged to express their views. When teams become dominated by one particular approach (Whyte and Brooker, 2001), this can become difficult. If the MDT is functioning well, then responsibility for safeguarding will genuinely be shared.

It is not unusual for social care professionals in teams with a predominately medically oriented majority to adopt the language and approach of this model as a means to enable effective communication and acceptance within the team, (Shaw et al., 2007; Davies et al., 2006). The challenge is to ensure that responsibility is genuinely shared rather than becoming synonymous with one discipline, as has been reported:

> Social work has become identified with child protection work; and finally child protection work has become the equivalent to social work, despite repeated efforts to establish the reality of the former as a 'multi-agency' responsibility.
>
> (Cooper, 2012) - Page 152

Working with families

Families and friends of people receiving institutional care are key partners in harm prevention and safeguarding. In high secure settings, contact with a family may be limited or absent for the individual and also the care team. Regular contact with families through email, telephone, Skype or even home visiting may provide opportunities for concerns regarding care to be raised. The importance of carer feedback was highlighted by the recent report on the Princess of Wales and Neath Port Talbot Hospitals in Wales (Andrews and Butler, 2014), which emphasised the importance of taking feedback and complaints seriously.

Co-production – working with residents

Co-production is defined as 'professionals and citizens making better use of each other's assets, resources and contributions to achieve better outcomes and/or improved efficiency' (Bovaird and Loeffler, 2013). Bovaird (2007) has previously described a continuum of co-production from co-delivery of services designed by professionals to full user and professional co-production. The process assumes that individuals and communities have:

> ➤ Assets that can be engaged in achieving self-actualisation,

> ➤ Potential for reducing reliance on formal care and agencies, and

> ➤ Potential for increasing independence and 'citizenship' (Reilly, 2014).

High and medium secure facilities particularly are affected by the need to balance the therapeutic environment with the duty to maintain safety. In these environments co-production may be a way of working to develop trust. Enabling people to move towards self-motivation and establishing personal outcomes can help an individual develop lasting skills and behavioural change (Ryan and Deci, 2000). Co-production develops partnerships where the assets of carers, patients and staff have equal importance. It encourages contributions from the entire system to improve care for a patient and (if successful) creates an open and enquiring environment which welcomes change.

Supervision and training

Effective supervision of staff has been repeatedly highlighted as an important safety and quality factor (Kalaga and Kingston, 2007; White et al., 2002; Wardhaugh and Wilding, 1993) and has been adopted throughout health and social care. Quality, however, varies and supervision systems that undermine autonomy or are cumbersome can have a negative effect:

> In effect, bureaucratic decision making can undermine moral responsibility with practitioners following procedures regardless of whether they are lawful and/or moral.
>
> (Preston-Shoot et al., 2010) - Page 10

Due to ongoing financial austerity, it is increasingly the case that staff with the greatest amount of contact with residents, usually health care assistants and housekeeping staff, are the least well-paid and trained

(HIS, 2014: Sykes and Groom, 2011). As a result of reducing budgets and the need to redesign services to make them sustainable, those who spend the greatest amount of time with people but have little autonomy are vulnerable to being perpetrators of harm, either deliberately or inadvertently, as they 'get through their day' (White et al., 2002). Effective supervision by experienced and compassionate staff is crucial in maintaining care standards in the face of such pressures.

Outward looking culture

Inward looking cultures do not generally evolve or promote professional learning and development. They concentrate on their own norms and practices and resist changes suggested by others, such as new members of staff. Ranks may close and workers become isolated until they conform or leave (Cambridge, 1999). Institutions with well-established cultures, low staff turnover and 'long stay' residents may be particularly at risk. An outward looking organisation in contrast generates learning from complaints (Andrews and Butler, 2014), seeks to develop multi-disciplinary working rather than a mono-working culture (Bradshaw, 2000) and is conscious of the need to monitor the shift patterns most commonly associated with harm (night shift, weekend and 'back' or afternoon/evening shift) and to engage positively with external visiting professionals (White et al., 2002). It also supports external learning and mentoring, secondment and shadowing.

Regulation and commissioning

Health and social care undertaken in institutions is registered, monitored and inspected by national bodies in England and Wales (Care Quality Commission, Monitor, Healthcare Inspectorate Wales (HCIW)), in Scotland (Social Care and Social Work Improvement Agency (SCSWIS)) and Northern Ireland (Regulation and Quality Improvement Authority (RQIA). Both announced and unannounced visits by inspectors form part of the regime and providers are measured against explicit accepted standards. Information from carers, staff, family and friends may prompt unannounced inspections if there are particular areas of concern and are always part of an inspection. Inspection on its own, however, only provides a snapshot, as with an MOT for a car. Scrutiny systems, just like an MOT, will only provide confidence at the time of the test that all is well. They are no guarantee of greater confidence as the inquiries at Mid Staffordshire and the Princess of Wales Hospitals show (Andrews and Butler, 2014).

Conclusion

Some of the most vulnerable in our society are in institutional care. Facilities have varied substantially over time, between areas and between patient groups. Safeguarding is key in all, however, and many of the deficits contributing to high-profile failures are universal, or at the very least cross many geographical and temporal boundaries. The potential remedies do also. Effective supervision, listening to and working with patients and families, and having inspection regimes for individual workers and for overall providers can all work together to reduce risk. However much our institutions have improved and the fact that most people get good care (they really have and they really do), this chapter illustrates clearly that abuses and acts of omission are still regularly occurring.

It is increasingly important that we harness new technologies that allow greater communication and more rapid and accurate feedback in parallel with our traditional interpersonal, legal and bureaucratic mechanisms to work alongside those in our care and their families to reduce risk. The last few years have seen an explosion in the use of technology in everyday life to promote independence, and this is now beginning to trickle into health and social care. Innovative apps allow families and professionals to collaborate in care and communicate rapidly about concerns or things that are going well. Patient feedback websites collect instant data that can longer be 'missed' by those looking for different answers.

Safeguarding, like health and social care in general, is increasingly a partnership in which we work with patients and families to promote safety, often using innovative technology. Alongside robust systems of scrutiny and regulation, thorough reviews when things go wrong, and 'good practice' in terms of supervision and team working this suggests that the future of safeguarding in institutions may be more positive than the past.

Implications for practice

➢ Those living in long-stay institutions might be particularly at risk of harm. It is therefore crucial to have effective, multi-disciplinary safeguarding processes in place.

➢ The provision of independent advocacy is vital to ensure that individuals and family members have their voices heard and that any concerns are taken seriously.

➤ Within institutions a robust supervision process alongside effective monitoring and inspection is important in ensuring that safeguarding issues are not simply viewed as poor practice.

References

ADASS. (2011) *Carers and Safeguarding Adults: Working Together to Improve Outcomes*. Available at https://www.adass.org.uk/adassmedia/stories/Policy%20Networks/Carers/Carers%20and%20safeguarding%20document%20June%202011.pdf [accessed 19 September 2017].

Andrews, J. and Butler, M. (2014) *Trusted to Care: An Independent Review of the Princess of Wales Hospital and Neath Port Talbot Hospital at Abertawe Bro Morgannwg University Health Board*. Available at http://gov.wales/topics/health/publications/health/reports/care/?lang=en [accessed 19 September 2017].

BBC. (2014) Behind Closed Doors: Elderly Care Exposed. In *Panorama*. Aired 30 April 2014. Available at http://www.bbc.co.uk/iplayer/episode/b042rcjp/panorama-behind-closed-doors-elderly-care-exposed

Bovaird, T. (2007) Beyond engagement and participation: User and community co-production of public services. *Public Administration Review,* 67(5): 846–860.

Bovaird T. and Loeffler E. (2013) *We're All in this Together: Harnessing User and Community Co-production of Public Outcomes,* Birmingham: Institute of Local Government Studies.

Bowers, L., Simpson, A., Alexander, J., Hackney, D., Nijman, H., Grange, A. and Warren, J. (2005) The nature and purpose of acute psychiatric wards: The Tompkins acute ward study. *Journal of Mental Health,* 14(6): 625–635.

Bradshaw, D. (2000) Preventing the abuse of vulnerable adults. *Journal of Adult Protection,* 2: 25–38.

Burgess, A. W., Dowdel, E. B. and Prentky, R. A. (2002) Sexual abuse of nursing home residents. *Journal of Psychosocial Nursing and Mental Health Services,* 38(6): 48–49.

Cambridge, P. (1999) The first hit: A case study of the physical abuse of people with learning disabilities and challenging behaviours in a residential service. *Disability and Society,* 14: 285–308.

Care Quality Commission (CQC). (2012a) *Time to Listen in NHS Hospitals.* Available at http://www.cqc.org.uk/sites/default/files/documents/time_to_listen_-_nhs_hospitals_main_report_tag.pdf [accessed 19 September 2017].

Care Quality Commission (CQC). (2012b) *Time to Listen in Care Homes.* Available at http://www.cqc.org.uk/sites/default/files/documents/time_to_listen_-_care_homes_main_report_tag.pdf [accessed 19 September 2017].

Cooper, A. (2012) 'How to (almost) murder a profession: The unsolved mystery of British Social Work', in Adlam, J., Aiyegbuisi, A., Kleinot, P., Motz, A. and Scanlon, C. (eds), *The Therapeutic Milieu Under Fire: Security and Insecurity in Forensic Mental Health,* London: Jessica Kingsley.

Davies, J. P., Heyman, B., Godin, P. M., Shaw, M. P. and Reynolds, L. (2006) The problems of offenders with mental disorders: A plurality of perspectives within a single mental health care organisation. *Social Science and Medicine*, 63: 1097–1108.

Department of Health (DoH). (2000) *No Secrets: Guidance on Developing and Implementing Multi-agency Policies and Procedures to Protect Vulnerable Adults from Abuse*, London: The Stationery Office.

Department of Health (DoH). (2002a) *Mental Health Policy Implementation Guide: Adult Acute Inpatient Care Provision*, London: The Stationery Office.

Department of Health (DoH). (2002b) *Mental Health Policy Implementation Guide: National Minimum Standards for General Adult Services in Psychiatric Intensive Care Units (PICU) and Low Secure Environments*, London: The Stationery Office.

Department of Health (DoH). (2005) *Mental Capacity Act*. Available at http://www.legislation.gov.uk/ukpga/2005/9/contents [accessed 19 September 2017].

Department of Health (DoH). (2006) *Safeguarding Vulnerable Adults (SVA) Act 2006*. Available at http://www.legislation.gov.uk/ukpga/2006/47/contents [accessed 19 September 2017].

Department of Health (DoH). (2012) *Transforming Care: A National Response to Winterbourne View Hospital*, London: The Stationery Office.

Dergal, J. and de Nobrega, P. (2000) Dealing with the problem of elder sexual abuse. *Canadian Nursing Home*, 11(2): 11–16.

Francis, R. (2013a) *Report of the Mid Staffordshire NHS Foundation Trust Public Inquiry*, London: The Stationery Office. Available at www.midstaffspublicinquiry.com [accessed 19 September 2017].

Francis, R. (2013b) *Executive Summary: Report of the Mid Staffordshire NHS Foundation Trust Public Inquiry*, London: The Stationery Office. Available at http://www.midstaffspublicinquiry.com/sites/default/files/report/Executive%20summary.pdf [accessed 19 September 2017.]

Goffman, E. (1961) *Asylums: Essays on the Social Situation of Mental Patients and Other Inmates*, New York: Anchor Books.

Halamandaris, V. J. (1983) 'Fraud and abuse in nursing homes', in Kosberg, J. (ed.), *Abuse and Maltreatment of the Elderly: Causes and Interventions*, Bristol: John Wright.

Harris, D. K. (1999) Elder abuse in nursing homes: The theft of patient's possessions. *Journal of Elder Abuse and Neglect*, 10(3/4): 141–152.

Harris, D. K. and Benson, M. L. (1999) Theft in nursing homes: An overlooked form of elder abuse. *Journal of Elder Abuse and Neglect*, 11(3): 73–90.

Herman, H., Trauer, T. and Warnock, J. (2001) The roles and relationships of psychiatrists and other service providers in mental health services. *Australian and New Zealand Journal of Psychiatry*, 36: 75–80.

Health Improvement Scotland (HIS). (2014) *It's All in the Detail*. Available at http://www.knowledge.scot.nhs.uk/media/CLT/ResourceUploads/4046468/SPSP-MH%202014%20Leaflet.pdf

Health and Social Care Information Centre (HSCIC). (2013) Mental Health Bulletin: Annual report from MHMDS returns – England, 2011–12: Further analysis and organisation-level data. Available at http://www.hscic.gov.uk/ catalogue/PUB10347 [accessed 19 September 2017].

HM Government. (2000) *Care Standards Act*, London: The Stationery Office. Available at http://www.legislation.gov.uk/ukpga/2000/14/contents [accessed 19 September 2017].

HM Government. (2005) *The Kerr/Haslam Inquiry*, London: The Stationery Office.

Kalaga, H. and Kingston, P. (2007) *A Review of Literature on Effective Interventions that Prevent and Respond to Harm against Adults*. Scottish Government Social Research. Available at Killapsy, H. (2007) From the asylum to community care: Learning from experience. *British Medical Bulletin*, 79/80: 245–248.

McNicholl, A. (2013) Protecting our adults: Why England should follow Scottish lead on adult safeguarding. Community Care. Available at http://www. communitycare.co.uk/2013/05/23/protecting-our-adults-why-england-should-follow-scottish-lead-on-adult-safeguarding/ [accessed 19 September 2017].

Mental Welfare Commission/Social Work Services Inspectorate. (2004) *Investigations into Scottish Borders Council and NHS Borders Services for People with Learning Disabilities: Joint Statement from the Mental Welfare Commission and the Social Work Services Inspectorate*. Available at http://www.scotland.gov. uk/Publications/2004/05/19333/36719 [accessed 19 September 2017].

NHS England. (2013) *NHS Standard Contract for Medium and Low Secure Mental Health Services (Adults)*. Available at http://www.england.nhs.uk/wp-content/ uploads/2013/06/c03-med-low-sec-mh.pdf [accessed 19 September 2017].

Preston-Shoot, M., Roberts, G. and Vernon, S. (2010) Values in social work law: Strained relations or sustaining relationships? *Journal of Social Welfare and Family Law*, 23(1), 1–22.

Prins, H. (1987) Literature review: Understanding and managing insanity: Some glimpses into historical fact and fiction. *British Journal of Social Work*, 17, 91–98.

Ramsey-Klawsnik, H. (1993) Interviewing elders for suspected sexual abuse: Guidelines and techniques. *Journal of Elder Abuse and Neglect*, 5(1), 5–19.

Ramsey-Klawsnik, H. (1996) 'Assessing physical and sexual abuse in health care settings', in Baumhover, L. A. and Beall, S. C. (eds), *Abuse, Neglect, and Exploitation of Older Persons: Strategies for Assessment and Intervention*, London: Jessica Kingsley.

Reilly, F. (2014) *Co-production in Secure Mental Health Settings*, unpublished MPhil chapter, School of Social Policy and Social Work, University of Strathclyde, Scotland.

Rogers, J. W. (1815) *A Statement of the Cruelties, Abuses and Frauds Which are Practiced in Madhouses*, London: Baldwin, Craddock and Joy.

Ryan, R. M. and Deci, E. L. (2000) Self-determination theory and the facilitation of intrinsic motivation, social development, and well-being. *American Psychologist*, 55: 68–78.

Scottish Executive. (2000) *The Same As You: A Review of Services for People with Learning Disabilities*. Available at http://www.gov.scot/resource/ doc/1095/0001661.pdf [accessed 19 September 2017].

Scottish Executive. (2001) Regulation of Care Act 2001. Available at http://www.
  legislation.gov.uk/asp/2001/8/contents
Scottish Government. (2007a) *Protection of Vulnerable Groups (Scotland) Act 2007*.
  Available at http://www.legislation.gov.uk/asp/2007/14/contents
Scottish Government. (2007b) *Adult Support and Protection (Scotland) Act*.
  Available at http://www.legislation.gov.uk/asp/2007/10/contents [accessed
  19 September 2017].
Scottish Government. (2008) *HM Chief Inspector of Prisons for Scotland: Out
  of Sight: Severe and Enduring Mental Health Problems in Scotland's Prisons*.
  Available at http://www.scotland.gov.uk/Publications/2008/11/10131239/6
  [accessed 19 September 2017].
Scottish Independent Advocacy Alliance. (2016) *Providing Advocacy*. Available
  at http://www.siaa.org.uk/us/independent-advocacy/providing-advocacy/
  [accessed 19 September 2017].
Select Committee Report. (1816) *The Better Regulation of Madhouses in England*.
  First Report, PP 1816 (227) VI 249, p. 191.
Shaw, M., Heyman, B., Reynolds, L., Davies, J. and Godin, P. (2007) Multidisciplinary
  teamwork in a UK regional secure mental health unit: A matter for negotiation?
  Social Theory & Health, 5: 356–377.
Sykes, W. and Groom, C. (2011) *Older People's Experience of Home Care in
  England, Equality and Human Rights Commission, Research Report 79.* Available
  at https://www.equalityhumanrights.com/sites/default/files/research-
  report-79-older-peoples-experiences-of-home-care-in-england.pdf [accessed
  19 September 2017].
Turner, J., Hayward, R., Angel, K., Fulford, B., Hall, J., Millard C. and Thomson,
  M. (2015) The history of modern mental health services in modern England:
  Practitioner memories and the direction of future research. *Medical History,*
  59(4): 599–624.
Wardhaugh, J. and Wilding, P. (1993) Towards an explanation of the corruption
  of care. *Critical Social Policy,* 13: 4–31.
Whistleblowing Commission. (2013) *Statutory Whistleblowing Code of Practice
  Will End Culture of Silence Says New Independent Whistleblowing Commission
  Report*. Available at http://www.pcaw.org.uk/whistleblowing-commission-
  public-consultation
White, C., Holland, E., Marsland, D. and Oakesy, P. (2002) The identification
  of environments and cultures that promote the abuse of people with
  intellectual disabilities: A review of the literature. *Journal of Applied Research
  in Intellectual Disabilities,* 16: 1–9.
Whyte, L. and Brooker, C. (2001) Working with a multidisciplinary team in
  secure psychiatric environments. *Journal of Psychosocial Nursing and Mental
  Health Services,* 39 (9): 26–34.
Wing, J. K. and Brown, G. W. (1970) *Institutionalism and Schizophrenia: A
  Comparative Study of Three Mental Hospitals, 1960–1968,* Cambridge:
  Cambridge University Press.

11

Conclusion and Key Messages

Ailsa Stewart and Gillian MacIntyre, University of Strathclyde; Pearse McCusker, Glasgow Caledonian University

This final chapter aims to bring together some of the key messages that have emerged throughout the book. While each of the preceding chapters has taken a different focus exploring particular conceptual frameworks or issues for specific service user groups, a number of common themes have emerged across the chapters which can help us to better understand the complex field of adult safeguarding as a whole. This chapter will discuss these themes and will attempt to address some of the ongoing complexities in this field. It will aim to provide clarity around what adult safeguarding is and how this can be understood before considering key ethical dilemmas and issues for practice that have emerged during the course of this volume.

What is adult safeguarding?

Adult safeguarding can be considered to concentrate on the provision of support and protection of adults who meet specific criteria laid down in various policy and legislation across the UK. This criteria is likely to include the inability of those adults, for a range of reasons (including lack of capacity), to protect themselves or act in their own best interests despite retaining the right to autonomy and self-determination (see Chapter 2). This potentially includes a broad range of adults as, arguably, this definition could apply to all adults at some point in their lives. Within this volume, for example, we have considered the protection of adults with learning disabilities, older adults, those who lack capacity and those with mental health problems as well as those where none of the above apply but whose context creates the potential for them to be at risk without external support and protection (see Chapters 7–10).

This volume highlights that there remains a range of perspectives on the extent and parameters of adult safeguarding across professions, agencies and jurisdictions, alongside underlying concerns of the appropriateness of any intervention in the lives of adults and any associated reduction of rights. It therefore remains a contested concept and area of practice (Pritchard, 2008) with multi-disciplinary working at the core to ensure rigorous and appropriate consideration of an adult's health and social care needs (Greenfields et al., 2012 as identified in Chapter 5 by McGregor et al). Jurisdictional differences are also highlighted within this volume with contributions from across the UK. These differences relate to different levels of professional and organisational responsibility and such basic concerns as language. This is significant in considering the extent to which we can develop a shared understanding of adult safeguarding across the UK.

The experience of serious inquiries and other forms of investigations into poor practice have clearly aided in informing the development of practice in adult safeguarding. A variety of inquiries (see Chapter 10, for examples) evidence the importance of regulation and inspection of services as well as rigorous monitoring and review procedures to ensure the evolution of effective practice that does not reduce the rights of the individual. Recent activity around the Cheshire West case (DoH, 2014b) and the attendant consideration of what constitutes illegal and legal deprivation of liberty within the parameters of adult safeguarding is a useful example of this. There is evidence from a range of professional perspectives that practice is evolving to take account of the challenging ethical dilemmas raised throughout this book. This involves working to support people in an empowering way in order to ameliorate any potential reduction in their rights. There also appears to be an increasingly shared conceptual understanding of adult safeguarding with common elements emerging across the UK (see Chapters 7–10). These are outlined in more detail later in this chapter and throughout the preceding volume.

Collaborative working and the emphasis on its importance to ensuring effective provision are enshrined both in policy and in some circumstances legislation across the UK jurisdictions and have aided knowledge exchange and mobilisation around adult safeguarding (Stewart, 2016). This focus has facilitated the emergence of a shared understanding, to some extent, among professionals that coalesces around vulnerability, however defined, risk of harm and the threshold at which the adult's insight into the consequences of particular behaviours requires intervention (Davidson et al., 2015; Davidson and Campbell, 2010). The differing responsibilities across disciplines, it could be argued, appear to maintain a fault line between professions and agencies amidst concern that without a joint responsibility, adults who require safeguarding may fall between the service gaps or perhaps more importantly receive inconsistent support and protection. Whilst a single agency retains the lead responsibility for adult safeguarding it is therefore perhaps inevitable that differing priorities will be afforded to adult protection across other agencies and professions and fault lines will persist.

As noted earlier, the broad population under consideration brings with it challenges concerning the extent to which any intervention under the adult safeguarding umbrella may reduce the rights and associated citizenship of the individual adult. If we accept that any adult can be at risk of harm, often due to a confluence of ecological factors outwith their own control or due to a specific medical condition, then any attempt to reduce the breadth of this population is accompanied by the disquiet that potentially vulnerable adults may be excluded from having access to the support and protection they require. This dilemma remains at the axis of adult safeguarding – do we risk reducing the autonomy of the adult in the short term to ensure their protection in the longer term? On balance, this volume suggests that the answer to this question is yes and that in fact we have a responsibility to do so to avoid harm to our citizens, arguing that a short-term paternalistic approach is justifiable if there is a consequent increase in autonomy in the longer term.

The focus for policy makers and practitioners therefore must be on the way in which practice can take a rights-based approach that promotes independence and empowerment through the adult safeguarding process, such as the use of underlying principles and the requirement (in some cases) to have the consent of the adult in any intervention where practicable. The six principles for safeguarding developed in the guidance for the implementation of the Care Act (DoH, 2014a) are a very useful illustration of how these various issues can be brought together and a framework for practice developed. These principles are empowerment, proportionality, partnership, protection, prevention, accountability and it is useful to consider these principles across the examples provided in this volume.

Alongside these principles it is important to reflect on some of the discussions on vulnerability and abuse throughout this volume. The nature of vulnerability and the extent to which it can be considered to be inherent to the individual or as a result of context or other external factors is a key consideration in adult safeguarding (see Chapters 2 and 4 for example). Determination of vulnerability can be viewed as paternalistic and patronising by both professionals and those whose use supports, therefore an agreed paradigm which acknowledges the impact of context is essential to reducing the potential to disempower adults, reducing their rights as citizens thus further marginalising already excluded groups. The range of harm/abuse considered within this volume is extensive and includes physical, emotional, sexual and financial harm. There is evidence that the type of abuse/harm being explored within adult safeguarding processes is fairly consistent across the UK but that there are particular types associated with different populations; people with learning disabilities, for example, are more likely to experience financial, sexual and physical abuse (Khalifeh et al., 2013; Hughes, et al., 2012).

Legislative and political frameworks

Noted within this volume are the political conditions which influence the consideration and development of adult safeguarding. As Mackay notes in Chapter 3, the prevailing political ideology will both influence the extent to which the government has the appetite and willingness to intervene in what could be considered a broadly private sphere in the lives of its citizens and the resources it consequently attaches to pursuing this agenda. In a financial climate with ever-reducing resources and no end in sight to these reductions, it is of some concern that responsibility for adult safeguarding be maintained in the public sector and as a policy priority to ensure adults at risk of harm for whatever reason continue to be protected. The alternative approach, however, suggested by a neo-liberal agenda is to attach this responsibility to citizens rather than organisations, reducing the role of state involvement. As many of the examples in this volume evidence, providing effective support and protection requires independent oversight and careful consideration of complex ethical dilemmas to ensure appropriate practice and maintenance of individual rights.

The influence of wider international developments on how adult safeguarding is conceptualised and practised is also illustrated, for example, through the Convention on the Rights of Persons with Disabilities. As has been shown, this statute brings to the fore and questions concepts of capacity and incapacity, which underpin much of adult safeguarding work. Previous discussion in this volume identifies that the principle of legal capacity, regardless of type or level of disability or mental distress, is now enshrined in international law through Article 12. It thus places emphasis on ensuring that means of supported decision making are implemented, which in practice requires public bodies and professionals to demonstrate how they have determined and upheld adults' past and present wishes. This sets up considerable tension between the need to provide and fund robust mechanisms for supported decision making and moving away from existing practices, which are largely predicated on substitute decision making. The CRPD's impact is also reflected in discussion of the Northern Ireland Mental Capacity Act 2016, which represents the latest UK legal development to grapple with the balance between protecting adults against harm and upholding their rights to self-determination, as outlined in detail in Chapter 6 of this volume in relation to adults experiencing mental distress. As well as addressing matters in relation to adults perceived to lack capacity, the contributors to this volume have also considered the issue of safeguarding adults who have capacity and consequently the unqualified right to make decisions for themselves. The question of what to do, as a professional, in situations where adults decide not to accept help and support to prevent harm is acknowledged throughout as extremely challenging.

Key ethical dilemmas

From reading this edited volume, the inherently ethically complex nature of adult safeguarding becomes abundantly clear. Regardless of care group or context, making decisions to intervene, or not to intervene, in situations where adults are perceived to be at risk of harm is accompanied by ethical dilemmas. Furthermore, the outcomes of any decisions taken have been shown to be difficult to predict. Discussion clearly illustrates that ethical sensitivity is embedded throughout safeguarding work, centred on the need to balance adults' rights to self-determination with the State's duty to protect people from harm. A further level of complexity is added by the fluid nature of societal views and expectations surrounding questions of risk and safety. As such, thresholds of what is considered acceptable in terms of risk to adults have been shown in this collection to differ across jurisdictions, professions, cultures and eras, influenced by factors including advances in knowledge and prevailing political discourses, which in turn shape legal frameworks. The shifting nature of the moral and legal landscape is illustrated in today's safeguarding thresholds and practices becoming tomorrow's unacceptable infringements of people's civil liberties or failures to provide adequate levels of protection. This process of ongoing ethical and legal change is reflected in discussion throughout this book of developments in the statutory frameworks of the four UK jurisdictions.

Despite our shifting understanding about the nature and acceptable levels of risk, the central dilemma or tension for practitioners working in this complex field remains the same over time, namely the extent to which the duty to protect adults at risk of harm can be balanced with their right to self-determination as highlighted above. The duty to protect from harm is embedded in legislation across the four countries. Yet there is growing recognition that statutes which adopt a blanket approach to adult protection are in danger of contravening human rights legislation that sets out the rights of an adult to make their own decisions as well as their right to privacy. Rather than conceptualising protection and self-determination as areas of conflict and tension therefore, adopting a rights-based approach to adult safeguarding may be useful in overcoming some of the dilemmas highlighted in this volume.

The duty of professionals to protect vulnerable adults can be reframed in terms of the adult's right to protection. Campbell et al., in Chapter 6 of this volume draw on service user perspectives that highlight that those subject to compulsory measures in the form of compulsory treatment orders as set out in S.63 of the Mental Health (Care and Treatment) (Scotland) Act 2003 may find it easier to accept these measures if they are viewed as part of their *right* to treatment as opposed to a more paternalistic approach that might suggest that these measures are enforced on an individual because it is in their *best interests*. Similarly in Chapter 9, McCusker and Jackson discuss the dilemmas involved in safeguarding those where there is a risk of suicide or self-harm, a particularly challenging area of practice, especially where the individual concerned might retain capacity. They suggest that involving people as far as possible in decision making and care planning might be the most effective way to reduce risk.

Promoting participation amongst service users and carers has been identified throughout this volume as being crucial in ensuring effective safeguarding practices across the UK. In order to do this effectively, it is argued that the concept of inter-dependence and the inter-dependent nature of everyday living and care-giving must be acknowledged (Rabiee, 2013). This involves accepting that we all have the potential to be vulnerable at various points across the life-course (Beckett, 2006). In doing so, we begin to question the binary notion of the self-reliant citizen on the one hand and the vulnerable adult in need of protection whose right to self-determination is compromised on the other.

Within this context, a shift towards a model of supported decision making that explores the ways in which people – be they individuals who use services, family members or professionals – can contribute in a meaningful way to the decision-making process makes sense. It is argued that the current legislative framework across the UK does not necessarily support this new way of working, although Northern Ireland is leading the way in this regard and the concept of supported decision making has been enshrined in the *Adult Safeguarding Policy for Northern Ireland* (DHSSPS, 2015). A model of supported decision making allows practitioners, in partnership with people who use services. to explore the ways in which they can contribute to the decision-making process, identifying the support that they might need to do so. Adopting this model has the potential to reduce power imbalances by acknowledging that different participants have different knowledge, skills and expertise to bring to the decision-making process. This is in line with theories of recognition (Anderson and Honneth, 2004) which aid this discourse by allowing us to consider the ways in which communities (and organisations) value and recognise the contribution made by different participants (or citizens) regardless of their particular circumstances.

Implications for practice

The contributors to this volume have offered both conceptual and practical discussion that it is hoped will provide practitioners with useful ways of interpreting and approaching safeguarding work. A number of consistent themes have been shown to underpin good practice in adult safeguarding, and it is fitting to revisit them briefly here.

First, regardless of care group, discussion throughout this volume highlights the importance of having sound legal and ethical knowledge. Inadequate safeguarding practices have been explored in detail in this volume and have been shown to thrive in contexts where there is a lack of training and awareness of safeguarding responsibilities among professionals. It is highlighted that professionals' 'duty of care' includes safeguarding and that good quality training needs to be provided on an ongoing basis to ensure that a commitment to ethical safeguarding is woven into organisational cultures. Moreover, the narratives explored here indicate that sharing knowledge of safeguarding law and policy with service users and carers and informing them of their rights is essential in enabling them to exercise those rights. In particular, advocacy services have been identified as an important means of supporting adults through the complexities of safeguarding interventions. As indicated, however, policy has impacted on the resources available to fund such services with the result that access varies across the UK.

All of the practice examples explored here indicate that legal knowledge on its own is not sufficient to protect adults from harm. They have shown that the law cannot predict the myriad ways in which safeguarding concerns arise for individuals and families, and as such professionals are required to interpret where thresholds for intervention are met. The examples given in this volume confirm that it is often difficult to arrive at clear assessments of risk or of how to proceed. Increasingly, however, legal frameworks are being drafted in ways that seek to aid the professional decision-making process through the use of legal principles, which in effect act as signposts to help practitioners weigh up often competing imperatives. As such, principles, including intervening in the least restrictive way possible, have been shown to provide an essential counterbalance to the understandable personal and professional desire to prevent someone coming to harm. Relatedly, this volume also reminds professionals of the need and value of referring to their respective codes of practice, in addition to attending to relevant statutes.

Arguably, the pivotal theme concerns the general approach that should be taken to adult safeguarding work. The narratives relating to all of the care groups discussed in this collection signal relationship-based practice as crucial to achieving successful safeguarding outcomes. This aligns with the recognition that people are experts in their own lives and, accordingly, their views and preferences must take centre stage in decision making about any aspects of care, support and protection. The importance of exercising agency and choice in life is increasingly recognised in law and policy, as reflected in discussions throughout this volume. In essence, the collective message from the practice examples reported here is that effective safeguarding is built on trusting relationships between services users, carers and professionals. Discussion has illustrated that it is often the quality of these interactions rather than legal measures that leads to successful outcomes. This is illustrated in Chapter 8, in the course of assessing thresholds of risk posed by carers and determining whether undesirable behaviours constitute intentional harm or understandable reactions borne out of stress and frustration with the caring role. The ability to make such finely balanced professional judgements is greatly enhanced by getting to know the carer and service user well and gaining a clear understanding of the nature of their relationship.

Central to ethical adult safeguarding is effective multi-disciplinary working, as highlighted above. Discussion has signalled the requirement to share the duties and responsibilities of safeguarding across professions if adults are to be provided with the types and levels of support and protection required. As well as lessening the likelihood of failures in care, timeous and collective multi-professional discussion and decision making have been demonstrated as key to managing the dilemmas and anxieties that safeguarding work often precipitates. The seemingly intractable and irresolvable nature of some safeguarding concerns is well documented in this volume and, in each example given, the achievement of desired outcomes is shown to be made more likely by the pooling of resources and knowledge that good multi-professional working constitutes. It is also clear, however, that there are very real impediments to effective inter-agency communication and collaboration, reflecting broader literature on this subject (see, for example, Petch, 2014). This is where legislation and policy frameworks have been demonstrated as providing the necessary impetus for consistent and systematic multi-professional responses to safeguarding concerns. This is illustrated, for example, in the establishment of adult safeguarding committees to coordinate and monitor safeguarding practices in local areas; however, as contributors to this volume have also indicated, such initiatives need sufficient legal sway and resourcing to improve safeguarding cultures and practices.

Commentary in this volume also attests to the importance of having effective mechanisms of support in adult safeguarding. This is essential given the above noted complexities and level of interpretation involved in assessing risk thresholds and arriving at ethically and legally justifiable responses. As illustrated, this type of work can also generate considerable emotional upheaval, given the implications of making decisions about whether or not to intervene in an adult's life. As such, suitable supervisory and peer-support arrangements are needed to enable practitioners to think through decisions and make sense of, and manage, the feelings associated with them.

The insights provided in this volume clearly signal the importance of not shying away from the societal and professional responsibility to safeguard adults from harm. The implications of not doing so are illustrated lucidly in discussion of recent abuses within institutional settings, discussed in Chapter 10. The examples contained in this collection also reflect the often partial nature of resolutions and the frustration of not being able to safeguard someone when they are at obvious risk of harm but do not wish to engage with the care plan being proposed. In acknowledging the uncertainty and challenges of adult safeguarding work, however, it is hoped that together they offer helpful illustrations of how professionals, service users and carers have grappled with the particular issues and dilemmas they faced and found unique responses to improving protections and quality of life for people at risk of harm.

Rather than positioning the inherently messy, difficult and changing nature of adult safeguarding in negative terms, this book signals why it is important to continually reflect on and revise expectations, standards and practices at national, organisational and practitioner levels. In essence, it suggests that practitioners frame adult safeguarding as a cornerstone of professional practice and both welcome and seek to build on the developing knowledge base and legal frameworks that have emerged in the last two decades. This requires an acceptance that safeguarding will continue to pose significant challenges and a commitment to using best available knowledge and approaches to intervene in ways that are both ethically and legally defensible.

References

Anderson, J. and Honneth, A. (2004) 'Autonomy, vulnerability, recognition, and justice', in Anderson J. and Christman J. (eds), *Autonomy and the Challenges to Liberalism: New Essays* (pp. 127–149), New York, NY: Cambridge University Press.

Beckett, A. E. (2006) *Citizenship and Vulnerability: Disability and Issues of Social and Political Engagement,* Basingstoke: Palgrave Macmillan.

Davidson, G. and Campbell, J. (2010) An audit of assessment and reporting by Approved Social Workers (ASWs). *British Journal of Social Work,* 40(5): 1609–1627.

Davidson, G., Kelly, B., MacDonald, G., Rizzo, M., Lombard, L., Oluwaseye, A., Clift-Matthews, V. and Martin, A. (2015) Supporting decision making: A review of the international literature. *International Journal of Law and Psychiatry,* 38: 61–67.

Department of Health (DoH). (2014a) *Care and Support Statutory Guidance. Issued under the Care Act 2014,* London: Department of Health.

Department of Health (DoH). (2014b) *Department of Health Guidance: Response to the Supreme Court Judgement/Deprivation of Liberty Safeguards,* London: Department of Health.

Department of Health, Social Services and Public Safety (DHSSPS). (2015) *Adult Safeguarding Policy for Northern Ireland: Adult Safeguarding: Prevention and Protection in Partnership,* Belfast: DHSSPS.

Greenfields, M., Dalrymple, R. and Fanning, A. (eds) (2012) *Working with Adults at Risk from Harm,* Maidenhead: Open University Press.

Hughes, K., Bellis, M. A., Jones, L., Wood, S. and Bates, G. et al. (2012) Prevalence and risk of violence against adults with disabilities: A systematic review and meta-analysis of observational studies. *The Lancet,* 379: 1621–1629.

Khalifeh, H., Howard, L. M., Osborn, D., Moran, P. and Johnson, S. (2013) Violence against people with disability in England and Wales: Findings from a National Cross-Sectional Survey. *PLoS ONE,* 8(2): e55952. doi:10.1371/journal.pone.0055952.

Petch, A. (2014) *Delivering Integrated Care and Support,* Glasgow: IRISS. Available at https://www.iriss.org.uk/resources/reports/delivering-integrated-care-and-support

Pritchard, J. (ed.). (2008) *Good Practice in Safeguarding Adults,* London: Jessica Kingsley.

Rabiee, P. (2013) Exploring the relationships between choice and independence: Experiences of disabled and older people. *British Journal of Social Work,* 43(5): 872–888.

Stewart, A. (2016) *The Implementation of the Adult Support and Protection (Scotland) Act (2007),* Glasgow: University of Glasgow.

GLOSSARY

Adult safeguarding – A continuum incorporating within its parameters a range of interventions and safeguards to prevent adults from harm including compulsory treatment at one end and traditional welfare supports at the other. This may include those who are unable to protect themselves by virtue of mental disorder, learning disability, physical disability and/or physical frailty.

Deprivation of Liberty Safeguards (DOLS) – Safeguards that are part of the Mental Capacity Act 2005 and aim to ensure that people looked after in care homes and hospitals are not looked after in a way that restricts their freedom.

Direct payments/Self-directed Support (SDS) – Money in lieu of services to meet assessed needs so the person or their proxy can arrange and manage their own support.

Libertarian – A person who believes in free will for all, where individuals are sovereign over their own lives and not subject to the will of others including governments.

Neo-liberalism – The prevailing global ideology that views the welfare state as inefficient, ineffective and paternalistic and therefore develops policies that promote the use of markets in service delivery to create self-reliance in the citizen.

Protection plan – Arising from investigations under the Adult Support and Protection (Scotland) Act 2007 with the aim of identifying and coordinating services in protecting the adult from harm.

Social model of disability – Suggests that disability is caused by the way society is organised rather than by a person's impairment or difference.

United Nations Convention on the Rights of Persons with Disabilities (UNCRPD) (CRPD) – Statute that signalled a paradigm shift in conferring equal human rights and fundamental freedoms on all people with disabilities. Of particular relevance to adult safeguarding, capacity and mental health laws are Articles 12 and 14. Article 12 enshrines equal recognition before the law (i.e. that people with disabilities have legal capacity on an equal basis with others in all aspects of life), which confers a duty on countries to provide people with disabilities with adequate support to ensure they can exercise their rights. Article 14 refers to the liberty and security of people with disabilities and stipulates that the existence of disability alone cannot justify deprivation of liberty.

INDEX